HUMAN DIGNITY AND LIBERAL POLITICS

Martin D'Arcy, SJ, Memorial Lectures

These books are based on lectures given at the Jesuit Campion Hall of the University of Oxford. The author of each book is a distinguished member of the Society of Jesus, and the goal of the series is to present the very best of Jesuit scholarship. The series honors Fr. Martin D'Arcy, SJ, the celebrated Master of Campion Hall from 1933 to 1945.

Human Dignity and Liberal Politics: Catholic Possibilities for the Common Good
Patrick Riordan, SJ

The Moral Life: Eight Lectures
James F. Keenan, SJ

HUMAN DIGNITY and LIBERAL POLITICS

CATHOLIC POSSIBILITIES *for the* COMMON GOOD

Patrick Riordan

GEORGETOWN UNIVERSITY PRESS / WASHINGTON, DC

© 2023 Georgetown University Press. All rights reserved. No part of this book may be reproduced or utilized in any form or by any means, electronic or mechanical, including photocopying and recording, or by any information storage and retrieval system, without permission in writing from the publisher.

The publisher is not responsible for third-party websites or their content. URL links were active at time of publication.

Library of Congress Cataloging-in-Publication Data

Names: Riordan, Patrick, 1950– author.
Title: Human dignity and liberal politics : Catholic possibilities for the common good / Patrick Riordan.
Description: Washington, DC : Georgetown University Press, 2023. | Series: Martin J. D'Arcy, SJ memorial lectures | Includes bibliographical references and index.
Identifiers: LCCN 2022045233 (print) | LCCN 2022045234 (ebook) | ISBN 9781647123680 (hardcover) | ISBN 9781647123697 (paperback) | ISBN 9781647123703 (ebook)
Subjects: LCSH: Christian sociology—Catholic Church. | Common good—Religious aspects—Catholic Church. | Political science—Philosophy. | Christian ethics—Catholic authors. | Liberalism.
Classification: LCC BX1753 .R488 2023 (print) | LCC BX1753 (ebook) | DDC 261.8—dc23/eng/20230601
LC record available at https://lccn.loc.gov/2022045233
LC ebook record available at https://lccn.loc.gov/2022045234

24 23   9 8 7 6 5 4 3 2   First printing

Printed in the United States of America

Cover design by Jeremy John Parker
Interior design by BookComp, Inc.

To the new generation, Charlotte, Martha, Nick, Ross, Barra, Sula, Dylan....
May they never lack the common goods of freedom, family, and friendship

CONTENTS

Acknowledgments ix
List of Abbreviations xi

Introduction 1
1 Three Lenses to View Common Goods 9
2 Aristotle Reconstructed 30
3 Does Political Augustinianism Help? 49
4 Aquinas and Analogy: The Limits of Bounded Rationality 70
5 Is Liberalism the Enemy? 92
6 The Role of Conflict in a Political Account of Common Goods 114
7 Utopia and Apocalypse 136
8 Is Talk of the Common Good Inevitably Paternalistic? 156
9 Fraught Common Goods: Integral Ecology, Humane Economy 176
10 Culture as Common Good 201
Epilogue 223

Bibliography 229
Index 239
About the Author 243

ACKNOWLEDGMENTS

This book grew from the Fr. Martin D'Arcy Memorial Lectures delivered at Campion Hall, University of Oxford, in Trinity Term of 2021. While the D'Arcy Lectures have been held since 1978, this is the first time that they were delivered online. The absence of a live audience was conditioned by the circumstances of the COVID-19 pandemic that both limited our academic activities and opened new opportunities. Sincere thanks, therefore, are due to the members of Campion Hall who rose to the challenge—notably, to Dr. Nicholas Austin, SJ, master of the hall, who gave the lead to the project on the recommendation of the members of the Academic Committee, Dr. Philip Kennedy, OP, and Professor Gavin Flood. The production relied on the expertise of Sarah Gray, events manager, and Yingying Jiang, communications officer. I am grateful also to the members of the Hall, Wilin Buitrago Arias, SJ, Jijimon Joseph, SJ, Dr. Frank Turner, SJ, Dr. Sèverine Deneulin, and Dr. Minlib Dahll, OP, along with the master, who expertly moderated the sessions. Conversations with colleagues in the hall helped to clarify the argument, and thanks are due to all colleagues, including Dr. Philip Moller, SJ, and Matthew Dunch, SJ, who provided theological and philosophical balance. Audience questions and email provoked further conversation that has made the book somewhat richer than the lectures, and I am grateful to those who took the time to engage.

That I had the opportunity to work in Oxford is due to the initiative of the former master, Dr. James Hanvey, SJ, who thereby enabled a resumption of our collaboration begun many years before in the Heythrop Institute for Religion, Ethics, and Public Life. Campion Hall in the years since has provided a grounded experience of common goods in our communal and academic life, for which I am extremely grateful.

The publication of this volume also marks a first for the Martin D'Arcy Memorial Lectures in that it initiates a collaboration between Campion Hall and Georgetown University Press. The plan is to hold the D'Arcy Lectures annually, to be published by the press. I am grateful to Al Bertrand and his team at Georgetown for their efficient editorial work and the support provided to an author who is all too aware of his limitations. The encouraging reports and suggestions from the readers were very much appreciated.

I am grateful to have had the opportunity to present the D'Arcy Lectures and to have them published by this academic press. I take the opportunity to acknowledge a debt to my fellow Jesuits in the Irish province who have been my support in the intellectual apostolate. The late David Tuohy, SJ (+ 2020), an educationalist, David Coghlan, SJ, specialist in action research, and James Murphy, SJ, philosopher, have been constant companions in our mission, without whose friendship the life of scholarship would not have been sustainable. I also acknowledge the support of my many friends, not least Dr. Joel Tabora, SJ, president of Ateneo de Davao University in the Philippines, whose repeated invitations enabled me to address a wider audience and engage with a richly different culture. More than one hundred participants in the Philippines engaged in two online seminars on the topic of common goods, having watched video recordings of the D'Arcy Lectures.

Finally, I do not know how to thank my family, Donal, Frances, and Liam, their spouses, and their children, except with the token of dedicating this book to the newest generation. So many goods in common that we have enjoyed and want to share: "We should never stop thanking God!"

LIST OF ABBREVIATIONS

CST   Catholic social teaching
ECtHR European Court of Human Rights
GDP   gross domestic product
SAT   Scholastic Aptitude Test
SPE   Special Purpose Entity
UDHR   Universal Declaration of Human Rights

INTRODUCTION

There has been a resurgence of interest in "the common good" as a topic in political philosophy and social ethics, as well as in public theology and Christian ethics. Many critiques of contemporary culture and politics also invoke the concept. In much of the literature about common goods, whether secular or religious, authors present readers with a choice. Regimes of liberalism and neoliberalism are deemed so inhospitable to a decent human or Christian existence that readers are challenged to opt instead for the common good. This may include the encouragement to opt out, to take the "Benedict Option." The hegemony of an economic and political liberalism in our Western societies provokes the critique of many who bemoan the lack of shared values, the absence of a sense of communality, and the resultant divisiveness of a society that fosters competitiveness. The critics' use of common good language appears to situate them as opponents of the established order. In a social and political milieu widely acknowledged to be polarized, I find it regrettable that even discussions invoking what is common among us contribute to exacerbating the divisions instead of bridging them. The thrust of my argument in this book is to explore what is common, even where there is difference and division. In this brief introduction I note some recent significant contributions that invoke the common good or common goods as representing a vision of an alternative, in contrast to the approach ambitioned here, where the common is sought also in the actuality of what is, and not only in the vision of what might be aspired to.

RECENT DISCUSSIONS OF COMMON GOODS

The renowned political commentator Michael Sandel, in his book *The Tyranny of Merit: What's Become of the Common Good?* (2020) bemoans the loss of the common good as something displaced from public political culture. He claims that a formerly shared vision of the purpose of human life and of social cooperation has been lost. Our modern world offers instead an economic standard of well-being focused on the satisfaction of consumer preferences via markets delivering goods and services. He targets an economic interpretation of the common good whereby it is understood as gross domestic product (GDP), the summation of the satisfaction through market exchanges of the needs and desires of consumers. The political competence required by government for the sake of such a common good is technocratic, the mastery of means. Opposed to the technocratic approach is a concern with purposes and ends, not primarily means. But purposes are not predetermined; they must be chosen, and that presupposes a form of politics that facilitates deliberation about purposes. If citizens are to engage in deliberation and debate about the purposes of common life, they will require civic virtue and practical wisdom. Traditional approaches exemplified by philosophers like Aristotle and the founders of the American republic are acknowledged for their emphasis on the moral education of citizens and the inclusion of this task among the common goods of the polity. Where the dominant style of politics is the pursuit of interest, a collaborative deliberation about purposes has no place. I completely endorse the need to resource our collaborative deliberation and hope that this book provides some material for that.

The former chief rabbi of the United Kingdom (UK), Jonathan Sacks, in his 2020 book *Morality: Restoring the Common Good in Divided Times*, fears that the cultivation of individual liberties has undermined a shared morality, and that the toxic quality of public debate and the resultant divisiveness is regrettable. He argues that there can be no real freedom without morality and without the acceptance of responsibility. The good to be fostered is a common moral foundation for social order. Common good as he invokes it is subversive of the present established order, and not defensive. The analysis of such a shrewd and experienced commentator as Jonathan Sacks must be taken seriously, but the proposed strategy provokes a question: How can we overcome the problematic divisiveness by further polarization?

A similar case is made by a theologian, Jake Meador, in *In Search of the Common Good: Christian Fidelity in a Fractured World* (2019). His title reflects the same regret: that the dominant culture of liberalism has led to a polarized and hateful public discourse, a fracturing of society, and a widening of differences and inequalities. His recommendation is that the unity of a society depends on a shared story, and that the Christian story can provide a vision for a renewed common life. Here, again, the common good is invoked in opposition to a dominant narrative. While my arguments will draw from the Catholic intellectual tradition, and I will not deny my own espousal of a Christian vision, the substance of my contribution is intended to be both intelligible and acceptable to reasonable fellow citizens of other faiths or of no faith. The secular vision that I offer has its ancestry in a faith community's experience, but it is explicitly secular without denying or attempting to conceal its roots.

It is understandable that many of the contributors to this discussion refer to distinctive American experiences, which undoubtedly have their counterparts in Europe and the UK. Robert Reich, in his book *The Common Good* (2018), points to the vicious cycle of deterioration of public culture in the United States and argues that a virtuous cycle is required to restore a shared sense of what really matters. He picks out the need to clarify how honor, shame, patriotism, truth, and the role of leadership should function in the public culture. This is another example of how the common good of the title is not aligned with the establishment but invoked to support a project of replacement and reform.

Colin Woodard offers another distinctively American analysis. His *American Character: A History of the Epic Struggle between Individual Liberty and the Common Good* (2017) interprets the history of the country in terms of the polarization between individualism and collectivism, between individuals' rights and the good of the community. His account of this continuing tension, with one or another position dominant at different times, illustrates the challenge, if not the impossibility, of finding a sustainable balance between these two standpoints. It confirms my impression that many who write about the common good locate it as one pole in a juxtaposition.

From the perspective of Catholic reflection on social and political reality, it is worrying that the notion of common good in these debates is usually associated with one side or the other. The Catholic intellectual tradition hopes to speak of realities that apply to all, and so it typically avoids taking sides in specific ideological debates. The Second Vatican Council's approach in its Pastoral Constitution on the Church Today, *Gaudium et spes*, is to invite all to a dialogue about the common good as the set of economic, political, legal, and cultural conditions for the flourishing of human beings, whether as individuals or communities. It remains a challenge to present and explain this intellectual tradition of the common good in the context of contemporary debates. But at least now it has become permissible to write and speak of common goods, and of the human good, so there are opportunities for raising serious questions and proposing possible solutions. The lively contemporary debate also raises questions for the adequacy of the Catholic position: Does it sufficiently account for the extent of real conflict in social and political life, beyond the kinds of disagreements that can be accommodated in a university common room?

Some tendencies in these publications exaggerating a contrast distort the possibility of a balanced account of common goods. Sometimes the notion of common good is invoked in favor of civil authorities and the general welfare; sometimes it is employed to protect individual freedoms and human rights. I argue that the concept of the common good within Catholic social teaching (CST) combines both aspects, since the rights and freedoms of individuals are common goods of our societies. Partisanship for one pole or the other is foreign to the Catholic concern for the whole.

A further concern is the tendency in some explicitly Catholic literature to invoke a Catholic notion of common goods in the critique of liberalism and neoliberalism that suggests that a Catholic must be opposed to any and every liberal philosophy or regime. The markedly anti-liberal account of common goods is not consistent with the Catholic tradition. I am concerned that the church's position may be misrepresented in these discussions. I defend the view that the evolved teaching of the church does not oblige believers to embrace any one political philosophy or support any specific constitutional form. Church teaching insists on the fundamental dignity of the human person, which should be respected by all state forms and actual regimes. It also teaches that civil authorities should serve the common good and adhere to the requirements of solidarity and subsidiarity. These high standards can provide grounds for a critical review of the functioning of any regime, and that can lead to a lively debate among believers who legitimately take up opposing positions.

SUMMARY OUTLINE OF THE CHAPTERS

Chapter 1 presents the three lenses through which the topic of common goods is analyzed. Aristotelian practical philosophy provides the basic account of action and cooperation as oriented to the good and the good in common. Twentieth-century pronouncements of CST highlight human dignity and the common good, and accommodate such modern themes as democracy, human rights, and religious liberty, evaluating them in terms of dignity and the common good. During the twentieth century, developments in political thought moved beyond a comprehensive liberalism that was hegemonic in its conception to a more political liberalism that could facilitate the collaboration in political life by exponents of many different worldviews and religious doctrines. These three lenses illuminate the challenge of explanation addressed in the book. A heuristic concept of the common good is identified, along with two criteria for clarifying claimed candidates: first, no systematic exclusion of any individual person or group, and second, no systematic exclusion of any genuine dimension of the human good.

Chapter 2 revisits the option for an Aristotelian approach and considers the enormous differences between the world of modern liberal politics and Aristotle's Greek city-state. Three major elements in Aristotle's account of politics would seem to make it irrelevant. First is his assumption that a political community is united in sharing a view of what is good; second is the expectation that rulers in the city are concerned about the good characters and virtues of citizens; third is the teleological perspective that both individuals and the community are oriented to their fulfillment. In a modern approach the expectations are very different. Conflict is presupposed and not harmony, a minimum of conformity to the law is expected and not the internalization of virtues and values, and the currency of debate is persons' rights rather than the ultimate end, or telos, of life. However, this chapter attempts to reconstruct the modern view in terms that approximate the Aristotelian. While there is conflict, there is also agreement on how the conflict is to be handled. While the minimum is enforced, the visions driving the expanding regulations are maximalist. While rights are legislated for and secured, they express real human goods and so are open to further reflection on the grounds and ends of those goods. This reconstruction enables the retention of key Aristotelian elements while the limited and constrained aspects of modernity are accommodated.

Chapter 3 follows the many Christian theologians who turn to Augustine for an account of the political and the relationship between the sacred and the secular. A revision of Augustine's thought permits a different understanding of the secular, considering it a spectrum of positions rather than an extreme of exclusion of and separation from the sacred and the divine. In several contemporary debates I review and endorse the rejection of forms of illiberal secularism that would deny religion a place in public life.

Chapter 4 takes Aquinas's discussion of law in relation to the common good to clarify the analogical use of the term. The theological presuppositions of the medieval discussion must be considered for an adequate grasp of what is at stake. Often treated as simply a philosophical examination of law, there is a real danger of distortion leading to a neglect of Aquinas's intellectualism, his privileging of the theological horizon, and his analogical use of terms such as "society," "law," "common good," and "promulgation." Clarification helps to illustrate misuse and confusion in some current uses of the term "common good" when it is identified, for instance, with "commons" or "public goods."

Chapter 5 contains the heart of the argument. It notes the very bad reputation that liberalism has had historically and in the present debates, but makes the case that liberalism as a doctrine for government predicated on the centrality of human freedom is not the enemy of the common good. Following the Second Vatican Council's strong affirmation of religious liberty and its grounds in the dignity of the human person, we can ask which forms of state and government are compatible with this central value of human dignity, and with fundamental liberties. A brief survey of Pope Benedict's practice of addressing political leaders in New York, London, and Berlin proposes the Pope Benedict Option, which advocates a spirited engagement with the world, celebrating its recognition of human dignity and the importance of human freedom but pointing beyond to that unlimited horizon of truth and goodness to which it can be open. The Pope Benedict Option outlines an alternative to the Benedict Option.

Chapter 6 asks about the role of conflict in politics and whether the understanding of common goods can accommodate the reality of conflict. Given the prevalence of conflict in social life, how do human communities succeed (when on rare occasions they do succeed) in managing their conflicts such that they do not erupt in violence? How do societies institutionalize the peaceful and peace-reinforcing handling of conflict? Understanding the political as a distinct form of rule, based on a commitment to manage conflict by talking, its conditions are elaborated. Among these conditions are persons, with character and virtue, and appropriate skill and knowledge, supported by relevant institutions. These common goods of persons, skills, knowledge, and institutions facilitate all our goods in common.

The argument to this point, following a clarification of the secular in chapter 3, the limited purposes of human-made law in chapter 4, and the nature of politics in chapters 5 and 6, requires of states that they recognize the limits to their competence, notably regarding common goods. The political common good is the set of conditions for individual and communal flourishing, while the more extensive common good of ultimate fulfillment exceeds the competence of the state. However, history provides many examples of states that have claimed for themselves the right not only to define the ultimate end of humankind but to impose it coercively on their members. The themes of utopia and apocalypse addressed in chapter 7 allow for an examination of the distortion of the political common good and an illustration of the lack of openness to the transcendent that conditions how some political leaders and institutions use their power. The espousal of a common good vision must be aware of the danger of succumbing to utopianism.

Where chapter 7 considers temptations of the state to overstep its competence, chapter 8 considers a possible objection that the church, in specifying the purpose of the state, is unjustifiably paternalistic. This challenge leads to a clarification about solidarity and what is entailed in working for the good of others. The meanings of "good for" and "the good of" are refined, such that greater precision in talking about common goods is attained. How medical practitioners, entrepreneurs, and politicians might justify their claims to serve the good of others and the common good is explored. Reliance on procedural correctness alone is not sufficient to ensure the justifiability of policies. The task of engaging in the evaluation of proposals and policies in terms of common goods cannot be avoided. In that evaluation, the two criteria of the common good—no exclusion of persons (solidarity) and no exclusion of dimensions of human good (subsidiarity)—are found to be relevant.

Fraught common goods of a humane economy and integral ecology provide the topic of chapter 9. In the book's argument to this point I take issue with authors who present the common good as a sectarian or ideological concept in a polarized debate in which liberalism is seen as the enemy. Here I defend the notion of "experiments in living" proposed by John Stuart Mill, which is pilloried by some critics. Showing the usefulness of this notion in challenging people and cultures to reflect on and learn from their experience, I apply this strategy in reviewing recent experiences with deregulation, one of the foremost policies of neoliberalism targeted by its critics. The experience underlines the necessity of some regulation and highlights the wisdom of Pope John Paul II's insistence that the free market needs to be constrained within a strong juridical system.

In chapter 10, attention is turned to some of the intangible common goods that have been mentioned in earlier chapters. Sandel's criticism of meritocracy highlights the distortions that can arise from an educational system, worsening social division and exacerbating inequality. This occasions the exploration of education as a private, club, public, and common good. Three authors are considered who in different ways underline the importance of character formation for politics. They do not argue that the state should take on itself the necessary moral formation, but that the state, in its own interests, should respect those agents in civil society—parents, families, churches, and organizations—that can and do provide for the formation of citizens.

An epilogue adds to the conclusion of chapter 10 with a brief summary of the book's argument and illustrates it with a reflection on the life and work of Ernst-Wolfgang Böckenförde. In his work as a jurist on Germany's constitutional court and in his publications, he exemplifies the Pope Benedict Option—namely, the spirited engagement with liberal institutions and liberal ideas from a Catholic standpoint with a view to facilitating a more adequate achievement of common goods.

CHAPTER 1

THREE LENSES TO VIEW COMMON GOODS

The revival of interest in the topic of the common good is due in no small measure to Alasdair MacIntyre. His combination of explanatory terms of practice, goods both external and internal, virtues, and tradition, developed in *After Virtue*, provides the intellectual resources for a provocative argument.[1] MacIntyre concludes that the common good, understood as the flourishing of a community that has developed its vision through a history of reflection and conversation, is only possible in a relatively small-scale local community. He gives examples of Scottish fishing communities, Irish cooperatives, weavers in Lancashire. Such communities value traditional skills and the persons who exhibit them, whose characters and virtues have been shaped by submission to standards of performance. Members of such communities are united in accepting standards of excellence and appreciating the goods that they make possible as pursued in their forms of life. The conceptions of those standards and goods are extended over time as persons achieve excellence, both in performance of their characteristic activity and in formation of character. MacIntyre asserts that such a concept of the common good is not achievable in a liberal democracy and that the forms of political community constructed around markets are inimical to the common good. In fact, he writes, the dynamics of the market and of bureaucratic government are the principal threats to the common good of such local small-scale communities as he describes.[2]

LIBERALISM AND COMMON GOODS: TWO OPPOSED VIEWS

The plausibility of his criticism of liberal democratic states appears in MacIntyre's analysis of the standard liberal rationale for the state. The state is explained as a necessary means for the delivery of certain essential goods and services such as security, and the protection of rights and liberties. The thinness of such a rationale leaves no grounds for the virtue of patriotism. Why should citizens risk their lives in defense of such an entity? As MacIntyre formulates it, it is like being asked to die for the telephone company![3]

It was because of such criticism of liberal analysis and liberal institutions that MacIntyre was frequently labeled a communitarian, giving priority to he social and the communal over the emphasis on individualism in liberal thought. However, he always rejected this label, denying that he was a communitarian.[4] The polarity in this debate, he thought, was on the question of the modern state: Was the state grounded on the interests of individuals whose consent was the source of legitimacy, or was the state ideally grounded on a preexisting community, whether formed around ethnic or religious bonds? MacIntyre rejected both positions, wanting to uphold an Aristotelian vision of political community.

I have learned a lot from MacIntyre and have found his radical stance challenging. However, I have often wondered how he could manage to reconcile this philosophical position with his Catholic allegiance. In the twentieth century, the social teaching of the church addresses citizens and politicians in modern states, challenging them to consider their responsibilities in terms of service of the common good. The assumption implicit in this teaching, expressed in the documents of the Second Vatican Council and in many papal encyclicals and speeches as well as publications by bishops' conferences, is that the modern liberal democratic state is obliged to serve the common good. *Should* implies *can*. Is it possible to integrate these two apparently contradictory propositions in a coherent vision? "The liberal state should serve the common good"; "The liberal state cannot possibly have a common good." MacIntyre himself has not resolved this tension explicitly, but I have tried to do so by relying on an understanding of the analogical use of such terms as "common good." The same term can be used in a range of different cases such that its meaning changes from case to case—not arbitrarily, but systematically. The challenge is to provide an account of that operative system grounding the varied uses of the same term. This challenge has motivated my previous publications on the topic of common good.[5]

The same problem is appearing again but in a new guise. The Catholic church's invoking of the common good in addressing economic and political issues suggests that the addressees, both individuals and institutions, not infrequently fail to live up to those normative demands. But to persist in preaching that the market, or the state, should serve the common good, the church must hold that what is prescribed is, in principle, possible. That it should be done implies that it can be done. If it is not doable in principle, there can be no obligation to attempt to do it.

One possible escape route is to suggest that the references to common good may be intended not as normative prescriptions but as criticisms exposing the inadequacies of modern institutions and their officers. Those inadequacies might not be the moral failure to do what can be done, and ought to be done, but has not been done; instead, the problem could be that the institutions and their officers are not appropriate for the proposed purpose. The criticism directed at the liberal state may be intended to show not that the liberal state fails to achieve what it ought to achieve—namely, the service of the common good—but that it is unable to do so because it is a completely inappropriate instrument for achieving that task. William Cavanaugh succinctly formulates this stance in the subtitle of one of his publications: "Why the Nation-State is Not the Keeper of the Common Good."[6] Sharing a platform at Trinity College in Dublin with both William Cavanaugh and Patrick Deneen addressing the role of the church in a pluralist society, I gradually came to realize what was at issue between us. I found their analysis of the malaise of contemporary liberal institutions persuasive. With regard to determining the facts, there was no disagreement between us. I could accept the point that instead of facilitating pluralism, the economic and political pressures in modern life tend toward homogenization and the elimination of difference. I could accept the direction of influence of optionality, that freedom is increasingly seen in terms of having consumerist choices. These pressures are analyzed as intrinsic to the liberal establishment in market and state, and that, too, is persuasive. The disagreement arises about whether these developments are inevitable or irreversible, and whether the modern state could function differently.[7]

The fear expressed by many critics of liberalism is that many ordinary people, including believers, accept the standards of the civil law as equivalent to the demands of morality; if it is legal, it is morally permissible. Where the legal standards establish a minimum and moral standards are taken from an appreciation of excellence, the discrepancy can be considerable. On issues such as the protection due human life, the separation of the legal and the moral can have enormous consequences, as in relation to abortion. Similarly, on other matters such as truth telling and fidelity, the same danger of subversion of high moral standards arises. The accommodation of many Christians to a culture of liberty, hedonism, and consumerism has resulted in a practical atheism whereby the God of Christian revelation is replaced in practice by the benefits of comfort and wealth.

The response to this situation embraced by some Christians is to opt out of the system. The opt-out pathway has been given the name of "the Benedict Option," and has a book with that title.[8] The idea was originally suggested by MacIntyre, who writes inspiringly of the common goods that are achievable in such communities: "What matters at this stage is the construction of local forms of community within which civility and the intellectual and moral life can be sustained through the dark ages which are already upon us."[9] He writes this at the end of his book *After Virtue*, reflecting on the depressing failures of socialism as exposed by Trotsky, suggesting the need to wait for a new St. Benedict. Patrick Deneen, despairing of the liberal establishment, also recommends the Benedict Option as an explicit strategy for citizens concerned with living faithful Christian lives amid the consumerism and dishonesty of modern circumstances.[10] The strategy is to build local small-scale communities that are united in practices that conform to the strictures of the Gospels. This should enable people to conduct a different style of life more in accord with the faith community's values than those of the surrounding culture. For long this has been a temptation for religious people, to seek to establish their preferred form of communal life away from the messy, sinful, and broken situations that are the products of our histories.

I do not deny the attractiveness of the vision of authentic living in community, nor do I deny the plausibility of MacIntyre's analysis of the common goods of practices. What I challenge is the implication that the Benedict Option or its equivalent is mandated (either required or encouraged) by the church's teaching on common goods. I also challenge the implication that the liberal democratic state cannot have a common good. I want to make a case for an engagement in liberal institutions for the sake of common goods, appropriately understood. I will attempt to explain the assumption in the church's position on common goods that the modern state could function differently, that it could be an instrument for common goods and not only a threat. In doing so, I hope to secure the traditional teaching from the misunderstanding that it essentially posits a radically alternative vision of economic and political matters. In other words, the intellectual resources from Catholic tradition should enable us to discover goods in common wherever humans and human communities cooperate. Finding the good in the midst of brokenness, fragility, and failure is a very different approach to one that identifies a polarity, an either-or, a binary of good and bad.

I want to present an account of common good and common goods that avoids unnecessary polarization with liberal political philosophy and that remains faithful to the tradition of Catholic reflection on political and social reality. The notion of common good is not confined to only one discipline, whether political philosophy, social ethics, moral theology, or the philosophy of law. There is a real danger of distortion if attention is restricted to only one narrow set of issues. That is why my approach encompasses theological, philosophical, and political aspects of the notion.

ARISTOTLE, GAUDIUM ET SPES, *AND POLITICAL LIBERALISM*

My topic is the goods that are, could be, or should be common. Common to you and me, common to all those with whom we actually or potentially cooperate, common to all humankind. Even beyond that, we could consider what is common to all beings, and beyond that, considering all beings as creatures, what is common to Creator and creature. The mention of Creator provokes a question: Is the discussion theological or philosophical? My intention is to argue both philosophically and theologically, but when writing theologically, I will not be assuming that readers have faith, that they share my Christian worldview. However, I will assume good will on their part, and the willingness to give a charitable interpretation of what they read. I will not expect them to agree with my position; my hope is to explain it so that readers can understand the arguments that are made and determine for themselves the extent to which they are persuaded by them.

Philosophically I draw on Aristotle, and many others who have learned from him. Aristotle is the outstanding philosopher of ethics and politics, whose questions and distinctions remain provocative and fruitful almost two and a half millennia since they were first voiced. If I invoke Aristotle, you will not be surprised if Plato before him, and Aquinas after him, get a mention. Aristotle's thought is my resource for reflecting on our contemporary experience. Perhaps you are surprised that Augustine is not immediately listed as a source. Admittedly, the burgeoning literature on political Augustinianism makes him an interesting figure for this topic, and in a separate chapter I will explain why I do not think it helpful to begin with his rich theological thought.

Theologically I draw on *Gaudium et spes*, the Pastoral Constitution on the Church Today, the influential declaration by the bishops of the Catholic church assembled at the Second Vatican Council in the 1960s. Subsequent papal encyclicals and declarations by bishops' conferences are also among my resources when thinking about common goods. Mostly I cite these sources from the Vatican website.

The third lens in my approach is political liberalism, and for this I find the work of John Rawls, among others, useful, even if not completely satisfactory.

The extensive literature provoked by his writings allows for amendments and developments of a liberal philosophical position suitable for my task.

Right at the beginning I place my cards on the table, acknowledging my standpoint and my sources. I hope to be transparent on these, and will have to return to this more personal acknowledgment at various points as my assumptions and commitments shape my argument. I am a Jesuit priest who takes seriously the intellectual heritage of the Catholic church in which the concept of "the common good" has a place. To understand the richness of this concept of common good I draw on Aristotle's practical philosophy, and to face the challenge of relevance to contemporary political and economic reality I elaborate a liberal stance.

Why Aristotle?

I seek a way of speaking about our experience without having to use the jargon or constructs of some theory or other. Aristotle seems to articulate the natural orientation of human reason undistorted by ideological positions. He believes that we can learn something about reality by attending to the way we spontaneously talk about things. So, for instance, his analysis of the four causes proceeds by attending to the use of the term in ordinary speech as well as to the use made of it by various thinkers. Aristotle's approach, which adverts to our ordinary, spontaneous way of speaking as disclosing the structure of reality, is attractive for equipping citizens in democratic regimes for the exercise of their responsibilities.

The mention of responsibilities provides another indication of why Aristotle is a useful guide. In both his *Ethics* and *Politics*, he challenges his students to take a stance on questions that will affect how they live and how they shape their lives. The classification of types of constitution in the *Politics*, for instance, is framed by the question of how each one would wish to live. An analysis of tyranny is offered, but not in the manner of a distanced, neutral observer. Instead, the question is posed whether one would prefer to live under a tyrannical regime, or in some other.[11] The theoretical analysis is for the sake of an existential, practical choice. Similarly, the question in the *Ethics* about the ultimate purpose of life is raised to help young Athenian men choose for themselves how they would wish to live, whether trapped by illusory promises of satisfaction, or critically aware of the limitations of what popularly passes for success in life.

The mention of young Athenian men warns us that Aristotle's thought is conditioned by his time and place. We must be aware of his limitations and be critical of the views he held. In this we can sometimes turn his own critical thought against him. Allowing for these reservations, Aristotle's empiricism, his attention to spontaneous speech, and his framing of study in a wider practical context make him useful for my approach to understanding common goods. An incidental benefit is that this pre-Christian philosopher writes about politics in terms of common goods, and so provides support in answering those who would dismiss talk of common goods as purely of Catholic interest, a sectarian concept. The notion of common good is not theological in origin, but philosophical, introduced by Aristotle in his *Politics*.

As Aristotle sees it, human action is always for some good, or something that is perceived to be good. The maker of flutes sees something worthwhile in the product, in enabling good and beautiful music and allowing the excellence of the performer to appear. Flute maker and flute player cooperate; they act together for a good in common. Note here that the understanding of cooperation as "acting together" is not to imply "at the same time" or "in the same place." The maker of the instrument must complete their task before the musician can perform. And yet the performance cannot take place unless there is an available instrument. Among the goods at stake in their activity is their own excellence and flourishing, even if they do not think about this. An excellent instrument and an excellent performance are complemented by the excellence of the flute maker and the well-being of the musician. Here we have a distinction between two meanings of the good that are related in Aristotle's view: the practical sense, as that objective of action that is pursued because it is considered good, and the good of the agent, who is fulfilled and perfected in the activity of pursuing worthwhile objectives. This is achieved without it necessarily being the direct intention of the agent. Aristotle is aware that there are many instances of cooperation and many organizations and institutions facilitating collaboration, whether business, sporting, cultural or religious, each of which has its distinctive activities oriented to its purpose, constituting common goods. There are as many common goods as there are forms of cooperation: "Since there are many actions, arts and sciences, it follows that their ends are many too—the end of medical science is health; of military science, victory; of economic science, wealth."[12]

For Aristotle, there is always the valid question of whether the good pursued by people collaborating is a genuine good, and whether it is truly for their good—that is, whether its achievement will accomplish their excellence or perfection. Aristotle always allows for the possibility that people can be mistaken about their good, both in what is worth pursuing and what is good for them as contributing to their fulfillment.

Aristotle's basic line is that just as all action is for some good (or perceived good), so all cooperation is for the sake of a good in common. "Common good" is not only or primarily designated in the singular as *the* common good. He introduces the singular, with definite article, when discussing *the* good for the sake of which the political community cooperates. Against the background of the Greek city-state such as Athens, he considers that the highest possible good of cooperation which best perfects the collaborators is the good achieved in politics. As the city is taken to represent the highest possible form of cooperation, so its good is taken to be the highest possible good. In other words, the highest possible achievement for humans, the most fulfilling accomplishments, and the best they can be and become, is as engaged citizens participating in the life of their city. We may not want to follow Aristotle in drawing this conclusion, and Christians will not, but his path to it is interesting.

Aristotle, in his analysis of any matter, takes his standard from the best case, whether an object of botany or zoology, or of ethics or politics. He explains that the nature of any kind of thing is to be read from its completion, or maturity—that stage of its existence when it has achieved what it is capable of being. So the seed or the sprouting plant are to be understood in terms of what they are on the way to becoming. It is similar with forms of cooperation. In the development of forms of human collaboration, the political is understood as that which can be the end of a process, a stage of self-sufficiency, at which nothing is lacking that might yet complete the development: "Whatever is the end-product of the perfecting process of any object, that we call its nature, that which man, house, household, or anything else aims at being. Moreover the aim and the end can only be that which is best, perfection; and self-sufficiency is both end and perfection."[13] In his short genealogy at the beginning of the *Politics* he describes a process of development of forms of human collaboration for common advantage, from the partnership of pairs (male and female, master and servant) to the formation of households, the emergence of villages, and associations of villages. At every level, the collaboration is for the sake of something worthwhile. The city/polis emerges when the collaboration is sufficiently sophisticated to provide the association with everything it needs to achieve the good life. There is nothing more to wish for. However, the household is not presented here as merely a stage in the evolution of the polis, as the caterpillar is a stage in the life cycle of the butterfly. He stresses this when considering the relationship between them. Aristotle makes this point relying on the distinction between life itself and the good life. He writes, "The final association, formed of several villages, is the city or state. For all practical purposes the process is now complete; self-sufficiency has been reached and so, while it started as a means of securing life itself, it is now in a position to secure the good life."[14] The household nurtures life on a daily and generational basis. The city pursues the good life. The "good life" is the notion Aristotle uses for that form of cooperation in which "nothing is lacking." The good life, realized in politics, is contrasted with life itself, which is secured in the household. There is a parallel distinction between necessity, the satisfaction of need, and liberty, freedom from necessity.

Aristotle here is echoing Plato in *The Republic*: the construction in thought of the best possible city faces the fact that people will not be content with merely having their physical needs satisfied. The discussion becomes polemical in agreeing that such a society would be no better than a city of pigs. Beyond necessities of life are the enrichments of culture and luxury, and people living together would also demand these. Aristotle's term for this more luxurious and cultured existence is "the good life," and he identifies this as "the" common good of the city. In trying to say what exactly constitutes the good life, Aristotle relies on a contrast with alternative views of politics. The political association is *more than* a set of nonaggression pacts, it is *more than* a mutual guarantee of rights, and it is *more than* a set of contracts for the exchange of goods and services, all possible forms of association recognized in his day. But what that "more" is, Aristotle does not explain in detail. However, he does provide some pointers which allow us to understand in outline what he means. He points out that communities based on nonaggression or mutual benefit in trade are not interested in fostering the character and virtue or well-being of the citizens of partner cities. "But a state is something more than an investment," he writes. "Its purpose is not merely to provide a living but to make a life that is worthwhile."[15] In a mature political community, the legislators in pursuing the common good would be primarily concerned about the development of citizens' characters and would make laws with the purpose of training the citizens in virtue. "But all who are concerned with lawful behaviour," he says, "must make it their business to have an eye to the goodness or badness of the citizens. It thus becomes evident that that which is genuinely and not just nominally called a state must concern itself with virtue."[16] By "virtue" Aristotle means the capacity for noble actions, excellence in the performance of distinctive human actions, among which he lists the activities of friendship and the doing of justice as a member of the citizen body. The notion of "the good life" is constructed by a process of expansion of the conception of the human good. "Always more than" points beyond what spontaneously comes to mind in specifying the purpose of social cooperation: wealth, security, and now an additional dimension of human well-being in terms of character and virtue, so that friendship, justice, and wisdom in ruling are realized. The good life, therefore, as the common good must be read as a *heuristic*, naming something aimed at that is not fully comprehended.

A heuristic is something we rely on to help and guide the process of discovery. It is like the symbols we use in mathematics when we say, "Let x be the unknown quantity" and construct equations that we work on to discover the value of x. Aristotle's "good life" names such a reality, which we are in the process of discovering, but the process is the common life we make together. Our life together is like a conversation we engage in but cannot say in advance where it will lead.

Aristotle had surveyed the constitutions known in his world, and he observed that the constitution of every city encapsulated some conception of the good, and of the good life. The basis for political community, he believed, was the sharing of a view of what was good and worthwhile, what was noble and just, and what was lawful. Without agreement on such fundamentals, an association of people would not constitute a political community. Just as we can hardly imagine a tennis club without a commitment by its members to the sport of tennis, Aristotle thought no one could conceive of a polis without agreement among its citizens about the shared vision of the good life. Harmony and agreement are at the heart of his account of the common good. Still, Aristotle concedes in the *Politics* that there are many possible conceptions of the good life, each with its own characteristic form of constitution and a corresponding criterion of justice. So, for instance, in oligarchy, the unifying vision regards the good life as a life devoted to the pursuit and enjoyment of wealth. In a city like Sparta, renowned for its military prowess, the characteristic virtues to be fostered in the citizenry were military virtues.[17]

Aristotle inquires of any constitution whether rule is exercised for the common good, the good of all, or only the good of the rulers. This allows him to distinguish between good and bad extremes. Rule by one for the common good is termed monarchy; rule by one in the interest of the ruler only is tyranny. Aristotle's objection to democracy as he understands the term is that it is rule by the many, the majority, in their own interests, and not in the interests of all. That is a very contemporary concern—the majority using their power for their own benefit and not for the good of the whole country.[18]

Even though it may not be possible to anticipate the preferred outcome of the conversation that is the pursuit of the good life, it must be possible to identify unacceptable results. Conversations that end in bullying or shouting down or the silencing of some contributors are unsatisfactory. Hence, it is possible to formulate two criteria for the common good, based on Aristotle's own distinctions. If the purpose of the political community is to be a *common* good, then it can only be such if it does not systematically exclude any individual or any group of persons from a fair share in the good for the sake of which they cooperate. This is the first criterion, modeled on Aristotle's concern that rule be for the good of all and not merely for the good of the rulers, whether one, few, or many. And if the ultimate purpose is to be a common *good*, then it can only be complete if it does not systematically exclude or denigrate any genuine dimension of the human good. Recall the additional meaning of the agent's good as not the object pursued but the fulfilment of the agent, as in the accomplishment of the flautist in the earlier example. This second criterion is modeled on Aristotle's evaluation of different constitutions in terms of their conceptions of human good, whether expansive or constricted. He relies on the phrase translated as "always more than" to identify the conception of the human good that will be satisfactory and comprehensive without being able to say exactly what it is. It is something striven for in political life; it would be more than a mutual guarantee of rights, a set of nonaggression pacts, or treaties to exchange goods and services. Pointing beyond suggests a *heuristic* understanding of the common good, the good life. That is, it names something that is only vaguely known, which has yet to be fully discovered but which would have to meet the two criteria.

The application of these two criteria is not intended so much to validate some version or candidate as a genuine common good; instead, their relevance is to guide the deliberation and conversation as proposed goods or visions of the good life are tested for their adequacy. The inability of any candidate to answer challenges couched in terms of the two exclusions would suggest that the proposed candidate could not qualify as satisfactory, and so would need to be corrected or qualified. Success in meeting the challenges as formulated at any particular place or time would not in itself guarantee the proposed candidate as a common good. Because even in applying the criteria we may be handicapped by limited awareness of the people affected or of the dimensions of the human good to be realized. Given the heuristic nature of the notion, and the fact that the search in history also involves correcting presuppositions and blind spots, it is conceivable that those formulating the challenges need to be made aware of the full range of groups affected by any proposal, or become attentive to some neglected dimension of human well-being. The criteria express the rationality of development and make sense of the self-corrective process of abandoning visions once considered justified.

Catholic Social Thought

Let us take an imaginative leap over millennia from the Athens of Aristotle to the Catholic church in the twentieth century. In both contexts we find mention of common goods. Could they possibly be speaking and writing about the same reality? MacIntyre warns against assuming that the same term in use in different contexts carries the same meaning. He illustrates the difficulties arising when the same term—in his case, "virtue"—is used in different senses in different situations.[19] Care must be taken also with the notion of "common good."

When the Catholic church in the mid-twentieth century writes and speaks of *the* common good, it does not refer to an ultimate or a highest good, as one might expect from Aristotle's coining of the phrase when discussing politics. Instead, it focuses on means and conditions. For the context of the collaborative shaping of common life, the authoritative instances in the church concentrate on the appropriate means for a decent human life and not on the ultimate ends of human life. This is a very important contrast, and relevant for clarifying many misunderstandings. Of course, the church does have a vision of the ultimate and highest good; it affirms its responsibility to preach the Gospel with a doctrine that points toward an ultimate end, but for this purpose it does not—any longer—use the language of common goods.

Pope John XXIII's encyclical letter *Mater et magistra* ("Mother and Teacher") (1961) writes of the common good to refer to the conditions and resources that would facilitate the achievement of a decent human life.[20] This usage is borrowed by the Second Vatican Council in *Gaudium et spes* (1965): "The common good embraces the sum total of all those conditions of social life which enable individuals, families, and organizations to achieve complete and effective fulfillment."[21] This shift of perspective is rooted in the recognition of the dignity of the human person, a dignity expressed both in theological terms as *imago Dei*, "bearing the divine image," and in philosophical terms as having both intelligence and freedom. Respect for that freedom motivates the caution in stressing the set of conditions for human fulfillment rather than the nature of human fulfillment itself. The council regards the pursuit of the full set of conditions that would enable persons and groups to flourish as the common economic, social, and political project of humankind. This extends across the full range of human activities and human aspirations. No list, however long, would be exhaustive, and that is not just because it is hard to think of everything. It is also because human ingenuity is constantly creating new possibilities and so new conditions, coming up with new fields of endeavor, new areas of scientific exploration, and new possibilities of medical and surgical intervention and care. Accordingly, the complete set of conditions for human flourishing, including economic, social, cultural, legal, political, international, and global, reveal how complex the challenge is. And in each of these areas we can expect lively debate about what needs to be done.

In the mid-twentieth century the church saw the need to move from a defensive and fearful stance to a more positive engagement with the world. The council wanted to address all people—not just believers in Christ, or in

God, but everyone, including atheists. Hence the recognition that while these addressees would not all share the same ultimate vision, they might nonetheless be able to agree on what conditions and resources would help people achieve their vision of the good life, whatever it might be. Here we see the council's opening to the world: the desire to have a basis for cooperation with people of goodwill who might not share in the church's ultimate convictions but could still be partners in working for human development.

One such debate about human development concerns workers. Since the engagement of Pope Leo XIII with the phenomenon of modern capitalist economic systems in *Rerum novarum* (1891), the popes have repeatedly insisted that human work should not be treated just as a factor of production with a cost, a cost which employers are constantly motivated to minimize. Culminating in the letter of Pope John Paul II explicitly devoted to the topic of work, *Laborem exercens* ("On Human Work") (1981), the popes have maintained a constant insistence that work and the status of the worker is at the heart of the social question.[22]

Concern for workers demands solidarity. Pope John Paul II writes in his encyclical letter *Sollicitudo rei socialis*, ("On Social Concern") (1987) that solidarity "is not a feeling of vague compassion or shallow distress at the misfortunes of so many people, both near and far. On the contrary, it is a firm and persevering determination to commit oneself to the common good; that is to say to the good of all and of each individual, because we are all really responsible for all."[23] Pope John Paul is clear about the need on the part of the church and all Christians for a firm commitment to changing the circumstances that deprive people of their humanity and deny them the prospect of a decent life. In the Catholic tradition of upholding the common good, the focus can be directly on those groups that are vulnerable to exploitation or discrimination. Hence the adoption of the language of "the preferential option for the poor." The church wants to place itself at the side of those who are victims, who suffer, who bear a disproportionate burden either because of natural catastrophe or human irresponsibility.

Solidarity is paired with another important principle related to the common good—namely, subsidiarity. The principle of subsidiarity insists that assistance motivated by solidarity should not replace the efforts of recipients themselves to address their problems and find solutions. It entails a willingness to help, with an expectation that those being helped take responsibility to find and implement their own solutions to their problems. In a hierarchically structured governance system, the principle of subsidiarity requires that the higher-level authorities assist but do not replace those operating on the ground. This is opposed to all centralizing tendencies that are inclined to draw all power to the center of institutions or organizations, depriving the so-called grass roots of opportunities to manage their own affairs. Of course, it should also apply to the church itself. So, we can understand what Pope Francis is trying to do with his emphasis on synodality as the implementation of this vision of subsidiarity.

It is also Pope Benedict's vision. In his 2009 encyclical letter, *Caritas in veritate* ("Love in Truth"), Benedict writes, "*The principle of subsidiarity must remain closely linked to the principle of solidarity and vice versa,* since the former without the latter gives way to social privatism, while the latter without the former gives way to paternalist social assistance that is demeaning to those in need."[24] By "social privatism" Benedict means the attitude that everyone should be left alone to mind their own business, and by its opposite, "paternalistic social assistance," he means the paternalistic attitude of acting on the assumption that one knows what is best for others. This statement is made originally in the context of reflection on international development aid. There are two important values which are to be respected, and disregard of one in favor of the other can lead to distorting or objectionable outcomes.

Political Liberalism

The selected aspects of common goods are viewed through the three lenses of Aristotelian philosophy, Catholic social thought, and political liberalism. With this last lens, political liberalism, I draw on the philosophy of John Rawls, who has a famous book with that title. John Rawls has effectively set the agenda for my discipline of political philosophy throughout my working life. His *A Theory of Justice* appeared in 1971 when I was an undergraduate, though at that time studying economics and geography. It still set the agenda ten years later in 1981, when I was writing my doctorate in Innsbruck on the philosophy of justice. His later writings, *Political Liberalism* (1993, 1996) and *The Law of Peoples* (1999), were targets of my attention in my books on the common good in 2008 (*A Grammar*) and 2015 (*Global Common Goods*). I was stimulated by his thought, but mostly I was critical. Like the Irish police officer who said to a tourist lost in the west of Ireland, "If I were going to Dublin, I wouldn't start from here," I had questions about his starting point. I am critical of Rawls, but at the same time I was not and am not in agreement with many of his better-known critics, Michael Sandel among them.[25]

My task is to present and defend a philosophical and theological account of common good that is consistent with the position espoused by the Catholic church, but that, I fear, is in danger of distortion at present. The possibility of distortion arises because of a polemical stance being taken, whether against meritocracy (Michael Sandel), ethical pluralism (Jonathan Sacks), or liberalism (Patrick Deneen). These authors share one thing in their varied concerns: they invoke the common good as naming an alternative to their targeted opponent. This is a crude summary, already sketched in the Introduction, but it sets the agenda for the argument to be presented in the following chapters.

Right at the beginning I can formulate a question that will be addressed more fully in chapter 5—namely, is liberalism the enemy? If I am committed to the common good, may I not also be a liberal? As a Catholic, endorsing the church's position on the common good and common goods, I want to affirm that I am philosophically and politically liberal. Central to my approach is a positive evaluation of liberalism, understood as a tradition of thought about how societies should be governed that is predicated on the centrality of human freedom. And human freedom is a fundamental good, and any form of government that respects and promotes and facilitates human freedom is capable of being a common good, a good in common pursued together by all who work to construct and maintain structures of legal and political order. The strategy is not to accuse liberalism of lacking something, but to draw attention to what is already operative in the liberal perspective at its best, its grasp and valuing of what is humanly important—namely, persons' dignity and freedom.

Many of the authors I am reacting to are critical of liberalism as the dominant orthodoxy of political regimes, and neoliberalism in economics. I am mostly in agreement with them on the problems they identify, but my difficulties with their critiques are philosophical. Some authors challenge John Rawls's thought, taking him to be a representative of contemporary liberalism. One such critic is a fellow Jesuit, William R. O'Neill, whose 2021 book *Reimagining Human Rights: Religion and the Common Good* is critical of Rawls.[26] It is understandable that many see Rawls as a defendant—or worse, a creator of contemporary liberal regimes or neoliberal policies. I think it a mistake to take his thought as a presentation of the self-understanding of liberal regimes. Yes, he is a liberal, because he values liberty, and assumes that people would want their government to protect their liberties. But he has not shaped his country's constitution or system; he has inherited it and has attempted to resolve philosophical problems that arise when its difficulties are considered. As I see it, Rawls addresses the very same difficulty that many of his more recent critics face when they consider the actual political and economic situation. The United States is very divided. Democrats and Republicans seem poles apart on so many issues. They seem to take opposed stances on many practical matters, and what is more, they can mobilize sophisticated philosophical theories to support their practical interests. How does one find common ground in this situation, where even the common ground of philosophical reason is contested territory, as MacIntyre has so well documented?[27] Rawls should be understood as seeing the same divisiveness that the late Jonathan Sacks so eloquently describes in his book *Morality* and with which he attempts to find common ground through his approach. Rawls invites partisan listeners and readers to attempt to step back from their practical and theoretical commitments, and to consider how a social and political order could be constructed if no one were able to insist on their demands. The hypothetical constructs of *A Theory of Justice* and its follow-up, *Political Liberalism*, have been roundly and properly critiqued. But the basic concern driving these works is the attempt to find common ground in a furiously contested political context. William R. O'Neill is attempting something similar.

The long-running dispute between so-called liberalism and communitarianism largely instigated by Michael Sandel's attack on the unencumbered individual posited in Rawls's hypothetical contract in *A Theory of Justice* finally ran out of steam.[28] Many of those labeled as communitarians, such as Alasdair MacIntyre, refused the label; the thing in common on that side of the debate was their opponent, Rawls. And his account of the human chooser in the hypothetical original position was not intended to be a description of the human person, nor a phenomenology of choice, nor an ontology. I would want to defend Rawls and other liberal thinkers, not in terms of what they have achieved but in terms of what they have tried to do. And I want to make the case that what they have tried to do is very much in the cause of trying to find common ground in a very divided and polarized situation, and that I consider a common good.

The question posed is how the Catholic tradition of understanding political reality in terms of common goods might be compatible with a political liberalism. This is a challenge that must be met if a liberal Catholic voice is to be maintained and upheld against the tendency to resort to a right-wing conservatism as the only defensible position for a Catholic citizen. A plausible, defensible, and attractive account of a politics of the common good must be offered to meet the interest of the many people who are attracted by the distinctiveness, clarity, and seeming moral purity of the position embraced by the critics. That is what I attempt in this book.

As I see the issue, the challenge to Christians in a liberal democracy is to hold in tension the following propositions:

1. First, our faith conviction that all humans have offered to them an ultimate common good, or highest good, that is God, and the beatitude of life in God in the Resurrection.

2. Second, the facts that
   - the members of our political community do not all accept that there is or even could be a common ultimate purpose;
   - if we do think there is a common purpose, we do not all agree on what it is; and
   - if we do agree on what it is, we do not all agree on its implications for practical life.
3. Third, in the context of this plurality, we face the challenge to make and conduct a common life seeking peace, prosperity, and justice according to law.

Political liberalism as sketched by John Rawls provides a convenient philosophical apparatus for appreciating what is at stake.[29] This model appears satisfactory from a Catholic perspective because of how it sees the relationship between comprehensive doctrines and political institutions. Of course, political liberalism is an "ism," a body of thought, and it is not identifiable with any actual liberal regime. The attractive elements in Rawls's thought for the Catholic standpoint include the following:

1. No single worldview or comprehensive doctrine should dominate the political arena. Not only religious worldviews but also purely secular philosophies—such as a comprehensive or doctrinaire liberalism, secularism, and humanism—are denied dominance. Whatever arguments might be made on their behalf, they do not justify domination of the public arena.[30]
2. That arena must be equally accessible to representatives of all reasonable comprehensive doctrines, each worldview needing to find its own reasons in terms of its basic commitments and values for endorsing the political account of justice articulated within the public forum.[31]
3. Candidates for the political conception of justice can be proposed for agreement between participants. Rawls insists that there are many possible political conceptions of justice and so many forms of public reason. The *Theory of Justice* account is no longer proposed by Rawls as the best candidate, but only one among others. "There are many liberalisms and related views," he writes, "and therefore many forms of public reason specified by a family of reasonable political conceptions. Of these, justice as fairness, whatever its merits, is but one."[32] Rawls later includes within the set of possible political conceptions "Catholic views of the common good and solidarity when they are

expressed in terms of political values."³³ He also includes Habermas's discourse conception of legitimacy. Important in this quoted passage is the qualification about expression in terms of political values.

4. Espousal of the limited political notion of liberal justice for use within the restricted public space does not preclude holding a more comprehensive vision of justice, the good, and ultimate human fulfillment. Rawls agrees with David Hollenbach about the desirability of debate about ultimate ends, although this will not take place within the institutions of government. "It can occur," Hollenbach writes, "wherever thoughtful men and women bring their beliefs on the meaning of the good life into intelligent and critical understandings of this good held by other peoples with other traditions. It short, it occurs wherever education about and serious inquiry into the meaning of the good life takes place."³⁴

5. The constructivist approach to political order does not prevent one from holding a realist ontological account of ultimate goods and ends. As I have argued elsewhere, the process of construction can also be a process of discovery, as people learn from experience what best suits human needs and human aspirations, what is really in their interest and for their good.³⁵

6. This model allows, therefore, for an analogical account of common goods, one that can embrace the ultimate goods affirmed in the comprehensive doctrine and the limited goods in common that are the means and conditions for human fulfillment both individual and communal. At the same time, it allows for those institutions and meanings generated in the public arena to be analyzed and valued as common goods of political cooperation. We will return to the topic of analogy in chapter 4.

CONCLUSION

Drawing together the three lenses, we can project a kaleidoscope of rich interactions and overlaps, identifying similarities and differences revealed by the three lenses.

First, the differences: Aristotle stresses the hierarchy, the ultimacy and primacy of the good life, the highest good as the common good of the highest form of cooperation—namely, politics. Catholic social thought uses common goods to speak not of the ultimate end but of the means and conditions for the pursuit of ultimate ends—human fulfillment, both individual and communal. Where Aristotle is all-encompassing in his approach, the church's social perspective is confined to what can be common ground.

Second, the similarities: both Aristotle and Catholic thought are programmatic rather than substantive in their specification of common goods. I use the label *heuristic* to qualify the kind of concept that is generated. Both rely on operative criteria for determining whether any particular instance is in fact a genuine common good. And the criteria they generate exhibit remarkable parallels. Aristotle's "no person or group excluded" parallels the church's understanding of solidarity; Aristotle's "no dimension of human good excluded" parallels the principle of subsidiarity. While the parallels can be drawn to highlight the similarities between the Aristotelian and Catholic views, the differences remain to remind us that they are not completely identical.

With Aristotle we can understand cooperation in terms of goods in common. We can understand also why he might imagine the highest possible good in common that would be the purpose of the most developed form of human cooperation. A heuristic concept or ideal could name the goal of that cooperation that lacked nothing, that was completely self-sufficient. With the Catholic sources we can appreciate the reluctance to seek agreement in terms of such an ideal in a context in which people are divided on ultimate goods and the purpose of human existence. The church authorities seek common ground with those who are of a different persuasion about ultimate ends, so that a basis for cooperation for the sake of humanity can be found.

The church at the Second Vatican Council accepted the factual reality of plurality and diversity. It attempted to address this situation without succumbing to the relativism that would consider the Catholic worldview as one possible perspective, equally valid with others. It wanted to hold on to its mission to serve the truth of the Gospel while finding a basis of collaboration with others of different fundamental convictions.

The following chapters will attempt to explain and defend this vision, drawing from Catholic thought and relying on Aristotle's practical philosophy, and structured on the model of political liberalism as sketched by Rawls. Philosophical, political, and theological arguments will be adduced to make the case. This is a difficult and complex stance to manage, and it is not well served by slogans or shibboleths. The task of this project is to rescue Christians and other people of faith from simplistic sloganeering relying on "communitarianism" or "common good" versus liberalism when considering how to read the signs of the times, and how to analyze what is going on in cultural and political life. Of course, this will always be disputed terrain, and I do not expect to find complete agreement. However, I do hope to provide some resources so that citizens who wish to invoke a Catholic intellectual tradition will have sophisticated tools at their disposal and won't be easily dismissed as foolish or naïve. Those resources must be intelligible, and accessible to other citizens also. In the next chapter I explore more closely what we can take from Aristotle for our modern situation.

NOTES

1. Alasdair MacIntyre, *After Virtue: A Study in Moral Theory*, 2nd ed. (Notre Dame, IN: University of Notre Dame Press, 1984).
2. Alasdair MacIntyre, "Three Perspectives on Marxism: 1953, 1968, 1995," in *Ethics and Politics: Selected Essays*, vol. 2 (Cambridge: Cambridge University Press, 2006), 156; see also his more extensive elaboration of common goods in Alasdair MacIntyre, *Ethics in the Conflicts of Modernity: An Essay on Desire, Practical Reasoning, and Narrative* (Cambridge: Cambridge University Press, 2016), 176–83.
3. Alasdair MacIntyre, "A Partial Response to My Critics," in *After MacIntyre*, ed. John Horton and Susan Mendus (Oxford: Polity, 1994), 303.
4. Adam Swift, *Political Philosophy: A Beginner's Guide for Students and Politicians* (Cambridge: Polity, 2001), 134–35.
5. Patrick Riordan, *A Grammar of the Common Good* (London: Continuum, 2008); *Global Ethics and Global Common Goods* (London: Bloomsbury, 2015).
6. William T. Cavanaugh, "Killing for the Telephone Company: Why the Nation-State is Not the Keeper of the Common Good," in *In Search of the Common Good*, ed. Patrick D. Miller and Dennis P. McCann (New York: T&T Clark, 2005).
7. My contribution, "The Secular is not Scary," was published along with theirs in *The Church in Pluralist Society: Social and Political Roles*, ed. Cornelius J. Casey and Fáinche Ryan (Notre Dame, IN: University of Notre Dame Press, 2019).
8. Rod Dreher, *The Benedict Option: A Strategy for Christians in a Post-Christian Nation* (New York: Sentinel, 2017).
9. MacIntyre, *After Virtue*, 162.
10. Patrick Deneen, *Why Liberalism Failed* (New Haven, CT: Yale University Press, 2018), 191.
11. Aristotle, *Politics*, trans. T. A. Sinclair (Harmondsworth, UK: Penguin, 1962), bk. 7, c. 2.
12. Aristotle, *Ethics*, trans. J. A. K. Thompson (Harmondsworth, UK: Penguin, 1981), bk. 1, c. 1.
13. Aristotle, *Politics*, bk. 1, c. 2.
14. Aristotle.
15. Aristotle, bk. 3, c. 9.
16. Aristotle.
17. This treatment of different constitutions is a riff on Plato's dramatic presentation in the *Republic*, in which the different constitutions are represented by the characters of the dialogue, with Cephalus representing oligarchy, Polemarchus representing democracy, Thrasymachus depicting tyranny, and the brothers of Plato, Glaucon, and Adeimantus, representing a form of aristocracy based on the military virtues of honor and status.
18. Aristotle, *Politics*, bk. 3, c. 7.
19. MacIntyre, *After Virtue*.

20. Pope John XXIII, *Mater et magistra*, "Mother and Teacher," 1961, https://www.vatican.va/content/john-xxiii/en/encyclicals/documents/hf_j-xxiii_enc_15051961_mater.html.
21. Second Vatican Council, *Gaudium et spes*, Pastoral Constitution on the Church Today, §74, 1965, https://www.vatican.va/archive/hist_councils/ii_vatican_council/documents/vat-ii_cons_19651207_gaudium-et-spes_en.html.
22. Pope John Paul II, *Laborem Exercens* [On human work], 1981, https://www.vatican.va/content/john-paul-ii/en/encyclicals/documents/hf_jp-ii_enc_14091981_laborem-exercens.html.
23. Pope John Paul II, *Sollicitudo rei socialis*, "On Social Concern," §38, 1987, https://www.vatican.va/content/john-paul-ii/en/encyclicals/documents/hf_jp-ii_enc_30121987_sollicitudo-rei-socialis.html.
24. Pope Benedict XVI, *Caritas in veritate*, "Love in Truth," §58, 2009, http://w2.vatican.va/content/benedict-xvi/en/encyclicals/documents/hf_ben-xvi_enc_20090629_caritas-in-veritate.html, emphasis in original.
25. Michael Sandel, *Liberalism and the Limits of Justice* (Cambridge: Cambridge University Press, 1982).
26. William R. O'Neill, *Reimagining Human Rights: Religion and the Common Good* (Washington, DC: Georgetown University Press, 2021).
27. Alasdair MacIntyre, the trilogy of *After Virtue; Whose Justice? Which Rationality?* (London: Duckworth, 1988); and *Three Rival Versions of Moral Enquiry: Encyclopaedia, Genealogy, and Tradition* (London: Duckworth, 1990).
28. Charles Taylor, "Cross-Purposes: The Liberal-Communitarian Debate," in *Philosophical Arguments* (Cambridge, MA: Harvard University Press, 1995); Swift, *Political Philosophy*, 134.
29. John Rawls, *Political Liberalism* (New York: Columbia University Press, 1996).
30. Rawls, *Political Liberalism*, 11–15, 154–58.
31. Rawls, *Political Liberalism*, 134.
32. John Rawls, "The Idea of Public Reason Revisited," in *The Law of Peoples* (Cambridge, MA: Harvard University Press, 1999), 141–42.
33. Rawls, "Idea," 142.
34. Rawls, "Idea," 134–35, citing David Hollenbach, "Civil Society: Beyond the Public-Private Dichotomy," *Responsive Community* 5 (Winter 1994–95): 22.
35. Riordan, *A Grammar*, 94–99.

CHAPTER 2

ARISTOTLE RECONSTRUCTED

Critics of the political-cultural situation of modernity identify a polarization that is persistent and even endemic. Many who write about the common good locate it as one pole in a juxtaposition. Their various proposals provoke the following questions: If the analysis of division is correct, and if the common good is identified with one pole in the division, how can it be a solution to the polarization as such to opt for one pole over the other? If Aristotle is identified with the common good, how can he help us to understand the opposing position? Since I rely on Aristotle for my analysis of contemporary politics, I will have to present a different account of his understanding of the common good than that typically invoked by the authors cited in the Introduction. This I attempt in this chapter.

Can we seriously expect Aristotle to have something useful to contribute to understanding the reality of politics today? Aristotle would seem to belong to a world that is long past, and his relevance to the world of today needs to be defended. The task is to generate a theoretical account that helps us make sense of our experience. I am not attempting to develop a practical stance on the basis of which citizens, politicians, or parties might campaign, offering voters a program for government, or a policy or set of policies relying on common goods as slogans. I concentrate instead on presenting an account of common goods that can be at the heart of a theoretical understanding of political affairs that might eventually ground a more practical stance. Aristotle is useful for this purpose.

Aristotle advises that the study of anything should begin with phenomena that seem to exemplify the object of study at its best, at its most-mature and most-developed stage, healthy and functioning well.[1] That approach requires an evaluative judgment about what is mature and well-functioning. The authors cited earlier, in the Introduction and chapter 1, offer a chorus of criticism of political institutions and practices as poorly functioning, distorted, and undeveloped. Taking examples from Western liberal democratic states as mature objects for study would beg the question. A preliminary remark will perhaps justify proceeding with an Aristotelian analysis even though the selection of the objects for study still needs to be justified.

I take as the "normal" case the way in which a society has articulated itself for action by developing institutions of a state, with ways of governing that include making, adjudicating, and enforcing law. It will also have institutions to secure and defend itself. Given the dimensions of power created by such institutions, the society will have developed means for the allocation of power and its limitation and removal, since conflict about power—who is to have it and how it is to be used—will be unavoidable. A useful lens for understanding what is at stake is to survey such an introductory account of the rule of law as presented by Tom Bingham.[2] Crises and problems occasioned by the abuse of power have provoked reaction and led to the securing of liberties and rights in law. We may be familiar with these elements in the liberal democratic states of the Northern Hemisphere and the so-called West. While we may draw on these states as useful examples for study of the nature of politics, none of them is perfect; while they may represent an advanced stage of development, I do not claim that they have achieved maturity or perfection.[3] At least on the issue of the allocation of power, its limitation, and removal from power, there is a possibility of generating a scale of development. Commentators have done so, such that instances of failed states can be identified: "Failed states," writes Rosa Ehrenreich Brooks, "... lose control over the means of violence, and cannot create peace or stability for their populations or control their territories. They cannot ensure economic growth or any reasonable distribution of social goods: They are often characterized by massive economic inequities, warlordism, and violent competition for resources."[4] Where the allocation of power or removal from power is uncertain, populations lack the security required for a decent human existence. The circumstances on which I base my analysis are not such as those in weak or failed states, but in which there is assurance about the location and responsibilities of power. That still allows a wide range of cases to which we might apply an Aristotelian analysis.

What are the aspects of contemporary politics on which Aristotle can help us? It may be more revealing to identify the dimensions of political experience on which Aristotle seems out of date and irrelevant. I focus here on three such aspects: conflict instead of harmony, a minimal agreement instead of a comprehensive moral vision, and concentration on rights instead of an account of the good.

LEARNING FROM ARISTOTLE

The language of common goods is borrowed from Aristotle and so is not the property of any church or faith community. But even if Aristotle precedes Christianity, is he not committed to a comprehensive doctrine of human fulfillment? And besides, isn't his comprehensive vision irrelevant to modern circumstances, in which conflict and difference instead of harmony and unity characterize political existence? Are not the differences such as to make Aristotle's thought irrelevant for our twenty-first century concerns? Since these are valid questions, Aristotle might not be the philosopher of choice to guide a citizen or politician who must engage in an explicitly secular public arena.

There is no denying the major differences between the polis as Aristotle understood it, and a modern liberal democratic state. Three are significant. First, Aristotle thought that it was a shared view of the good understood as a vision of fulfilment that constituted political community: "Our own observation tells us that every state is an association of persons formed with a view to some good purpose. I say 'good' because in their actions all [people] do in fact aim at what they think good."[5] What is claimed for our modern states is something quite different, if not opposed to it—namely, that the state's rationale is to manage conflict between adherents of different visions of the good life. Conflict and diversity characterize our modern states, not harmony and shared moral vision.

Second, Aristotle thought that the primary concern of the lawmakers in the polis would be the moral excellence of the citizens, because it was precisely the concern for the goodness and moral well-being of the citizens that made a community political in the full sense, and not simply a commercial or military undertaking: "All who are concerned with lawful behavior must make it their business to have an eye to the goodness or badness of the citizens."[6] Our modern states abjure any such moral task and confine themselves to the enforcement of a minimum, as required to ensure order and security. Modern lawmakers would reject any suggestion that their concern should be to make people good. They would more likely follow John Stuart Mill's "harm principle" and insist that state power should not be used to restrict human liberty except where the exercise of that liberty involves harm to others.[7]

Third, Aristotle's language is teleological, in contrast to the contemporary reliance on the language of rights. Aristotle understood human nature as oriented to a completion or fulfillment.[8] It followed from this that he took as a standard of action the best that could be done or achieved, in much the same way that athletes today would measure their performance against the established records, or at least against their personal best. The language of contemporary politics is based on rights, as limits on what states may do to citizens, and not on the good or the best achieved so far.

What should follow from this consideration of the three major differences: conflict as opposed to harmony, avoidance of harm and not promotion of moral excellence, and securing rights instead of facilitating fulfillment? One conclusion is to withdraw all Aristotelian endorsement from the modern state and deny that it could ever be the locus of rational approval or loyalty in Aristotelian terms. On such an account, the modern state could not possibly be the agent of the Aristotelian common good as the highest good embracing all other goods, as MacIntyre and others cogently argue. Alternatively, I suggest that the three points of contrast can be reworked to allow for an Aristotelian-style reading of our current situation without abandoning the sources of critique. But first it is necessary to consider what Aristotle says.

Aristotle: Key Ideas

Some preliminary remarks about Aristotle will help situate the discussion. I want to take him at his word in what he says in several key passages. The first is the remark early in the *Politics* that it is the sharing of a view of what is good and evil, right and wrong, just and unjust, that makes a household or a political community. Aristotle insists that shared meaning is essential to the existence of a political entity. And because shared meaning is so essential to political existence, Aristotle also remarks on the capacity for reasoned speech as the distinctive human capacity equipping the human for politics.[9] That capacity is exercised by participation in any manner of deliberation about what is beneficial or harmful, just or unjust. Deliberation may be ongoing, but it is oriented toward getting some answers, and adequate answers would be part of the common good of those engaged in the deliberation, the members of the polity. This is also implied, in part, by a second remark from Aristotle that I want to take seriously, which is that as all action is for the sake of some good, so, too, all action in common—cooperation—is for the sake of some good.[10] This needs to be qualified slightly by Aristotle's own remark, allowing for the possibility of error, that people act and cooperate for the sake of something that is thought to be good. And thirdly, we should take Aristotle at his word when he reminds us that it is not always the same good that is pursued in these forms of cooperation. The variety of human activities structured in arts and sciences has a corresponding variety of goods as their ends, as noted in chapter 1. The *oikos*, the household, has its own common good, different from that of the polis, the city. However, they are related in that the end of the city, the good life, is unattainable unless the purpose of the household, life itself, is already secure.

We are familiar from our experience with the myriad forms of cooperation, including political cooperation. What are the goods that are pursued in common in all these forms of cooperation? What are the shared views of those goods, the shared meaning that sustains the collaboration? And how might we engage in the reflection on that meaning along with the other participants, so that we pursue only truly valuable goods? Considering Aristotle's point about sharing a view of the good, is talk of the common good to be confined to communities of such a scale that all the participants can deliberate about their own goods in common? In other words, can a liberal democratic state with a market economy have a common good? Is it only the small-scale community, such as the Greek city-state with its restrictions on citizenship, that can realize the ideal?[11] As we have noted, MacIntyre reads Aristotle as saying as much, but his texts also provide resources for considering the common good of polities that fail to measure up to the highest standards. The nonideal cases do not appear in his examination *only* as examples of defect or deviance from the best-case scenario, although they are definitely that. They also can be analyzed as instances of cooperation in the pursuit of a good in common. I will take Aristotle at his word when he says that "*every* polis is an association of persons formed with a view to some good purpose."[12] Among the good purposes that Aristotle identified we can recognize themes that today figure in the analyses of political scientists. Security, the freedom from danger ambitioned by mutual nonaggression pacts, and prosperity, as achieved by treaties ensuring trade in goods and services, were as familiar to Aristotle as they are to us. But he thought that politics in the fullest sense would comprise something more. As noted in the previous chapter, his analysis is expansive rather than reductive. The horizon of the good is not confined to what is already achieved but is open to further accomplishment.

RECONSTRUCTING ARISTOTLE'S PROPOSITIONS

Even if we accept that the modern state is very different from the ideal polis envisaged by Aristotle and analyzed in books seven and eight of the *Politics*, it does not follow that we must abandon any investigation of the goods in common that are pursued and ought to be pursued in the forms of cooperation we now label political. In line with Aristotle's own usage, we should not confine talk of common goods to the best case. His generalization in the opening words of the *Politics* applies to all instances of cooperation and community—that all pursue some good, or something which appears to them to be good. We should be able to identify goods in common even in deficient and restricted instances of cooperation. Bernard Yack has convincingly made the case that Aristotle was concerned with the possibilities of achieving justice and virtue even in imperfect cities.[13] Imperfect cities are characterized by conflict and disagreement about the human good. Zoli Filotas considers the distinctive source of conflict that would arise in imperfect cities. The best forms of rule are those in which the very best people have charge of the city. Were an exceptional and outstanding individual to be found, then he (Aristotle's presupposition) should rule in a monarchy; a virtuous elite should rule in an aristocracy. The difficulty in imperfect regimes is that the citizens are more or less equal, and they are unable to agree on who among them is the more virtuous and therefore deserving of honors. Of Aristotle, Filotas writes, "Hierarchical rule is best, he says, just when the person ruled finds the superiority of the ruler 'to be evident and indisputable.' . . . When it comes to free adult men in the Greece of his time, Aristotle is clear that hardly anyone can be expected to agree with his neighbors about who is better than whom."[14] The evil of factionalism arises when people think that they are better and more deserving than others but that they are not given the honors to which they believe themselves entitled. "Cities whose members cannot agree about each other's worth," writes Filotas, "are powder kegs, prone to faction and then collapse, and Aristotle assumes this is disastrous for everyone, even people who would in principle have been better off under some other regime."[15] And so Aristotle advocates a form of rule in which people take turns in holding office. Acceptance of this, predicated on an asserted equality of citizens, is what Aristotle recommends to the young men who are his students: "Aristotle emphasizes the contrast between the arrangement that would be best if we could achieve it—uninterrupted rule by political experts—and the alternative practice that we must fall back on, granted our imperfect conditions."[16]

It is evident, then, that the tools of common good analysis can facilitate appreciation of the real good to be found in the cooperation among citizens of imperfect polities. At the same time, with an account of the best city available, it can identify and critique the relevant restrictions and deficiencies in actual polities. Hence the importance of not accepting the prescription that talk of the common good be confined to the best case or ideal, an implicit prescription in MacIntyre's approach and that of some of his followers.

First Divergence

Returning to the three major differences noted earlier, I will show that, far from being irrelevant to modern politics, Aristotle's thought illuminates what is going on in terms of the common goods of cooperation among the participants, citizens, and officials within democratic states. The first difference contrasts the reality of conflict with the harmony of agreement on what is good and just. However, even if we accept that government in liberal democracies is predicated on conflict, it does not follow that an Aristotelian analysis is irrelevant. To the extent that the conflict we encounter is managed politically—that is, by means that rely on talking and reasoning—the process of politics can be understood as oriented to attaining agreement on what is good, just, and lawful, even though that agreement and harmony is still a long way off.[17] One perennial basic conflict is the competition for power: power needed if one is to pursue any good policy. To the extent that majorities and powerful interests accept the obligation to allow minorities to have their say, to provide reasons to the defeated why the chosen policy is not unjust, and to respect constitutionally protected rights, their position in power is not purely coercive domination.[18] The acceptance of certain limits—the rule of law, constitutional constraints on power, and the myriad requirements concerning transparency and accountability—reflect a considerable degree of agreement about the manner in which conflict is to be handled. The extent of the good on which we already agree is not as broad as Aristotle would have ambitioned, but it is nonetheless a considerable achievement arising from a history of trial and error, of crises and problems. Adrian Vermeule makes a similar point about the tradition of understanding the purpose of law in terms of *Ragion di Stato*, seeing peace, justice, and prosperity as the goods to be achieved in law.[19] The historical development of the elements of the rule of law shows how solutions were developed to prevent the recurrence of problems already encountered.[20] Operative in this history is a vision of what is just and what is good, a vision that is vague and never fully articulated but finds concrete expression in the answers given to the actual problems faced. An Aristotelian can appreciate the forging of piecemeal and fragmentary agreement about the good and the just that sustains modern politics, even if it falls far short of the Aristotelian ideal.

However, as we can see in practice, not only is this agreement fragile, not to be taken for granted, but the systems of democracy and law are themselves liable to hijack, abuse, and distortion. Capture of the regulatory bodies is one familiar form of distortion; manipulation of the electorate through gerrymandering, redrawn constituency boundaries, and complexification of voter registration are also present threats. These two aspects must be addressed: the vulnerability of the systems to corruption or distortion and the fragility of the consensus about the value of the (admittedly always imperfect) systems of governance and law.

Critical voices like those of Patrick Deneen, William Cavanaugh, and the supporters of the Common Good Constitutionalism project with Adrian Vermeule and Conor Casey have drawn attention to the failures of our liberal regimes, and there is no denying the facts of capture, corruption, and distortion.[21] Safeguards to prevent these errors and solutions to remedy their harmful impact are sought. However, no matter how well we succeed in preventing and remedying corruption, our systems will always be vulnerable to distortion. A system guaranteed to realize "the common good" completely is illusory. Aristotle reassures us that even imperfect and defective systems will exhibit cooperation for goods in common. One advantage of an Aristotelian approach is the expectation to find cooperation for common goods in all forms of collaboration. Common goods are not to be found only in the best case.

Second Divergence

The second difference highlighted earlier is that the modern lawmaker does not have an eye to the character formation of citizens, and so does not conform to the measure Aristotle sets for a polis. I take it as read that this is the case. Once again, I suggest that an Aristotelian analysis is not therefore obsolete in this situation. One medieval Aristotelian provides a way forward. Thomas Aquinas remarks that the good is predicated in different senses, either simply, or qualified in some way. Aquinas declares that "leading its subjects into the virtue appropriate to their condition is a proper function of law. Now since virtue is that which makes its possessor good, the consequence is that the proper effect of law on those to whom it is given is to make them good, either good simply speaking or good in a certain respect."[22] A qualified sense of goodness is the goodness of conformity with the law's requirements, and a more complete goodness is realized when a virtuous character acts spontaneously in accordance with the law from a direct willing of the comprehended good.[23] Aquinas, following Aristotle, can confirm that the law's purpose is to make people good, and he qualifies Aristotle by noting that the attainable goodness (in many cases) is the minimal sense of conformity with the civil law.[24] If they conform their behavior to what the law commands, avoiding those actions that are prohibited and performing whatever actions are required, people are *in this sense* good. This meaning of goodness is the only one that human law with its instruments can attempt to guarantee, or at least address. The coercive force of law can succeed in effecting conformity but has no proper instrument for ensuring that the conformity springs spontaneously from virtuous character. Lawmakers can hope that habituation through the discipline of laws can lead to the formation of character, but they cannot make it happen.[25] Implicit in Aquinas's remarks that at least the lawmakers must be virtuous is the thought that no society that relies *solely* on the enforcement of law ensuring conformity can survive. The complete police state, regulating and monitoring everything, is doomed.

Aquinas's remarks point up the incoherence of the phenomenon associated with modern political culture, that the identification of a social problem inevitably leads to a demand for legislation. Law tends to be seen among the first rank of solutions, despite the fact that the only thing the institutions and officers of the law might be able to achieve is the prosecution of those who violate it, relying on officers and institutions of enforcement (courts and prisons) that are already overstretched. For compliance with the spirit of the law and the achievement of goods intended by law, other realities are needed: virtue and character, acceptance of duty and responsibility, and an intelligent grasp of the full range of goods at stake. These cannot be produced by legislation.

In taking this position Aquinas manages to combine what he learns from his two great authorities: Aristotle as the philosopher and Augustine as the Christian bishop and theologian. Augustine remarks on the wonder of divine providence that permits the control of evildoers and the limitation of the harm they might do by putting political power in the hands of people whose reliance on domination and coercion rather than love shows that they, too, are infected with the same disorder as found in the criminals whose behavior is to be controlled. But the effect of limiting destruction is beneficial to the social order. With Aquinas's distinctions of the two forces of law—directive and coercive—on the one hand, and his distinction of the two senses of goodness—good simply and good in some respect—on the other, Thomas succeeds in bringing into one comprehensive account the views of both Aristotle and Augustine.

From an Aristotelian perspective it is noticeable that the lawmaking of our modern democratic states is oriented to the regulation of behavior in the greatest detail. The law specifies where one may and may not smoke, how fast one may drive, how one may or may not redesign or paint the house facade, who (and under what conditions) may become employers of other people, and so forth. One can think also of the excesses of consumer protection legislation lampooned by Roger Scruton in his 2012 book on the common good, *Green Philosophy: How to Think Seriously about the Planet*. All these regulations are introduced for some purpose and deemed good and worthwhile by their proponents, but those who advocate and introduce the laws are motivated by something more than simply effecting material obedience. They have a vision of the good, which they hope to realize via the instruments of the law—for instance, protecting the health of workers by prohibiting smoking in the workplace, or protecting lives jeopardized by speeding traffic. This becomes articulated to some extent in the debates for and against some bill. The good (or the presumed good) is what is at stake in the making and enforcing of the law. So, while in the previous point I suggested that our modern political societies do operate with a shared view of the good—namely, a minimum of agreement on how conflict is to be managed—here I draw attention to the way in which our various efforts to legislate result in setting standards to which citizens are expected to conform in exercising their responsibility toward others. The law does attempt to make people good, in the qualified sense sketched by Aquinas.

Third Divergence

Aristotle considered the capacity for reasoned discourse to be the feature that equips humans for politics, and he expected the relevant conversation to be about the human good. However, in modern politics the language of rights, not that of the good, predominates. This is the third major divergence from the Aristotelian standard highlighted earlier. But again, there is a possibility of revision. Alasdair MacIntyre has shown convincingly that Alan Gewirth's attempt to provide a philosophical grounding for rights has failed.[26] He has also remarked on how liberal political systems continue unfazed by such failure. How can this be? I suggest that the dilemma evaporates once we realize that the language of rights is not what it claims to be. Introduced to deal with the lack of a shared language of the good, it pretends to be an alternative, rooted in something incontrovertible and agreed upon, but in fact it functions as it does to the extent that it is a way of expressing and protecting human goods.

For instance, consider John Stuart Mill's rejection of any account of rights as rooted in human nature or natural law.[27] On Mill's view, rights are instituted in society to facilitate the development of the human individual and human society. He appeals for his account of rights to the notion of utility, understood in the broadest sense, as the interests of the human as a progressive being. The law creates rights for the sake of some purpose, and the deliberation about that purpose should refer to human interests as expansive and transcendent. Those holding the opposite view insist that the law does not create rights as such but recognizes existing moral rights and institutionalizes them. With MacIntyre we can see that this debate is interminable, but perhaps we can also see that it is irrelevant. Neither position must prevail for the members of a liberal democratic state to continue successfully to use the language of rights. All it requires is that the rights identified and defended are sufficiently linked to genuine goods: human life, freedom of conscience, freedom of speech, religious liberty. The debate, then, is about the good, in the context of disagreement on the good but seeking to construct agreement. Note that I am not appealing to goods to justify rights claims but arguing that the meaning of the content of rights claims is rooted in the claims about related goods.

Nigel Biggar both challenges my optimism here and offers a solution.[28] Those who wish to bring all discussion to an end by appealing to their rights exhibit what he calls "rights fundamentalism." He regards this as an exaggerated emphasis on the existence of rights prior to all enactment in positive law and the preeminence of rights over concerns about public order and the common good. Biggar upholds an account of natural morality that acknowledges human goods, duties and obligations, virtues, and common goods. Rights are not exclusively foundational, but among the elements of natural morality they can mislead to an assimilation of legality to morality. And within the legal context, whether human rights, constitutional rights, or civil rights, countering rights fundamentalism involves resisting any attribution of absolute status to rights, since they are all conditional on their legal context, the availability of enforcement mechanisms, and the related goods of public order and the common good.

Biggar argues against natural rights as given or absolute. When natural rights are invoked to critique legislation or political regimes, they can be understood as appeals to moral standards that obtain independently of positive law. A review of modern Catholic considerations of rights leads to a conclusion confirming Biggar's own stance: "The modern Catholic tradition of rights does display a superior ability to recognize the larger, multifaceted moral order of which 'rights' are only a part; and it does recognize that morally justified positive rights are the socially contingent products of political deliberation about the common good."[29] Emphasis on "right order" as distinct from "an order of rights" characterizes this tradition. My suggestion here is that within the Catholic context rights are used as shorthand for identifying important human goods as aspects of well-being and flourishing. It is in the name of some neglected good that campaigns are launched to secure rights. This approach is not universal within the human rights community. For to the extent that "rights fundamentalism" holds sway, and rights are grounded in an assertion of essentially unconstrained human autonomy, there is a fundamental tension between these two views, a tension well-analyzed by Biggar's book.

ARISTOTLE RESCUED?

I am attempting to offer an Aristotelian version of what we find in modern democratic states, to provide a context for understanding the common goods of politics in a secular sense. Although the modern state does not exemplify the Aristotelian polis, it nonetheless can be appreciated in Aristotelian terms for what it does achieve. Despite its fundamental divergences from the Greek polis, the modern state exemplifies the key ideas of shared meaning as sustaining the political cooperation; the concern of lawmakers that participants in the political cooperation achieve qualities of character, as shown by their abiding by minimal standards; and the purpose of cooperation as the good life, as itemized in the many factors for which people are said to have rights. Although diverging from Aristotle's own application of these ideas and his conclusions, my reworking of his analysis allows us to see the essential core of the modern state. At the same time, this use of Aristotle's ideas allows us to recapture an essentially modern concern, which is to limit the power of the state. Aristotle's ideas, when applied to the modern liberal state, allow us to recognize certain limits to the state's competence.

Although the modern liberal state is based on shared meaning, the content of that meaning is inevitably limited to what can be achieved in public deliberation among persons and groups whose comprehensive doctrines are diverse. Although aspiring to equip people for a life in freedom, the goodness of character the state can affect by its own instruments is confined to compliance with the minimal requirements of the civil law. And although avoiding the danger of imposing a particular conception of human fulfillment on its citizens, the state nonetheless requires acceptance of a set of minimal standards for human behavior as formulated in the sets of human, civil, and political rights. The limits implicit in these positions make it possible for the state to remain free from domination by any sectarian doctrine, even one of a nonreligious nature such as atheistic humanism.[30] While ensuring the independence and freedom of the liberal state, these limits also allow for the criticism of the state and its officers whenever they might attempt to overstep the limits and take on an inappropriate role, for which they are not competent, in specifying the ultimate good of humans and their societies, and in specifying the standards of moral fulfillment and goodness.

Contrary to what Aristotle considered the purpose of politics—namely, the good life as the achievement of excellence in performance of distinctive human activities, both theoretical and practical—my argument points to the necessity of confining the purposes of modern politics. Explicitly religious concerns and theological content are to be excluded from the liberal democratic state's understanding of its nature and purpose. Of course, this does not preclude citizens, including theologians, having a faith-based perspective on the state. It is simply that the state cannot include such a perspective in its own self-understanding and in its understanding of its appropriate common good. However, the state is not compromised by allowing for the maintenance of other fora for the debate about the highest good and the pursuit of the unrestricted common good, even if these are not its proper business.

This account of Aristotle suggests that the search for the common good as the good life is ongoing. Accordingly, the label of "the common good" names something being sought but which is not yet known, although enough about it is known to be able to direct the program for its discovery. This specifies the concept of "common good" as heuristic in the context of a project of discovery. However, Aristotle's ontological commitments go beyond such a purely practical understanding, and the question arises whether the practical approach compromises the ontological. In my view, the program of construction can be at the same time a process of discovery. As we deliberate about what makes for our human good, we can at the same time be learning about the ends that correspond to our human nature. Discovering through trial and error what works and what does not work for us, we can be learning about the limits of our humanity. Bernard Yack separates the project of construction from one of discovery: he understands "common good" as something to be negotiated by citizens themselves in their deliberations, instead of something "that can be discovered by applying philosophical knowledge of the human good to particular situations."[31] Aristotelian scholar Richard Kraut, in his mainly positive review of Yack's book, argues that "if the common good is whatever emerges from political negotiations, and if the philosophical study of the human good and human virtue are irrelevant to ordinary political life . . . then Aristotle would have no reason to combine the study of happiness, virtue, and politics in the way that he does."[32] We do not have to choose between the practical and the ontological. More on this in chapter 8.

Faith-Based, but Not Theocratic

I suggest that the earlier reworking of Aristotle's thought is compatible with what the Catholic church has formulated as its view of a modern state committed to protecting human liberty, and its own relationship with such a state. This involves a recognition of the autonomy of the secular, as well as a commitment by the church not to use state power to achieve religious objectives. That this development in the mid-twentieth century involved a radical turnaround in the church's political understanding cannot be denied. It should be emphasized that the church's position is rooted in a theological stance, and so it does not amount to an acceptance of a relegation of religion to a purely private sphere. The acceptance of the possibility of cooperation for establishing and maintaining the conditions for the flourishing of human persons and their communities is compatible with tolerance for diverse religious faith communities, with their comprehensive doctrines. It does not insist on agreement on ultimate goods before engaging in cooperation on more instrumental and conditional goods.

Some theocratic positions take the opposite view. Taking Aristotle's assertion that the good life pursued in the polis is the highest good that embraces all the rest, they fill their notion of the highest good with content from their religious faith. They conclude that the political authorities have responsibility to pursue that highest good so understood. Then the authorities are understood to be obligated to bring about harmony and unity in society in the shared acceptance of this good, and to legislate to make people good and equip them for salvation. Not every religiously grounded position on politics is theocratic in that sense. There are other theologically grounded positions that can support the exclusion of concern with God as the highest good from the agenda of the state. Early in the Christian tradition Augustine realized that the instruments available to civil authorities, typically coercive force, were inappropriate and inadequate to the task of making people good. In fact, he generalized his view that only God could make people good according to the divine standard of goodness, and hence that it could not be the responsibility of political authorities to make people good.[33]

This position receives a more nuanced reworking by Aquinas, who is reluctant to abandon so much of Aristotle. Aquinas can retain the insights of both his mentors, Aristotle and Augustine, by relying on distinctions such as that invoked earlier between the different senses of "good." John Finnis draws on Aquinas to show that there is a perspective on the good relative to the state which does not exhaust the human good and leaves scope for other agents and authorities.[34] In particular, since the interior attitude and virtue of agents is a major dimension of their goodness or holiness, and this is not accessible to the instruments of the human lawmaker and enforcer, it follows that the human authorities cannot have the unrestricted common good as their appropriate goal. Their object is the domain of means and conditions, facilitating the pursuit of the good by persons and groups. The delineation of religious liberty helps to mark this distinction, since it specifies limits to what the state may do in interfering, either positively or negatively, with the freedoms of people to follow their religious conscience.[35]

Drawing on this account of goodness and of the limited capacities of the modern state, I argue against theocrats that the instruments of the state are unsuitable for making people good and getting them to conform to the requirements of their religious worldview. Without wishing to consider the validity of the ends proposed, I concentrate on the inherent limitations of the modern state, which, both in Aristotelian terms and in terms of its own self-understanding, is not designed to deliver the kinds of effects that Aristotle and the theocrat hope for.

CONCLUSION

Thomas Hobbes denied an ultimate end (*finis ultimus*) or highest good (*summum bonum*) as the purpose of the commonwealth, or state.[36] He had Aristotle's *Politics* in his sights as he asserted his great break with antiquity. Is it now the case that we must concede victory to Hobbes? Has the church succumbed to pressure and sold the pass to the prophets of enlightenment? A fundamental distinction is required here. Of course, the teachers of the faith continue to uphold a *finis ultimus* and a *summum bonum* for humankind and for all created reality; what they deny is that it is the business of the state or commonwealth to fit people to their ultimate end and highest good. Nor is it within the competence of the civil powers to specify what that end consists of. On this point they have learned already, if not from Saint Paul then from Augustine, that the instruments available to the civil authorities cannot possibly achieve the ultimate fulfillment of human beings.

The discussion of Aristotle shows that a religious vision of the *summum bonum*, or unrestricted common good, is not an appropriate common good of the modern liberal democratic state. It is worth recalling that the common good is understood here in a practical—as distinct from an ontological— sense, as that good in common for the sake of which people knowingly cooperate. While a liberal democratic state can have an appropriate common good of its own, this will be understood not in terms of policies designed to bring about human flourishing but in terms of policies securing the means and conditions for people and groups to pursue their own flourishing. The processes of liberal democratic politics can be understood as the search for and facilitation or provision of those conditions, ever changing as elements of human flourishing are discovered and clarified. For instance, the invention and development of the language of human rights can be understood in terms of this dynamic. In that context, current debates about the relative weights of equality and liberty exemplify the search for the appropriate conditions to allow individuals and groups to pursue their own visions of the good life.[37]

Will the debates within a pluralist society in a liberal democratic state never address questions of the ultimate human good? Of course, there are such further debates—aesthetic, cultural, anthropological, philosophical, and theological—about what constitutes human well-being and human flourishing, and these need to be fostered and facilitated in the broader political culture of civil society, in institutions of education, academia, publishing, and churches. The availability of the language of common goods will prove useful for communicating a faith-based vision of human fulfillment, but such a vision will be offered for consideration and free acceptance or rejection. But as argued above, the business of the liberal democratic state in providing conditions for flourishing does not have to await the resolution of such debates. Its business can be carried on while allowing the debates to continue, leaving open the determination of what would constitute human flourishing. A liberal democratic state that attempted to fix policies according to one preferred answer to the questions about the highest good would be exceeding its proper limits and violating liberties.

In practice, however, it is more likely to be the case that appeals to the common good do not invoke some ultimate good but are holding public authorities to account for their failure to provide the conditions for the flourishing of everyone and every group. That failure can be due to a deliberate or unintended exclusion of some from a share in the benefits of social cooperation, as when some groups suffer disproportionately from austerity policies, or it can be due to an imbalanced emphasis on some aspects of human good to the detriment of others, as when economic efficiency is measured only in terms of abstractions such as GDP, or the performance of the stock markets. When institutions of various kinds, including sporting associations, broadcast media, fashion houses, churches, and religious associations, are found to have protected their own interests in preference to caring for the victims of sexual abuse, the criteria of the common good are also invoked. In such cases, the appeal to common goods holds the authorities to account for their responsibility in providing for everyone and every group the conditions for their well-being. Responsible politicians will not hesitate to accept the validity of the concept of common good and its criteria, even if they might wish to engage in reasoned discourse about the goodness of the disputed measures.

Many aspects of Aristotle's view seem to be incompatible with politics today. However, Aristotle's discussion is sufficiently programmatic that elements of it can survive to guide our discussion of other conceptions of the common good. The key ideas are the heuristic nature of the concept, pointing to what is only partly known and still in the process of being discovered, and the two criteria of nonexclusion of persons and nonexclusion of dimensions of the human good.

NOTES

1. Aristotle, *Politics*, trans. T. A. Sinclair (Harmondsworth, UK: Penguin, 1962), bk 1, c. 2.
2. Tom Bingham, *The Rule of Law* (London: Allen Lane, 2010).
3. I accept the point made by Adrian Vermeule against John Stuart Mill, whose understanding of progress is ideological and even racist. See Adrian Vermeule, "All Human Conflict is Ultimately Theological," *Church Life Journal* (July 2019), https://churchlifejournal.nd.edu/articles/all-human-conflict-is-ultimately-theological/.
4. See Rosa Ehrenreich Brooks, "Failed States, or the State as Failure?" *University of Chicago Law Review* 72 (2005): 1159–60. The clarification of political reality takes place against the background of the real possibility of social and political chaos. In recent decades this has become a distinct object of study, as scholars of international relations consider the issues associated with failed states. See John Rawls, *The Law of Peoples with "The Idea of Public Reason Revisited"* (Cambridge, MA: Harvard University Press, 1999), considering how the application of liberal principles to international relations is obliged to acknowledge the issues raised by what Rawls calls "Outlaw States" (90) and "Burdened Societies" (105–7).
5. Aristotle, *Politics*, bk. 1, c. 1. The original translation is adjusted to avoid gendered language.
6. Aristotle, bk. 3, c. 9. Compare bk. 7, c. 8.
7. John Stuart Mill, *Utilitarianism, On Liberty and Considerations on Representative Government*, ed. H. B. Acton (London: Dent, 1972), 79.
8. Aristotle, *Politics*, bk. 1, c. 2: "whatever is the end-product of the perfecting process of any object, that we call its nature, that which man, house, household, or anything else aims at being."
9. Aristotle, bk. 1, c. 2: "Nature, as we say, does nothing without some purpose; and for the purpose of making man a political animal she has endowed him alone among the animals with the power of reasoned speech.... Speech... serves to indicate what is useful and what is harmful, and so also what is right and what is wrong. For the real difference between man and other animals is that humans alone have perception of good and evil, right and wrong, just and unjust. And it is the sharing of a common view in these matters that makes a household or a city." The date of the translation (1962) explains the gendered language.
10. Aristotle, bk. 1, c. 1.
11. Alasdair MacIntyre raises such concerns. See his "Politics, Philosophy and the Common Good," *Studi perugini* 3 (1997), reprinted in *The MacIntyre Reader*, ed. Kelvin Knight (Cambridge: Polity, 1998).
12. Aristotle, bk. 1, c. 1, emphasis added.
13. Bernard Yack, *The Problems of a Political Animal: Community, Justice, and Conflict in Aristotelian Political Thought* (Berkeley: University of California Press, 1993).

14. Zoli Filotas, *Aristotle and the Ethics of Difference, Friendship, and Equality: The Plurality of Rule* (London: Bloomsbury, 2021), 123.
15. Filotas, 125.
16. Filotas, 135.
17. Bernard Crick, *In Defence of Politics*, new ed. (London: Continuum, 2005).
18. J. R. Lucas, *On Justice* (Oxford: Clarendon, 1980), 16–18.
19. Adrian Vermeule, "Common-Good Constitutionalism," *Atlantic*, March 31, 2020, https://www.theatlantic.com/ideas/archive/2020/03/common-good-constitutionalism/609037/. The periodical gives the title "Beyond Originalism" to this article, but Vermeule refers to it by its original title, given here. For *Ragion di Stato* Vermeule draws on Giovanni Botero, *The Reason of State*, ed. Robert Bireley. Cambridge Texts in the History of Political Thought (Cambridge: Cambridge University Press, 2017).
20. Bingham, *Rule of Law*.
21. Conor Casey, "Common Good Constitutionalism and the New Debate over Constitutional Interpretation in the United States," *Public Law* 4 (2021).
22. Thomas Aquinas, *Summa Theologiae*, vol. 28, ed. and trans. Thomas Gilby, OP (London: Blackfriars, in conjunction with Eyre and Spottiswoode, 1966), pt. 1–2, q. 92, a. 1.
23. Joseph Raz draws a similar distinction between compliance and conformity: conformity is doing what the law requires while compliance is doing what the law requires because the law requires it. Joseph Raz, *Practical Reason and Norms*, 2nd ed. (Oxford: Oxford University Press, 1999), 178–79. The distinction is similar, but not the same. Aquinas's distinction does not focus on the fact of the law's command (what the law requires), but the reasons for the sake of which the law is enacted.
24. Aquinas, *Summa*, pt. 1–2, q. 92, a. 1 ad3m: "The political commonwealth cannot flourish unless its citizens are virtuous, at least those in leading positions: it is enough for the good of the community if others are so far virtuous that they obey the commands of the ruling authorities."
25. Considering the need for human law, Aquinas writes, "Some are bumptious, headlong in vice, not amenable to advice, and these have to be held back from evil by fear and force, so that they at least stop doing mischief and leave others in peace. Becoming so habituated they may come to do of their own accord what earlier they did from fear, and grow virtuous. This schooling through the pressure exerted through the fear of punishment is the discipline of human law." Aquinas, pt. 1–2, q. 95, a. 1.
26. Alasdair MacIntyre, *After Virtue: A Study in Moral Theory*, 2nd ed. (Notre Dame, IN: University of Notre Dame Press, 1984), 66–71; see also *Ethics in the Conflicts of Modernity: An Essay on Desire, Practical Reasoning, and Narrative* (Cambridge: Cambridge University Press, 2016), 78.
27. Mill, *Utilitarianism, On Liberty*, 79.
28. Nigel Biggar, *What's Wrong with Rights?* (Oxford: Oxford University Press, 2020).
29. Biggar, 92.
30. I note again Rawls's identification of secularism as a comprehensive doctrine, along with those of a religious nature, from which the overlapping consensus at the heart of a liberal polity should be independent: Rawls, 143, 149.
31. Yack, *Political Animal*, 170.
32. Richard Kraut, review of *The Problems of a Political Animal*, by Bernard Yack, *Political Theory* 23, no. 3 (1995): 550.

33. Augustine, *The City of God*, ed. D. Knowles, trans. H. Bettensen (Harmondsworth, UK: Penguin, 1972); R. A. Markus, *Saeculum: History and Society in the Theology of St. Augustine* (Cambridge: Cambridge University Press, 1970).
34. John Finnis, "Public Good: The Specifically Political Common Good in Aquinas," in *Natural Law and Moral Inquiry: Ethics, Metaphysics, and Politics in the Work of Germain Grisez*, ed. R. P. George (Washington, DC: Georgetown University Press, 1998).
35. Martha Nussbaum, *Liberty of Conscience: In Defense of America's Tradition of Religious Equality* (New York: Basic Books, 2008) offers a very helpful reworking of the value of religious liberty as safeguarding the liberal polity.
36. Thomas Hobbes, *Leviathan*, ed. J. C. A. Gaskin (Oxford: Oxford University Press, 1996), chap. 11.
37. Roger Trigg, *Equality, Freedom, and Religion* (Oxford: Oxford University Press, 2012).

CHAPTER 3

DOES POLITICAL AUGUSTINIANISM HELP?

Would it not be better to draw on the theologian, Saint Augustine, instead of the pre-Christian Aristotle, for a Catholic reading of political reality? In the context of heated arguments among American Catholics about what their faith obliges them to do as citizens and as politicians, many appeal to the authority of Augustine. These debates are not purely theoretical or abstract: they address issues of policy. For instance, President Biden, the second Catholic to be elected president of the United States, is a target of criticism by some, for failure to represent the church's stance on issues such as abortion and same-sex marriage. As documented by Julie Hanlon Rubio, these debates are painful for many believers, who become aware of the disjunct between the espoused language of common goods and the reality of conflict between opposed policy stances. Particularly frustrating is the fact that the elements of Catholic social teaching (CST) do not help to bridge the gulf between the parties, since "commitments to human life and dignity, the family and community, human rights, solidarity, subsidiarity, the dignity of work and workers, and stewardship of the environment can be honored by both liberals and conservatives with very different political commitments and thus do not often bridge the gulf between them."[1] It is ironic when the advocates of common goods who share a common faith and profess allegiance to the same church are unable to agree but find themselves mirroring the same divisions that exist in the wider society to which they offer thought on common goods. This situation presents the challenge addressed in this book. An additional concern is to resist the tendency of either side appropriating the notion of common good for its exclusive use. The two sides appear polarized, and there is an additional polarity for those who assume there is a distinctively Christian or Catholic way to respond to the reality. That polarity appears when the debate poses a radical choice. The present regimes of liberalism and neoliberalism are depicted as so inhospitable to a Christian existence that Catholics are faced with a stark choice: either opt for some form of theocracy, whereby religious authority directs the government, or opt out of the system to construct an alternative communal existence.

This is crudely formulated, but despite all the nuances in the texts referred to, this seems to be the principal message in the literature. The opt-out pathway has been given the name of "the Benedict Option" and is outlined in chapter 1. Dreher and Deneen advocate this approach, and other theologians, either wittingly or unwittingly, support this ambition with their exaggerated critiques of contemporary political and cultural life and their idealistic aspirations. The theocracy alternative is represented in the Catholic literature most explicitly by the movement of "integralism," which wishes to see the political realm subject to the rule of Christ.[2] The difficulty is that many authors who take this line deny that they wish to see theocracy established as the sovereignty of the church over the state, but the implication of what they embrace points in this direction. If they desire that all human affairs, including that of states, are subject to divine governance, how will they distinguish between what they envisage and theocracy? This is the critical question for believers who can see the positive side of integralism.

For instance, the emeritus archbishop of Philadelphia, Charles Chaput, OFM Cap., invokes Augustine as a model who defined "the ultimate priority of religious matters, but the practical autonomy of civil authority and religious authority."[3] These words are inspiring but ambiguous, since it is not clear how independent civil authority can become on this view. What domain of autonomous action is available to civil authority if religious concerns have ultimate priority? This is the issue that needs clarification if the conversation is to move beyond the polarizations that leave us with impossible options: either dominate or opt out.

CLARIFICATION OF SACRED-SECULAR

Augustine used the expression the *saeculum* to name the present age during which the people of God are on pilgrimage to their heavenly home. Our word "secular" in current usage is influenced by Augustine's term, and so in examining the concept pair "sacred-secular," it is necessary to turn to Augustine. In his famous book, or collection of books, *The City of God*, he contrasts two cities, the *civitas Dei* (City of God), and the *civitas terrena* (Earthly City), and this contrast is often used to give a theological reading of the sacred and secular.[4] The problem is that Augustine's description of the *civitas terrena* is so negative in theological terms—its citizens are motivated only by self-assertion, greed, the desire to exploit and dominate one another—that it hardly seems appropriate to characterize the world we live in, the city in history. Some authors have tried to conjure up a third term to speak of "the present age," in which the two conceptualized cities remain commingled. While they have been criticized for distorting Augustine's own position by introducing a third term, we can remain faithful to Augustine's thought by recognizing his two cities as ideal types or analytic tools to be used in understanding the complex dynamics at play in historical situations. Neither pole of the analytic contrast, the City of God or the Earthly City, can be univocally identified with any concrete political entity. Accordingly, the secular, as distinct from the sacred, cannot be identified with the *civitas terrena*. To avoid possible misunderstandings, I will avoid use of "the Earthly City," and will use the Latin label, *civitas terrena*, when referring to the analytic tool or ideal type characterized by Augustine. And I will use "the city in history" or a proper name such as Rome to refer to historical contexts that might be analyzed in terms of the two cities.[5] The city in history always comprises some admixture of the two cities.

A clarification of the term "secular" that allows for a gradation of cases along a spectrum, from a complete rejection of God at one pole to an openness to the transcendent at the other pole, would be useful. Pope Benedict envisaged such a regime in the speech he gave at the United Nations in New York marking the sixtieth anniversary of the Universal Declaration of Human Rights (UDHR): a demand not that states acknowledge God or his church but that they respect the transcendent value of human persons, whose fundamental openness to ultimate truth and mystery is key to their dignity and the basis of their entitlement to respect. This suggestion will be more fully addressed in chapter 5, but its foundations in a reading of Augustine will be laid here. A helpful rereading of his *City of God* shows the way. But first, before discussing the solution, let us revisit the problem.

Absolute Separation of Church and State

In his 2008 book *Render unto Caesar: Serving the Nation by Living our Catholic Beliefs in Political Life*, Archbishop Chaput accuses John F. Kennedy of absolutizing the separation of church and state so that the possibility of making one's faith commitment effective in public life is undermined.[6] A recent study of *Political Augustinianism* by Michael J. S. Bruno quotes with approval a paper by Archbishop Chaput, "The Vocation of Christians in American Public Life." It outlines what Christians are called to be and do. "What Augustine believes about Christian leaders, we can reasonably extend to the vocation of all Christian citizens," according to Archbishop Chaput.[7] The exhortatory tone implies that they are not doing it in sufficient numbers or with notable effect. The archbishop takes aim at the expressed self-understanding of one eminent Catholic in American public life, John F. Kennedy, who before his election as president in 1960 was obliged to allay the fears of fellow citizens, particularly Protestant citizens, that a Catholic leader would place the country under the influence, if not the power, of the Roman pontiff. Kennedy had to defend his faith in various fora and reassure voters that they had nothing to fear from his Catholicism. As part of his campaign for the presidency, Kennedy gave a speech to the Greater Houston Ministerial Association. In that address, Kennedy underlined his commitment to the First Amendment principle of separation of church and state:

> I believe in an America where the separation of church and state is absolute—where no Catholic prelate would tell the President (should he be Catholic) how to act, and no Protestant minister would tell his parishioners for whom to vote—where no church or church school is granted any public funds or political preferences—and where no man is denied public office merely because his religion differs from the President who might appoint him or the people who might elect him.[8]

The archbishop is critical of this stance for "absolutizing" the separation of church and state. Chaput invokes Augustine in criticizing Kennedy for his neglect of essential elements of any Christian's involvement in public life. The Christian is obliged to focus on the eternal ends of human life and to acknowledge that temporal goods such as political authority are to be subordinated to those ultimate ends. The Christian's conscience needs to be formed in relation to their eternal fulfillment, and to act virtuously toward that end. Kennedy is criticized for failing to highlight these significant elements of the Christian's vocation in public life and is faulted for fostering the very separation that minimizes the influence of religion on politics.

As an evaluation of the theological and philosophical coherence of Kennedy's statement, Archbishop Chaput's judgment is correct. The assertion that the president's oath of office has absolute priority over everything else is an exaggeration on Kennedy's part. And the similar assertion that the separation of church and state, politics and religion, is absolute is equally unjustified. As Mark Massa points out in his account of this issue in the presidential campaign, Kennedy did not perform as an exemplary representative of his church. But Massa also documents the extent to which Kennedy was obliged to address his religion as an issue in the campaign because of the organized Protestant movement to oppose his election. Massa makes clear that certain important Protestant voices such as those of theologians John Bennett, Reinhold Niebuhr, and Paul Tillich criticized the bigotry of socially conservative Christians who hid behind their Protestant allegiance to pursue a political agenda.[9] Nevertheless, Kennedy had to face a coordinated campaign that relied on such views as "it is inconceivable that a Roman Catholic President would not be under extreme pressure by the hierarchy of his church to accede to its policies with respect to foreign relations."[10] A document prepared for a meeting at the Mayflower Hotel that was unanimously accepted by participants as expressing their concerns included this statement. This document also asked whether it was "reasonable to assume that a Roman Catholic would be able to withstand altogether the determined efforts of the hierarchy of his church to gain further funds and favors for its schools and institutions, and otherwise breach the wall of separation of church and state."[11] In its conclusion the document expressed its fundamental concern: "That there is a 'religious issue' in the present campaign is not the fault of any candidate. It is created by the nature of the Roman Catholic church, which is, in a very real sense, both a church and a temporal state."[12]

This latter point echoes a theme from John Locke. His philosophy of legitimacy as rooted in the consent of the people shaped his opinion that Catholics ought not to be tolerated in a polity committed to the protection of liberties. He provided two arguments that would have shaped the views of Protestant citizens.[13] The first was that a liberal polity could not afford to tolerate those who on taking power would not tolerate others, and the record of the intolerance of Catholic rulers was taken to speak for itself. The second reason given by Locke was that Catholics, not having freedom of conscience, being bound by obedience to the pope, a foreign prince, could not freely take part in elections. This point has been influential for many Northern Irish Protestants, constantly expressed in the slogan opposing Home Rule for Ireland in the late nineteenth and early twentieth centuries: "Home Rule is Rome rule." No doubt Locke's influence also shaped the culture of some Protestant groups in North America. The history of anti-Catholic prejudice in the United States is part of this context.

Massa also reports how the print media shaped the debates in the campaign, choosing to publish photographs that drew attention to the religion issue, such as Kennedy meeting groups of nuns, and choosing to highlight issues linked to religion rather than his policies on labor or agriculture. Massa writes, "One newspaper's political analysis of Kennedy's campaign mentioned the word 'Catholic' twenty times in fifteen paragraphs."[14] Kennedy's absolutizing of the separation of church and state and his prioritizing of the president's oath over his conscience should not be read as the fruits of considered theological reflection but as a prudential response, in the heat of a campaign, to accusations and exaggerated fears that distorted the truth.

CAN AUGUSTINE HELP?

Dealing with this question of how to remain a faithful Christian in a world that accepts the separation of church and state, many Christians turn to Augustine to find guidance. In his writings they find a theological perspective that reinforces their condemnatory stance over against secular modernity, the excesses of neoliberalism, and the failures of liberalism to deliver on its promises. To defend my position adapted from Aristotle, presented in earlier chapters, I must consider Augustine and the question of whether his theological stance undermines my philosophical one.

The question of the relation of religion and rule is an old one. Augustine, in *The City of God*, identifies the problem and gives it its classical formulation.[15] He narrates the story of the pirate who has been arrested by Alexander's forces and is brought before the emperor. Challenged to explain what he is up to by engaging in piracy on the waters of the eastern Mediterranean, which Alexander dominates, the pirate answers that he is doing nothing different from what the emperor himself is doing. The only difference is one of scale. The pirate pursues a life of robbery and pillage on a single small ship, he says, and they call him a pirate, while Alexander pursues the same goals of conquest and theft with a vast fleet and a big army and is called commander and emperor. Augustine reflects on this story and asks if there is really any difference between the two: Isn't imperial power the same as organized crime, except on the largest scale? Isn't it simply domination and exploitation which can succeed because there is no higher power to control it?

Augustine affirms that there is no difference in principle between organized crime and power to rule unless the latter is characterized by justice: "In the absence of justice, what is power but organized crime?" To explain what he means by justice, Augustine draws on the Roman law tradition which sees it as the constant inclination to give each one their due. But Augustine makes a daring move at this point, drawing on Scipio's definition of "a people" as cited by Cicero: "a multitude bound together by a mutual recognition of rights and a mutual cooperation for the common good."[16] If a commonwealth is the "weal of the people," and a people is as defined, then, Augustine argues, Rome never was a city. A city that fails to give God what is due to God cannot claim to be just. And what is due to God is submission, obedience, and conformity to the divine will and purpose. What is due to God alongside obedience is worship, shown in the offering of sacrifices and the prayers of praise and petition. A political power that sees itself as sovereign—that is, as the highest authority—without the need to submit to the authority of God, cannot be just, since it fails to give each their due, and so is no different from organized crime.

We have to acknowledge the relevance of Augustine's answer for our contemporary situation. How can a modern secular state deserve respect and obedience if its claim to these is based solely on its ability to coerce its subjects with the threat of punishment? And if its claim to obedience is more positively based on its success in delivering benefits to its people, how far can such authority extend? As Alasdair MacIntyre puts it, how can a modern state that claims for itself no other grounding than the provision of services and security ask people to make sacrifices and even die on its behalf? It is like being asked to die for the telephone company! William Cavanaugh strengthens the point by asking how the state, so understood, can ask people to kill on its behalf.[17]

The dilemma deserves repetition. I do not want to take the simple implication of the story so far, that the state to deserve respect must give God worship and service and implement the divine will. I acknowledge the force of this argument, but at the same time I do not want to be a citizen of a republic nor a subject of a monarch that forcefully imposes a religious discipline on me or on my society. History has provided us with examples of such enforced orthodoxy. I see the value of liberal democracy and the self-restricting principles of constitutionalism, and I want to uphold these. The challenge is to articulate an understanding of my position that is respectful of both poles, the theological as well as the political.[18]

Since there are appropriate ways of speaking about both religion and politics, the question is how the two can be integrated in one single perspective. There can be no solution in denying the validity of one or the other. Both religion and politics must be respected. The familiar poles of theocracy and civil religion have in common the tendency to subject one dimension completely to the other. Theocracy makes the political subordinate to the religious such that lawmaking and social policy are driven primarily by the requirements of the revealed will of God. Civil religion, on the other hand, recognizes the important social contribution of religion in fostering social cohesion and civil virtues and so harnesses the religious dimension to serve the interests of the political.[19] Neither pole can be acceptable if we wish to retain respect for the validity of each dimension.[20]

Trainor's Reading of Augustine

There has been extensive discussion of Augustine—both how to interpret him and how to apply his analysis to our modern political situation. Negotiating my way through these largely theological discussions with a philosophical interest, I have found Brian T. Trainor's rereading of Augustine particularly helpful.[21] As noted, Augustine had set a very high standard with his remark about justice and the importance of giving to God what was due to God. Augustine was unhappy to end his reflections at this point, since he could not completely accept their implications. He did not shy away from facing them, however. He faced the conclusion that if Cicero's definition were accepted, that the city or political entity consisted of a multitude of reasonable beings united in agreement on what was required by justice and the common good, then the Roman Republic and the Roman Empire never were such political entities—the reason being that Rome never gave to God the submission due to God but worshipped idols and conducted its public life in violent conquest and conflict, contrary to God's command. As a former teacher of rhetoric in the Roman world, Augustine appreciated how shocking such a conclusion must have been.[22] He offered a way out by proposing to apply another definition, also rooted in Roman literature, which would allow him to make his critical case while at the same time preserving something of the respectability of Rome.

With an alternative definition of a city as a multitude of reasonable beings united in love of the same object, Augustine could distinguish between the City of God as the community of those who loved God and were thereby united, and the *civitas terrena* as the community of those whose love was of themselves. This latter form of love, while common to all, does not in fact foster unity, but leads to dissension and division. Contrasting the two forms of love, Augustine could highlight the worthiness of one city while exposing the flaws and shortcomings of the other. But this latter critique, unlike that based on the understanding of a city in terms of justice, did not require a dismissal of Rome's qualification as a political entity in the first place.

Augustine's conceptualization of the relationship between religion and politics was particularly privileged because he could be said to stand in both camps. As a scholar in the Roman cultural world, he had a deep appreciation of the history and ethos of the political.[23] As a bishop of the Christian church, he had a sound theological appreciation of created reality within the divine economy. Augustine worked out his position in response to the allegation that Christianity had destroyed the proper balance between religion and politics. Pagan refugees from Rome maintained that Rome's defeat was due to the city's abandonment of its traditional religious practices. Rome's divine patrons had supposedly withdrawn their favor and protection because the city had transferred its worship to the God of the Christians. Augustine's argument in *The City of God* hinges on a contrast between two communities, the City of God and the *civitas terrena*. The contrast is drawn in terms of the motivating goods and the typical psychological states of the members of both communities. Love of God is contrasted with love of self, the desire to serve and obey is contrasted with the desire to dominate, the pursuit of God's glory is contrasted with the pursuit of fame and honor, and the harmony of peace and justice is contrasted with the constant battling for domination among nations and within nations. These two cities are in conflict with one another, but it is a conflict of a different order to that found within the *civitas terrena*. The battle lines are drawn through the hearts of people as well as through societies and states. The victory is assured, the bishop Augustine affirms, but beyond history.

Within history, in this age, the *saeculum*, the human political community, is not identical to the *civitas terrena* but is a complex of the dynamics of both cities.[24] Far from denying the goodness of the historical community, Augustine acknowledges that it pursues temporal peace and justice, providing the conditions in which believers can pursue their calling to love their neighbor and serve God. The flaw in temporal peace and justice is that it must inevitably rely on domination, on coercion. The assertion of human will is at the core of Augustine's understanding of sin, and the rebellion of human will against the divine will is the ultimate source of the disorder he analyzes. But for order to be maintained in the political community, there must be a dimension of domination.

The question which arises for commentators on Augustine is whether the change of definition requires him to abandon the emphasis on justice as a defining element of a city. Oliver O'Donovan classifies the reactions as either "idealist" or "realist." Idealists want to stress that Augustine continues to hold the view that the true republic, to be just, must be Christian, or at least monotheistic, and committed to serving and implementing the will of God. A commonwealth united in love of its preferred objects would be a city only in name or appearance, not in reality. Realists, on the other hand, according to O'Donovan, see in Augustine's shift of emphasis an anticipation of the later modern understanding of the liberal polity as accommodating diverse comprehensive doctrines, and welcome it accordingly.[25] Trainor takes a typically Catholic "both-and" stance, recognizing the novelty of the shift to a more open definition without assuming the other understanding was abandoned. His task, then, is to explain how the two conceptions, idealist and realist, can be combined in a coherent understanding of the political entity. He attempts this by presenting Augustine's thought in such a way that the different distinctions and their coherence emerge.[26]

Following Augustine, a well-ordered city is one in which God's will is observed and the divinely intended order prevails. However, even for a city which would want to achieve this ideal, it is not possible within history given the condition of human fallenness and sin. It will be achieved in the *parousia*, beyond history. But within history there are different kinds of city: those which strive in various degrees to be well-ordered in the sense of giving each, including God, their due, and those which turn their backs on God. Trainor uses the convenient images of "facing towards" and "facing away from." The cities which deliberately face away from God, he suggests, are not on the scale of best-better-good-poor, but are to be characterized as "unjust/unrighteous, as beyond the sphere of the truly ethical/just, rather than as inadequate in light of the ideal."[27]

The issue is that if we insist on the definition of a political community in terms of justice in the full sense (including justice to God), we still have to account for the phenomena of some evidently unjust cities, which continue to exist as societies and function in maintaining some kind of order. How do they do it? Given the *libido dominandi*, the drive to dominate, we should expect chaos and disorder; why is there so much order?

On Trainor's reading of Augustine, it is helpful to make explicit two sub-distinctions, implicit in the argument of *The City of God* following the basic distinction between the two cities, the City of God and the *civitas terrena*. The first is the distinction between the City of God as it is in itself, and as it is in the form of church, the community of believers empirically, within history. The second is the distinction between the city in history as God-oriented, as receptive to God, and the city in history as God-denying, opposed to the true God and God's city. This allows Augustine to argue that the best city in history is the heavenly directed one, and the only one that can be considered (qualifiedly) just and in accord with the will of God.

With this complexity, then, we are not dealing simply with a two-term pair of "sacred" and "secular." The secular is not a univocal category but comprises a range of stances, which may be distinguished between those that are facing toward God and those that are facing away from God. Among those facing toward God are a great range of specimens, depending on how well they incorporate values and virtues. They recognize their condition as in progress toward an end, which may only be vaguely known. Trainor uses the term "heuristic" in this context to characterize this vaguely known end, without elaborating on it. But insofar as the common good is that end striven for (which may be understood as God as the highest good, or as the Good, simply, or as the human fulfillment of each and all persons), it might be named but will not be fully comprehended. All these forms of regime that face God realize justice in some degree, but within history, and given human sinfulness, their realization will be always incomplete.[28]

Their achievement of justice will always be restricted, relative to the justice of the City of God. But even so, they can be understood in terms of both definitions offered, as a multitude united in pursuing what is just *and* a community united in love of some good. In proportion as the good loved is superior or inferior in the hierarchy of good, so will the corresponding community be better or worse. It may seem strange to refer to such a good city as secular, since it appears possible for it to incorporate many religious elements—in the recognition of God as ultimate source of good, for instance. But secular is not distinguished from religious, necessarily, in Trainor's reading of Augustine. He is attempting to explain how Augustine's two definitions of "city" might be compatible and jointly applicable to some cities in history, but not all. That the members of the city are united in their pursuit of temporal and earthly goods (peace, justice, material well-being) does not preclude their being united also in doing the kind of justice that is prepared to give God what is due to God.

Some political communities are turned away from God, and they, too, can be labeled secular. At the extreme are cities whose existential orientation is away from the fullness of being, and truth and goodness. The good they pursue—perhaps power, domination over others, accumulation of wealth without regard for the needs of others—occupies the position of "highest good" for them and so is equivalent to a false god. For such cities their injustice is absolute, in contrast to the relative justice of other secular cities facing the other way. This is an analytic device. It remains a question whether any such city could possibly exist—namely, one in which there is no redeeming good present, in which the natural virtues of prudence, justice, fortitude, and temperance are completely absent. Doubtless there are and have been in history regimes in which the whole political and legal order is based on crime. The regimes responsible for the holocaust (Nazi Germany), the gulag (the Soviet Union), genocide (e.g., Rwanda) and the killing fields of Pol Pot's Cambodia spring to mind as possible candidates.

Many of Augustine's commentators have wanted to read him as generalizing this form of the secular as applicable to all political communities in history. Hence they have seen in him an anticipation of the stance of Thomas Hobbes. In their cases, the label "secular" is to be understood, Trainor notes, as meaning "*only* secular," or "secular *against* the sacred," or "intrinsically secular." But this reduction is false to Augustine's texts and his understanding of the city in history.

Trainor proposes the slogan "sacred reign–secular rule" to help explain how a secular regime could be open to the sacred and remain secular. Where the political authorities know themselves to be subordinate to higher standards that they do not set themselves, they acknowledge the limitations of their sovereignty. These standards are operative in citizens' expectations that their governments and legislatures will make and apply laws and edicts that deliver justice, respect human rights, and serve the common good. The exercise of rule in the presence of higher claims does not mean the enactment of revealed prescriptions from sacred scripture or the implementation of directives from religious authorities, but the exercise of political responsibility and practical reason in the consciousness of serving transcendent values.

Trainor contrasts his view of the Augustinian secular state with a theocratic state. Where the Augustinian regime is summarized as "sacred reign–secular rule," the theocratic state is summarized as "sacred reign–sacred rule." The contrast is illustrated in terms of two different ways in which religious law might be incorporated in civil law. Who decides on the incorporation, and for what reasons? The possible inclusion of religiously sourced law in the law of the state would be decided solely by the secular authorities in an Augustinian city in history, while in a theocratic state the religious authorities would decide. It is not difficult to imagine examples. For instance, religiously motivated groups in the mid-twentieth century campaigned for the recognition of conscientious objection to military service in the United States, the UK, and elsewhere. The legislators in these jurisdictions adopted the principle of religiously motivated conscientious objection, and eventually expanded the category. Their reasoning was based on the respect for individual liberty and the desire that no one should be forced against their will to undertake what they held to be morally objectionable. This was very different from a possible incorporation in the civil law at the behest of religious authorities for religious reasons.

Other examples might be found in the development of the principles and practices of punishment. The elimination of "cruel and inhumane" forms of punishment was argued for by religiously motivated groups. The Society of Friends has always been interested in reforming the practices of punishment. Religious conceptions of reconciliation may have inspired the development of practices of restorative justice, as well as contemporary explorations in transitional justice. But the decisions by lawmakers to adopt forms of restorative justice and ensure humane treatment of those punished were made for reasons perfectly accessible to nonbelievers (justice, respect for human dignity, effectiveness). They were made by secular authorities, and not by religious authorities for religious reasons.[29] Yet the human, secular reasons for the changes in law were such that they were open to the higher, more ultimate reality: human dignity, justice, solidarity of humankind, and divine mercy. We can take the adoption of the language of the dignity of the human person by the United

Nations in both the Universal Declaration of Human Rights (UDHR) and the subsequent conventions as exemplifying this point.[30]

There is a very similar vision of a possible relationship between the sacred and the secular in the Second Vatican Council's pastoral constitution when it speaks of the church and the political community as partners in service of the same human persons but offering different but complementary service. We read there: "The political community and the Church in their respective fields are independent and autonomous; but under different titles they are both helping the same people to fulfil their personal and social vocation. The more they co-operate reasonably, with an eye on the circumstances of time and place, the more effectively they will perform this service to everybody's advantage."[31]

Trainor argues that his reading of Augustine can be helpful in meeting the challenge formulated by Jürgen Habermas concerning the truth deficit of modern secular liberal democracies. Insofar as unease is widely experienced in Western polities because of the lack of grounding in substantive truth, the Augustinian model of sacred reign–secular rule is a source of reassurance. Also interesting is the argument Habermas makes concerning the attitude of Muslims to secular modernity. For many religious Muslims the operative model of Western liberal secularity is not attractive, seeming to foster practices and behavior that violate traditional moral, cultural, and religious norms. But if the secular is understood in an Augustinian sense, then the embracing of liberal democracy need not entail in principle an abandonment of religious conviction, and it offers a real and practicable alternative to a purely theocratic view of politics.

Trainor's rereading of Augustine is challenging, requiring us to move away from a simplistic conception of the secular as the arena opposed to the sacred. We are asked to consider the term as varied in meaning, as used analogously. This new look at Augustine suggests that a more complex comprehension is needed to understand one's dual position as believer and citizen. Being believer and citizen requires holding a view encompassing four perspectives: (1) there is the City of God in its completion; (2) there is the community of believers on pilgrimage through history; (3) there is the secular domain as oriented to and open to the sacred; and (4) there is the secular domain when it is opposed to and turned away from the sacred. This more complex model requires a broader vision. The familiar pair of church and state, for instance, can refer to a range of cases, depending on whether the state is open or closed to the transcendent—and even if open, there will be gradations in the extent to which the standards of justice and truth are incorporated in the entities within history.

It was certainly not Augustine's intention that good people would withdraw from the turmoil of the public arena, and it is certainly not the thrust of Pope Francis's engagement with important current issues such as global climate change. The model of "sacred reign–secular rule" advocated by Brian Trainor is a valuable resource for religious believers who are called to serve their communities in public life, whether as citizens or officials. It gives us the possibility of embracing our secular roles without a burden of guilt for failing to be faithful enough.

SECULARISM IN CONTEMPORARY DEBATES

Trainor writes as a theologian in presenting his interpretation of Augustine on the secular. But could his distinction between the two forms of secularism be accessible from within the secular domain when reformulated in secular terms? I suggest that we find a parallel distinction between liberal and illiberal secularism operative in secular debates about the secular. This distinction relies on the linked value of liberalism. Liberal secularism is tolerant of a wide range of possibilities for individuals and groups to exercise their liberty and is compatible with a pluralist society; illiberal secularism, by contrast, espouses a worldview and is intolerant of worldviews at odds with itself. Illiberal secularism is typically anti-religious.

Illiberal Secularism

The renowned British sociologist of religion, Linda Woodhead, comments on how an imperialistic secularism leads to distortions in the academic discourse when illiberal secularism is allowed to set the focus of discussion and the terms of the debate. Whenever the problems are so formulated that it appears as if religion were the main threat to liberalism, the religious perspective is placed on the defensive, needing to justify itself but allowed to do so only in terms permitted by the secularist. Woodhead defends the compatibility of religion with liberalism and sees anti-religious secularism as illiberal. Her principal target is the idea "that 'secular liberalism' is identical with liberalism."[32] She challenges two key elements of secular liberalism—namely, the agenda to keep religion out of politics and the agenda to achieve a strict separation between the state and religion, confining religion to a purely private sphere.[33]

Illiberal secularism is a comprehensive doctrine in Rawls's sense, but it is hegemonic and hence unreasonable, being unwilling to accommodate other reasonable comprehensive doctrines while at the same time claiming (explicitly or implicitly) to provide the neutral meeting ground in which all can express their views. It is for this reason that Rawls lists secularism as one possible comprehensive doctrine and denies it can fulfill the role of providing the content of the overlapping consensus.[34]

Justificatory Secularism

In these contemporary debates we find a distinction between different forms of secularism that parallels the distinction that Trainor argued for theologically. As Trainor underlines, when contrasting his preferred model with theocracy, secular rule means that only appropriate secular reasons may be given for laws and policies. In a theocracy, by contrast, rule itself is sacred, and the laws and policies of government are derived from religious sources. Political philosopher Cécile Laborde has argued for a defensible account of secularism that is both philosophically robust and politically viable. She defends a minimalist theory of secularism as a constraint on the reasons that might be invoked by states and their officials in justification of policy decisions. At its core is a norm that a state may not rely on religious reasons in support of legislation. It would be wrong to expect citizens in a pluralist society to accept reasons that can hold no weight for them.[35] She calls this a deflationary account of secularism, wanting to contrast it with those versions of secularism that present it as a comprehensive doctrine or a substantive project for the conduct of states. She distances herself from such substantive positions that would see secularism as anti-religious, and from supporters of secularism who look to it alone for the grounding of fundamental political values such as human dignity, equality, rights, or freedoms. Distinguishing the domains of opinion-forming and decision-making, justificatory secularism demands that decisions be *justified* using only nonreligious language, but opinions can be *influenced* and *formed* using any possible language, with images and values rooted in a speaker's worldview. As she puts it, the state is secular so that citizens do not have to be secular.[36]

She further distinguishes the stance of justificatory secularism from a similar line adopted by John Rawls in *Political Liberalism* and in later publications. Rawls considers that the requirements and constraints of public reason apply not only to officials but also to citizens when they engage in the public sphere.[37] Just like officials of the state and judges of courts, citizens are expected on the Rawlsian account to use only reasons that are accessible to all participants in a pluralist context. Even if Rawls had later modified this requirement by adding a proviso, to the effect that religious language might be used in public debate on the condition that it is translated into reasons acceptable to all, his position maintains a restrictive stance on what is permissible in public speech.[38] Laborde finds this excessive, arguing that while the state is required to be secular in its justification of its policies, there is no reason to demand the same stance from citizens. In this she joins other critics of Rawlsian liberalism who see it as making too many concessions to secularism in its illiberal form.[39]

Justificatory secularism is of value and interest to citizens of religious conviction because it both protects them from having imposed on them religious perspectives alien to their own convictions and provides them with the guaranteed freedoms of conscience and speech that will enable them to take part in public life and debate on the same terms as all other fellow citizens. This is an account of the secular that can be defended against many religiously motivated critics of secularism. It avoids the objection that secularism (in some of its forms) can function just like a religion in the sense of providing fundamental convictions and values for its adherents. It would be as wrong to impose such a worldview on citizens of a state as it would be to impose a religious worldview. Equally, it would be wrong to demand of all religiously motivated citizens that they refrain from the expression of religiously formulated opinions in public debate; those secularists who do so want the liberal state to abandon one of the key pillars of a liberal state in a pluralist society, the freedom of speech.

An anti-religious secularism jeopardizes liberalism because it distracts from the real threats to freedom, as exemplified in the totalitarianisms of the twentieth century. The question is not about the place of religion in a secular, pluralist society, but instead how a liberal society can deal with illiberalism in its various forms, whether religious intolerance, illiberal secularism, or anti-democratic ideologies.

Secular Neutrality

In the European context, the interpretation by the European Court of Human Rights (ECtHR) of the provisions of the European Convention on Human Rights concerning religious freedom has provoked a debate about secularity of the law. Ian Leigh has documented a tendency in the judgments of the ECtHR to endorse a radical secular conception of neutrality in decisions concerning religion, even though there is no mention of neutrality in the relevant articles of the convention.[40] The previous standard approach in the court's jurisprudence relied on an understanding of neutrality as equality of respect, but this has shifted toward a view of neutrality as equidistance. Equality of respect had allowed the court to recognize the so-called margin of appreciation in each

European state's particular circumstances, in which there are differing accommodations of religion and churches. Equality of respect had tolerated a positive attitude by the state toward religious communities without elevating any one church or religion to the status of established church. Equidistance, by contrast, conveyed a negative attitude of the state toward religion, reflecting more the American situation of constitutionally established separation than the complex European circumstances. Tacitly adopting the sense of neutrality as equidistance of the state from all churches and religions, the court was in danger of imposing a single model on the varied circumstances of European states.[41] Although Leigh documents that there is some evidence that the tendency has been halted, as, for instance, in the Grand Chamber's reversal of the Second Chamber's decisions regarding *Lautsi v. Italy*, it remains to be seen if this will be carried through in practice. Leigh quotes one of the judges giving reasons for overturning the lower chamber's judgment, adding emphasis with italics: "*Neutrality requires a pluralist approach on the part of the State, not a secularist one*. It encourages respect for all world views rather than a preference for one. To my mind, the [Second] Chamber judgment was striking in its failure to recognize that *secularism* (which was the applicant's preferred belief or world view) was, *in itself, one ideology among others. A preference for secularism over alternative world views—whether religious, philosophical or otherwise—is not a neutral option.*"[42]

This legal debate reflects an adjustment from the prescriptions of theory to the realities on the ground. Where theory prescribes that the state be secular and that there be a separation between the state and religion, the reality in many European societies is much more complex. The ECtHR has been obliged to recognize this complexity, and has adjusted its stance. Political scientist John Madeley has studied the complex network of relationships between states and the communities of their religiously affiliated citizens and attempted to map these relationships in a set of charts. His work is purely empirical, and he avoids evaluating both the claims of secular liberalism and their opponents. He bases his contribution on "a large amount of empirical research undertaken in recent years that has highlighted just how mutually entangled the fields of religion and politics actually have been and continue to be whatever the merits or demerits of such entanglement."[43] He formulates three propositions that reflect the findings of large-scale surveys conducted into the relations of state and religion in over fifty European territories. The first proposition is not surprising, that "most European countries continue to bear marks inherited from the era of the confessional state both in the religious demography of the countries and in the state institutions themselves." The second proposition notes the historical process of change in these relationships over time, but contrary to the expectations of increasing secularization and separation, state-religion connections "remain extremely common, in defiance of the modern assumption that state and religion should be kept separate." While the separation of state and religion is not the dominant model, the third proposition suggests that there may be a common pattern emerging characterized by the "commitment to recognise individuals' rights to religious liberty," and an associated privileging of mainstream religious groups as these exercise their acknowledged liberties.[44] Madeley concludes his observations with the remark: "The modern state in Europe, far from being ineradicably secular or essentially *laïque* can be seen to be 'more than a little religious.'"[45] What is true of European states does not apply to the United States, and the wall of separation there is much more impermeable.

With the variety of ways in which European states preserve a relatively secular space but yet manage to accommodate religious organizations, we can see the plausibility of Trainor's suggestion from a theological perspective—that the secular can include a range of stances of being closed or open to the transcendent.

CONCLUSION

Our topic is the common good. Were we to ask Augustine what the common good is, he would surely draw on his *City of God*, answering that God's glory is the only true common good. It is love of God, and the desire to serve God and do God's will, that unites the citizens of the City of God. They enjoy *concordia*, concord, unity of hearts, since each one loves the same ultimate Good, who is God. They also enjoy true peace since all sources of dissension are absent.

By contrast, the *civitas terrena* only appears to have a common good. The unifying desire is not a desire for a common good but is simply a similar desire motivating each of the members. Each one seeks their own advantage, as did Cain in killing Abel, and Romulus in killing Remus. The pursuit of individual advantage is the desire common to all, but as Augustine stresses, it is not a desire for a common good. The *libido dominandi* is the common factor, and where one or another domineering figure proves more successful in imposing their will on others, those who are dominated submit, seeing their advantage in doing so, hoping to survive. This is where some commentators have seen the similarity between Augustine's and Hobbes's analyses.

On this basis of this fundamental analysis from Augustine, the spontaneous answer to the question "What is the common good?" can only be along the lines that God, the Glory of God, the doing of God's will, is the *summum bonum*, the ultimate good, the only truly common good. Theological discourse influenced by Augustine is in danger of falling into this trap. Trainor's work suggests a way in which Augustine can be interpreted so that the trap is sprung. His analysis can be accepted without having to accept the relegation of all political goods as somehow tainted.

Even with the analytic tools employed by Augustine for the theological interpretation of historical events, it is possible to recognize the limited, temporal common goods achievable in politics. The theological discourse is not confined to the ultimate *summum bonum* as the only *bonum commune*. Pope Benedict XVI, before the United Nations in 2008, was able to speak of these temporal goods, but in such a way that their openness to more ultimate, transcendent goods was preserved. Even in the secular discourse of human rights there can be found the epiphany of the sacred. This will be explored further in chapter 5.

Various nontheological disciplines have been surveyed to find echoes of Trainor's theological distinction between different forms of the secular. Debates in political philosophy, jurisprudence, and sociology provide evidence that there is a form of the secular that is capable of accommodating religion without being threatened by it. In the sociology of religion, it is a distortion of the data to frame questions on the assumption that religion is illiberal: the secularist stance which does so shows itself to be illiberal. In political philosophy, justificatory secularism establishes standards for legislators and judges to justify their enactments and rulings but does not require the same standards of restraint of citizens and civil society. In jurisprudence, the important principle of separation can be institutionalized in various ways, and it would be an unwarranted imposition to require all liberal states to interpret their stance as one of neutrality understood as equidistance from all religions. Each of these contributions attempts to secure the entitlement of religion to a role in public life against tendencies to deny it that space in the name of secularism. They confirm, therefore, the relevance of Trainor's reading. There is a version of the secular and its relation to religion, which from the point of view of political philosophy is defensible and robust, and which from the point of view of religion and theology can be justified and defended as appropriate for rule of states, in which religious communities and churches can thrive and can contribute richly to a pluralist society. This version of the secular is a potential partner in cooperation with faith-based communities.

This theoretical and theological understanding, developed from a consideration of Augustine's thought, raises challenges for both the state and the church. Both are at risk of a utopianism, attempting to realize the ideal in history. Both are at risk of paternalism in taking charge of their respective constituencies and guiding them to their common goods, willing or not. These dangers will be explored in later chapters, also because they are real dangers for those preferring integralism or theocracy.

NOTES

1. Julie Hanlon Rubio, *Hope for Common Ground: Mediating the Personal and the Political in a Divided Church* (Washington, DC: Georgetown University Press, 2016), xv.
2. Thomas Crean and Alan Fimister, *Integralism: A Manual of Political Philosophy* (Neunkirchen-Seelscheid, Ger.: Editiones Scholasticae, 2020).
3. Charles J. Chaput, OFM Cap., *Render unto Caesar: Serving the Nation by Living our Catholic Beliefs in Political Life* (New York: Doubleday, 2008), 70.
4. Augustine, *The City of God*, ed. D. Knowles, trans. H. Bettensen (Harmondsworth, UK: Penguin, 1972).
5. It must be admitted that Augustine's usage is ambiguous, although his conceptual distinction between the *civitas terrena* and the city in history is clear.
6. Chaput, *Render unto Caesar*, 137.
7. Cited in Michael J. A. Bruno, *Political Augustinianism: Modern Interpretations of Augustine's Political Thought* (Minneapolis: Fortress, 2014), 294.
8. Cited in Bruno, 292. Kennedy's gendered language is explained by his context.
9. Mark S. Massa, SJ, *Anti-Catholicism in America: The Last Acceptable Prejudice* (New York: Crossroads, 2003), 95.
10. Cited in Massa, 92–93.
11. Cited in Massa, 93.
12. Cited in Massa, 93.
13. John Locke, *Locke on Toleration*, ed. Richard Vernon (Cambridge: Cambridge University Press, 2010), 35–36.
14. Massa, *Anti-Catholicism in America*, 98.
15. Augustine, *City of God*, bk. 4, c. 4.
16. Augustine, bk. 19, c. 21.
17. Alasdair MacIntyre, "A Partial Response to my Critics," in *After MacIntyre*, ed. John Horton and Susan Mendus (Oxford: Polity, 1994), 303; William T. Cavanaugh, "Killing for the Telephone Company: Why the Nation-State Is Not the Keeper of the Common Good," in *In Search of the Common Good*, ed. Patrick D. Miller and Dennis P. McCann (New York: T&T Clark, 2005).
18. Patrick Riordan, "Five Ways of Relating Religion and Politics or Living in Two Worlds: Believer and Citizen," in *The New Visibility of Religion: Studies in Religion and Cultural Hermeneutics*, ed. Graham Ward and Michael Hoelzl (London: Continuum, 2008).
19. Ronald Beiner, *Civil Religion: A Dialogue in the History of Political Philosophy* (Cambridge: Cambridge University Press, 2011).
20. Patrick Riordan, "Neither Theocracy nor Civil Religion Can Serve the Common Good," *Tambara* 32, no. 1 (2015).
21. Brian T. Trainor, "Augustine's Glorious City of God as Principle of the Political," *Heythrop Journal* 51 (2010); "Augustine's 'Sacred Reign–Secular Rule' Conception of the State: A

Bridge from the West's Foundational Roots to Its Post-Secular Destiny, and between 'the West' and 'the Rest,'" *Heythrop Journal* 56 (2015).

22. Rowan Williams, "Politics and the Soul: A Reading of the *City of God*," *Milltown Studies* 19–20 (Spring–Autumn 1987).
23. Eugene TeSelle, "The Civic Vision in Augustine's *City of God*," *Thought* 62 (1987).
24. R. A. Markus, *Saeculum: History and Society in the Theology of St. Augustine* (Cambridge: Cambridge University Press, 1970), 58.
25. Oliver O'Donovan, "The Political Thought of *City of God*," in *Bonds of Imperfection: Christian Politics, Past and Present*, by Oliver O'Donovan and Joan Lockwood O'Donovan (Grand Rapids, MI: Eerdmans, 2004), 55–56.
26. Trainor, "Augustine's Glorious City," 547.
27. Trainor, 549.
28. Trainor, "'Sacred Reign–Secular Rule,'" 375.
29. Trainor, 381.
30. Glenn Hughes, "The Concept of Dignity in the Universal Declaration of Human Rights," *Journal of Religious Ethics* 39, no. 1 (2011).
31. Second Vatican Council, *Gaudium et spes*, Pastoral Constitution on the Church Today, §76, 1965, https://www.vatican.va/archive/hist_councils/ii_vatican_council/documents/vat-ii_cons_19651207_gaudium-et-spes_en.html.
32. Linda Woodhead, "Liberal Religion and Illiberal Secularism," in *Religion in a Liberal State: Cross-Disciplinary Reflections*, ed. Gavin D'Costa et al. (Cambridge: Cambridge University Press, 2013).
33. Woodhead, 95–96.
34. John Rawls, *Political Liberalism* (New York: Columbia University Press, 1996), 154–58.
35. Cécile Laborde, "Justificatory Secularism," in *Religion in a Liberal State: Cross-Disciplinary Reflections*, ed. Gavin D'Costa et al. (Cambridge: Cambridge University Press, 2013), 167.
36. Laborde, "Justificatory Secularism," 185. See also Cécile Laborde, *Liberalism's Religion* (London: Harvard University Press, 2017), 125–30.
37. John Rawls, *The Law of Peoples with "The Idea" of Public Reason Revisited* (Cambridge, MA: Harvard University Press, 1999), 132.
38. Rawls, *Law of Peoples*, 143.
39. Nicholas Wolterstorff, "The Role of Religion in Decision and Discussion of Political Issues," in *Religion in the Public Square*, ed. Robert Audi and Nicholas Wolterstorff (London: Rowman & Littlefield, 1997), 81.
40. Ian Leigh, "The European Court of Human Rights and Religious Neutrality," in *Religion in a Liberal State: Cross-Disciplinary Reflections*, ed. Gavin D'Costa et al. (Cambridge: Cambridge University Press, 2013), 39.
41. Leigh, 62.
42. Leigh, 61.
43. John Madeley, "The European State: Ineradicably Secular or More Than a Little Religious?" in *Religion: Problem or Promise? The Role of Religion in the Integration of Europe*, ed. Šimon Marinčák, *Orientalia et Occidentalia* 4 (2009): 108.
44. Madeley, 127–28.
45. Madeley, 128.

CHAPTER 4

AQUINAS AND ANALOGY

THE LIMITS OF BOUNDED RATIONALITY

Given the complexity of the notion of common good, there is a need to clarify both the use of concepts and the limits of the various academic disciplines that employ the concepts. The first section that follows seeks clarification of concepts and disciplinary boundaries. In a second section I draw on Aquinas to establish the analogical use of terms and illustrate the disciplinary limits of the human sciences of law and politics. I present and comment on key texts from Aquinas on law and common goods. With the benefit of insights won from a reading of Aquinas, I outline in a third section some answers to the guiding questions and draw out some implications. This work should clear the ground for later chapters dealing with topics of integral ecology and humane economy, education, and culture.

QUESTIONS FOR CLARIFICATION

Talk about common goods in the plural and the common good in the singular, sometimes with an emphasis on *the*, as if intending to imply its singularity, its uniqueness, can be confusing. What is the relationship between *a* common good, common goods, and *the* common good? Many of the authors cited write of *the* common good, but it is not always clear if they intend a single unique referent.

A related question arises from the many kinds of things that are said to be common goods. For instance, institutions for handling conflict, such as courts and parliaments, can be identified as common goods, as I do in chapter 6 on politics and conflict. But also, the persons who build, maintain, and operate those institutions can be considered common goods, along with their skills and competencies. The culture of shared values and meaning that sustains all of this can also be included in the listing of common goods. How can that be meaningful, to use the same term and apply it to so many kinds of things, different phenomena?

A third question addresses the normativity of talk of common goods. Do we have obligations to provide for and care for common goods? Where do those obligations come from? Should something be said about duties? Surely it cannot be right to say it doesn't matter whether we care for the common good. And if we should care, if we do have duties and responsibilities, where do they come from? How are they grounded?

THOMAS AQUINAS ON LAW AND THE COMMON GOOD

To deal with these questions, I will turn to Thomas Aquinas to find some resources in the texts in which he wrote about common goods. A classic text for the notion of common good for Aquinas is his set of questions on law from the *Summa Theologiae*.[1] His Latin does not allow for definite ("the") or indefinite ("a") articles, so the English translation may be in danger of importing inappropriate emphases when translating *bonum commune*. In exploring these questions from Aquinas, I highlight four points: Aquinas's intellectualism, the complexity of the material, the different disciplines involved, and the use of analogy. I concentrate on this last one, and so mention the other three briefly, for the sake of completeness.

Aquinas's Intellectualism

In question 90, enquiring into the essence of law, Aquinas breaks it down into four aspects, asking whether law pertains to reason, what the purpose of law is, what the source of law is, and what the role of promulgation is. This discussion builds up a complex understanding of law that Aquinas can compress into a definition of law: "It is nothing else than an ordinance of reason for the common good, made by him who has care of the community, and promulgated."[2] He explicitly calls this a definition, and uses the phrase *nihil aliud est quam*, "nothing other than."

That law is a matter of reason requires that subjects of the law should have an intelligent grasp of the connection between what the law says it is good to do and what would constitute the well-being and flourishing of the community. The renowned Thomist scholar Brian Tierney sees in Aquinas's discussion a rejoinder to something cited from the jurist and encapsulated in what Tierney calls "the apparently, absolutist principle of Roman law, 'The will of the Prince has the force of law."[3] Tierney maintains that Aquinas concedes the point about the prince's will, but only under the condition that his will is in accord with reason. He points to Aquinas's argument: "The reason gets its motive force from the will, as we have shown. For it is because a person wills an end that his reason effectively governs arrangements to bring it about. To have the quality of law in what is so commanded the will must be ruled by some reason, and the maxim, *the prince's will has the force of law*, has to be understood with that proviso, otherwise his will would make for lawlessness rather than law."[4] This is the point also made, famously, by Augustine in his account of the reported encounter between the pirate and Alexander the Great mentioned in the chapter on political Augustinianism.[5]

The primacy given to the role of reason over the command of the ruler is the intellectualism of Aquinas stressed here. Reason grasps what is good, there is an intellectual comprehension of what is suitable or appropriate for achieving the intended good, and this lends the directive force to the rules and laws made. The contrast with a focus on the notion of command, rooted in the will of the ruler, is explicit in Aquinas. He does not deny the element of will and of command, also in the case of the individual agent, but these follow from a grasp of the appropriateness of what is commanded.

Complexity

In the second of the four articles in his question on the essence of law, Aquinas asks if law is always for the common good. The inclusion of the mention of the common good in the eventual definition quoted might be quickly glossed over unless one follows the discussion with care, and notes Aquinas's firm assertion that law is *always* for the common good.[6] Aquinas's answer will not be persuasive for many readers today, since the reasons he gives rely on contestable assumptions.

Aquinas presents two arguments in the body of the article. The first relies on the Aristotelian teleological conception of an ultimate end. Practical reason is, by its nature, oriented to an ultimate end. Following Aristotle who in his *Ethics* named this *eudaimonia*, Aquinas calls it *felicitas vel beatitudo*, "felicity or beatitude." The second argument relies on the relationship of parts to the whole. The parts of any complex structure are oriented to the whole, and the good functioning of any part contributes to the well-being of the whole. As human individuals are parts of a complete community, Aquinas maintains, the law which directs action toward their good must consider the shared well-being of all involved.[7]

Both arguments are likely to be challenged. On the first one there are those like Hobbes, who deny that there is a *summum bonum*, an ultimate end which is a common good of all reasonable beings. On the argument about parts and wholes there can be a double challenge. The first is more fundamental, inquiring whether the individual human being is properly understood as a part of something else. From a modern perspective, the characteristic of wholeness and identity belongs more to the autonomous individual person than to the political community. The second challenge might reluctantly concede the point borrowed from Aristotle about understanding the members of a polis, a political community, as parts of a whole, but deny that the analogy applies to the relationship between individuals and humankind. The human population of the world today is not a complete community in Aristotle's sense, nor is the human species over time. And yet that would have to be the presupposition on the basis of which the natural law might be defended in these terms as being for the common good. After all, Aquinas's thesis is that all law is for the common good of the relevant community.

Various Disciplines

One point in Aquinas's defense is to recall that his work is a compendium of theology, and that he can assume that the relationship between Creator and creation and creatures has been clarified in earlier discussions. Relevant points are (1) the dependence by participation of all that is in the pure act of being which is the Divinity; (2) the ultimate goodness of the Creator whose desire to share being, truth, and goodness is at the heart of the will to create; (3) the Creator's providential direction of all creation and especially humankind to an ultimate destiny; (4) and as Goodness itself God is the final cause of human beings and their actions. Aquinas's theological premises can provide filling for the seeming gaps in the argument that might otherwise be problematic for a purely philosophical reading of his text. Here we see the complexity of what Aquinas writes: taken out of context it might appear to be a standard discussion of law within a philosophical horizon, but attention to the context reminds us that it is part of a theological treatise. This is my third point, the importance of theology for understanding the account of law.

Analogy in Understanding Law and Common Good

Aquinas relates five terms in his account of law: (1) there is a community; (2) it has a common good; (3) there is some body (somebody) with care for the community (call it the authority); (4) there is law as a reasonable directive; and (5) the law must be promulgated, made known to the members of the community. In discussing the various kinds of law (q. 91) Aquinas notes that there are four kinds, and that for each of these kinds of law, there are the same five terms. This does not generate twenty elements, as we might at first expect, since there is overlap. The four kinds of law are eternal law, divine law, natural law, and human law. Corresponding to eternal law is the whole community of created being, which is governed by divine providence, divine reason, which orders all things to their end. Aquinas can refer to his discussion of creation and divine providence when he considers this example of law, so he does not need to elaborate. However, it may strike the reader that his use of the notion of "promulgation" in relation to eternal law is problematic. Aquinas notes that promulgation "is made by words spoken or written down; in both ways an Eternal Law is proclaimed by God's utterance, since the Divine Word and the Book of Life are eternal."[8] The Divine Word is the second person of the Trinity, "through whom all things were made," quoting the Gospel of John. The Word proceeds from the Father, who is the source of the wisdom that is cause of all that is. Even in the case of the eternal law there is a promulgation by way of the Word, the logos, but this Word is itself a divine person, so the meaning of promulgation is extended or stretched.

This theme carries over to the second article, concerning natural law, which Aquinas understands as reason in the human person, by which one can know what is good to be done and evil to be avoided. Here, too, promulgation is by creation—in this case specifically, the creation of beings of a rational nature. By virtue of their intellectual capacity, humans are understood by Aquinas to be images of the divine, God having created Adam and Eve in his own image, according to the Genesis narrative. Aquinas understands human reason as a participation in divine reason. So that orientation to the good rooted in human reason and will is the God-given natural law.

Human-made law is intimately linked by Aquinas to natural law, even to the point where he will say that law, to be valid—that is, binding in conscience—must be in harmony with natural law. It is not always so by deduction or derivation, but in many cases by determination, whereby authorities specify some manner in which goods are to be secured and protected from harm, it being important that all affected be aware of the appropriate directive (e.g., drive on the left).[9]

A point frequently overlooked by readers of Aquinas is that he understands legal validity to bind the consciences of addressees. He makes this an explicit question, whether human law binds in conscience.[10] Those kinds of law that have a divine source (eternal, natural, divine) bind in conscience, but what about human law? Aquinas is adamant that if the criteria for just laws are met, then they are binding. Those criteria include the law's purpose, its author, and its form. Unjust laws that are opposed to human good, or to the divine good, are not binding in conscience.

The implications for the relationship between law and common good are interesting. The community of humankind among whom the natural law (rooted in human reason) is promulgated has a common good, which is presumably the natural fulfillment (happiness, beatitude) of persons and their groups.

Human law, which is always addressed to a specific community, intends the common good, or fulfillment, of that community and its members. Human law is binding in conscience to the extent that it is in conformity with the natural law. It would seem appropriate, then, to conclude that the intended common good of human law would include virtue and virtuous actions, since these would be constitutive of the fulfillment of humans and their communities. But Aquinas explicitly excludes that human law should attempt to command acts of all the virtues,[11] and he also rules out that human law should attempt to prohibit all vices and vicious acts.[12] In giving his reasons, we find him using a conception of common good of human communities that is less than, or more restricted than, the comprehensive common good of humanity (whether considered naturally or supernaturally).

His use of the notion of common good in this consideration of legislating for either virtuous or vicious actions reveals the complexity of his reasoning. Aquinas explains, "Law is laid down for a great number of people, of whom the majority have no high standard of morality. Therefore, it does not forbid all the vices, from which upright [persons] can keep away, but only those grave ones which the average [person] can avoid, and chiefly those which do harm to others and have to be stopped if human society is to be maintained, such as murder and theft and so forth."[13] Noticeable here is the very constrained focus of concern: we have to prevent evil actions, but not all possible evil actions; there are some actions which, if tolerated, would make social life impossible, such as murder and theft. Murder and theft are Aquinas's examples, but societies in history have considered others, such as giving false witness (perjury), treason, blasphemy, corrupting the youth, adultery, and voter fraud. The deliberations among lawmakers would be different from those envisaged by Aristotle, whose main concern would be the moral character of citizens, to be formed by the normed practices in the city. By contrast, Aquinas's civil lawmakers would have as their principal (but not exclusive) focus the viability of the city, the maintenance of human society. Note the filter he uses: the evil actions to be prohibited are "chiefly those which do harm to others." The word "harm" (translating *in nocumentum aliorum*) resonates with John Stuart Mill's discussion of the grounds for restricting liberty. It is always worth drawing attention to Mill's formulation of his principle in his essay *On Liberty*, a principle he misdescribes as "simple" with a "single" end. Mill's ends are twofold:

both society's protection of itself and the prevention of harm to others. "That principle is," he writes, "that *the sole end* for which mankind are warranted, individually or collectively, in interfering with the liberty of action of any of their number, is self-protection. That *the only purpose* for which power can be rightfully exercised over any member of a civilized community, against his will, is to prevent harm to others."[14] Aquinas anticipates Mill by combining both these purposes in his formulation: certain acts that harm others are to be prohibited because if tolerated, social life would be impossible. They are distinguishable but linked ends.

Aquinas expands and contracts his focus when considering the common goods of overlapping communities. This gives the impression of an accordion effect of expansion and contraction. With narrowed focus he can consider the common good of a particular city, its survival and maintenance, but relativize that good as a means to the more extensive common good of humankind, especially as revealed in divine law. The narrower common good is certainly not a sufficient means, since the kind of regime that tolerates some vices and some evil actions is not identical with one that ambitions the moral fulfillment of every person and the whole person. The distinction between necessary means and sufficient means for the ultimate common good is vital here.

Note how this accordion-like changing of perspectives is invoked again in the treatment of human law's relation to virtues. Concern for virtue in total (what later will be called "morality") is not the principal concern of human lawmakers. Aquinas identifies their concern as the (limited) common good of the specific society. He writes, "Human law does not enjoin every act of every virtue, but those acts only which serve the common good, either immediately, as when the social order is directly involved from the nature of things, or mediately, as when measures of good discipline are passed by the legislator to train citizens to maintain justice and peace in the community."[15] The common good in question here cannot be that unrestricted common good which is the end of both natural and divine law. Human law is concerned with a more confined purpose, and two possibilities are envisaged. For instance, for the sake of its common good a republican regime following Rousseau might make the exercise of public duty obligatory—for example, in voting, jury service, or defense, since these are directly for the common good. At the same time, indirectly fostering the common good, the republican regime might require the attainment of literacy and familiarity with the civic order as objectives of educational policy. These are the concrete questions that any regime will have to face: what it should implement as requirements for the common good, recognizing that they will not be sufficient to achieve the desired good.

As noted, when considering law as binding in conscience, Aquinas acknowledges the possibility that human law might be unjust, and so not binding in conscience. But as many who have mocked his thought through the centuries have pointed out, the dismissal of an unjust law as "no law" because it is not binding in conscience does not let you off the hook when brought before the magistrate. Recall his listing of cases of unjust law. Law that is contrary to divine law is clear enough: commanding child sacrifice, or worship of idols. But human law can fail to be just on three scores—end, author, and form: "From their end, when the ruler taxes his subjects rather for his own greed or vanity than the common benefit; from their author, when he enacts a law beyond the power committed to him; and from their form, when, although meant for the common good, laws are inequitably dispensed. These are outrages rather than laws."[16] We have phrases for these three grounds of challenge: *Cui bono? Ultra vires!* Inequity!

Divine law refers to the law promulgated by Moses and Jesus and contained in the Torah and the Gospels, namely the Decalogue (old law) and the commandments of love (new law).

Surveying the four kinds of law (eternal, divine, natural, human) and the five terms (community, common good, authority, reasonable directive, promulgation), we see Aquinas operating with analogical usages of the terms. The authority, the one with care of the community, can be the Creator, the God of Revelation, or human civil powers. The relevant community can be the whole created order, the community of creatures, humankind enjoying the power of reason, a political community in some place and time, or the people of God, bound by covenant, whether the old or the new. These are very different communities and different kinds of community, with different laws and kinds of laws, differently promulgated. In all these cases, the same understanding of law is applicable once the analogical usage of the key terms is accepted.

Similarly, with the notion of common good, the end of the relevant community, we find analogy in play. "Good" is one of the so-called transcendental terms, recognized since Aristotle as exemplifying paradigmatically analogous usage. These terms—"one," "same," "good," "true," "object" (or "being")—do not belong among the categories and resist definition, being variously deployed in many different contexts.[17] The good generally is spoken of as the end of action, that which is desired, and which will vary, corresponding to the actor and the action in question. "Common" qualifies "good" where there is cooperation, and in each case the community has its own end, its completion or fulfillment. In the case of the law of a human society, its common good is an end, but at the same time it is instrumental to a more ultimate end. The fulfillment of the created order is difficult to specify or reconstruct, while the beatitude of life in the Resurrection with Christ, though mysterious, at least has the particularity of Christ's promise. The fulfillment of humanity is that it should flourish in achieving excellence in the activities appropriate to it, as Aristotle would say, but those activities and their corresponding excellence are revised by Christian revelation to a transcendent end and a graced existence. What, then, is the end or common good of civil community? If those charged with care of the community must formulate and promulgate directives of reason oriented to the common good, then they must have some idea of what that good is. What is it? How do they know it? I return to these questions in a later section of this chapter, and more extensively in chapter 6.

As Aquinas ranges over the different kinds of law, applying his five terms in the different cases, we note his facility in using terms with varying meaning, albeit within a range. A community of creatures is different from a community of rational beings, which is different again from a community of faith or a localized political community. In fact, in any one place—such as Oxford, to take a convenient example—all four kinds of community overlap, but they do not coincide with one another. To use the term "community" of all four requires a facility in analogy, not equivocation, since the variation in meaning is not arbitrary. It is similar with the other notions of law, authority, and common goods.

David Burrell emphasizes that Aquinas does not generate a theory of analogy, nor does he operate out of an implicit theory. Instead, his usage of important terms is analogous.[18] Some have attempted to provide an account of analogous predication by referring instances to a central case, but this strategy is risky. What instance of law would we take as core instance, from which the meanings of other instances could be determined?

In the selection of central cases, one might identify an instance that is studied in the process of discovery, or one might identify an instance particularly illuminating in the activity of exposition. Aquinas himself distinguishes these two pathways. In the construction of the *Summa* and in his theology of the Trinity, Aquinas distinguishes between the pathway of discovery and the pathway of exposition. The ordering of questions and material in the *Summa* follows the pathway of exposition. In presenting his compendium of theology, Aquinas as a teacher "postpones solutions that presuppose other solutions. He begins with the issues whose solution does not presuppose the solution of other issues."[19] The prologue of the *Summa* specifies this approach as appropriate to the instruction of beginners. Bernard Lonergan notes this distinction between the two orders when resolving difficulties in trinitarian theology: "When there are two systematic and inverse orders, necessarily what is prior in one order will be subsequent in the other."[20] Applied to the theology of the Trinity, Lonergan explains how in the *Summa* Aquinas is aware of a "twofold ordering of our trinitarian concepts. There is the order of our concepts *in fieri*. . . . There is the order of our concepts *in facto esse*."[21] The first records the narrative of our discovery of some matter—for example, how we came to understand the phases of the moon—and the second expounds what has been discovered—in this example, how the moon variously reflects the light of the sun as the moon orbits the earth.

The explanation of law in the relevant questions of the *Summa* follows the order of exposition, beginning with a question about the essence of law, proceeding to the kinds of law and the effects of law, and then focusing on eternal law, natural law, human law, and, finally, divine law, as in the two testaments. The presentation of law relies on an analogical usage of the terms, but if one is to explore the structure of the analogy relying on a central case, the question is which instance should be taken as the core or central case. The tendency for those coming as jurists to interpret Aquinas is that they take the instance closest to their experience—namely, human-made law as the exemplar. Aquinas's own approach is different, remaining as he does with the theological order of exposition, such that the eternal law is more appropriately the central case. But as Burrell has remarked, analogical usage is not typically or always best explained by reference to a core instance. Aquinas's own analogical predication enables him to write properly of the relations of the terms of "reasonable directive," "common good," "community," "the authority," and "promulgation" in the various instances without privileging one. In the order of discovery, we humans construct our concepts from what is familiar to us—namely, the experience of law in our human communities—and apply those concepts with relevant adjustments to the other instances. The risk in taking the case of human law as normative is that the distinctly theological perspective of the *Summa* is overlooked, and the ontological dependency of the created order on the Creator as its ultimate efficient cause and its final cause is neglected.

Thomas Gilby expresses the same concern in an appendix to the volume of the *Summa* on law, which he edited. Acknowledging their analogical usage and the sharing of terms between disciplines, he notes that "when the positive disciplines of law and politics, together with their ancillaries, discuss legality and the effective possession and performance of governmental powers they are not dealing precisely with the *lex* and *dominium* of the *Summa*."[22] This continues to be the case, Gilby maintains, also when the topic under discussion in the *Summa* is human legislation and political regimes. The presence of a moral element in law, especially natural law, may be found unacceptable to positive legal science. Gilby itemizes the tensions in relation to Aquinas's definition of law. A jurist may agree with the notion of law as a reasonable ordinance but will not see it as participation in divine wisdom. The common good to be endorsed will perhaps only be that commensurate with the competencies of the civil powers and not the ultimate common good, which is God. Similarly, with promulgation and the sense of the binding force of law, the jurist within the discipline of law will not have to deal with the way the law is addressed to and received by consciences that may be bound by it.

Perhaps J. Budziszewski slips into this tendency to base his interpretation on the human analogate when he presents Aquinas's analysis of law in terms of genus and species. Aquinas does not use these terms of genus and species when considering law, but the common notion of law and then its parts. Thomas Gilby, in a footnote to the Preface in his edition of the *Summa*, explains that the parts of law "are not kinds of law strictly speaking, for law is not divided like a genus into species; for example the Eternal Law is not one sort of law among many."[23] This thought is continued in Gilby's commentary on question 91 concerning the varieties of law. The variety, he writes, is not of species of a genus: "The Eternal Law is not a particular kind of law, but the exemplar transcending yet causing all laws." And further, in the same note, he writes that "the idea of law is analogical, and does not bear a fixed meaning which can be divided into separate compartments according to genera and species."[24] The same point is made again in Gilby's second appendix to the volume. Once again ruling out any reliance on genus and species, Gilby elaborates on the analogical use of "law," and explains it with reference to the Platonic notion of participation: "a more-and-less of being and truth and goodness which comes when a pure perfection can be communicated in various degrees by causality."[25]

Budziszewski clearly misses this point about analogical predication when he offers as introduction to the reading of question 91 the following commentary:

> In Question 91, St. Thomas considers the kinds, or varieties, of law. Although he does not continually remind us, we should bear in mind that for each of these to be a real species of the genus, "law," it must share in the essence of law, which he has just finished investigating in Question 90. For example, if there is such a thing as eternal law, it must be in some sense an ordinance of reason for the common good, made by public authority and publicly made known.[26]

Although he emphasizes on the following page that "the original, primordial law is eternal law" and considers the natural and divine laws to be reflections of eternal law, his language throughout is to identify the eternal law as the prime species of law. In the extended commentary on the question of the kinds of law, specifically eternal law, he persists in designating the kinds of law as "the species that belong to the genus of law."[27] On the question of whether there is an eternal law (q. 91, a. 1), he remarks that the "Angelic Doctor is simply asking whether any law has the property of eternity."[28] Such a formulation in a commentary is only possible for someone who reads these texts on law without appreciation of Aquinas's metaphysical commitments and his theological understanding that the eternal law is identical with God. There is no property of the divine which is separate from the divinity itself, whether it be eternity, divine reason, wisdom, or will.

This clarification about law can be offered also in relation to the other terms involved in the definition, such as authority, community, and, especially, common good. Good as a transcendental term exhibits the relevance of analogical predication, and the same is true of common good, but in relation to the various forms of community as instances of social cooperation.

ANSWERING THE QUESTIONS

Having looked at Aquinas's thought on law's relation to the common good, I return to the three sets of questions and see if adequate answers can be found.

1. Is it both singular and plural, and how are these related?
2. If it is many kinds of things, what is their common factor warranting the same label?
3. Is there some normativity about common goods, and if so, where does it come from?

Is "Common Good" both Singular and Plural, and How Are These Related?

I suggest that there is only one instance of a unique, singular referent for the term "*the* common good." That instance is when we speak of God (or cognate terms such as life in God, beatitude, the beatific vision, resurrection) as *the* common good. God as final cause is that which all creatures ultimately desire and is Goodness itself in which all created goods participate. Thomas Gilby formulates it thus in his commentary, having distinguished three meanings of *bonum commune* in the *Summa*: "The third *bonum commune*, the proper interest of theology, is the universal good transcending yet maintaining all particular goods. It is God himself."[29] God is the ultimate end, the final cause, of human action and cooperation.

There is a familiar and convenient distinction of two related senses of common good. On the one hand, it can refer to the ultimate ends of human fulfillment and flourishing, and on the other hand, it can refer to the means and conditions that enable humans as individuals and as societies to flourish. Ends and means are fluid notions, since something that is a means—for instance, a family home—can be pursued as the end of sets of activities of saving, borrowing, buying, and paying off a mortgage. And many subordinate goals or ends are not simply means to higher goals but can also be constitutive of the higher end. Continuing with the image of the pursuit of a family home, the constant activity of home making is not merely a means to the end of having a satisfied and contented family life, but is constitutive of that end. The activity of home making is not external as means to some end, but realizes the end. Much depends on the perspective of the speaker or author, therefore, so that what in one context appears as an end is in a larger context a means, a subordinate goal. Hence the use of the qualifier "ultimate" to signal an end that is not also a means. Further elaboration may be required when the standpoint of the analyst or speaker is factored in. What for Aristotle as political philosopher appears as an ultimate end, the happiness secured in the good life of the city, can be seen by Aquinas, the theologian, as means. From a theological perspective, the good functioning of human societies is not an ultimate good but is subsidiary to the transcendent interests of human beings.

Apart from the instance of the ultimate common good, God, all other references to "*the* common good" as singular presuppose a restriction of horizon, whether explicitly or implicitly. We see this occurring when Aquinas writes of the common good of a particular society; he brackets out, for the sake of clarity of focus, any consideration of more ultimate common goods, or, indeed, more restricted common goods, such as those of households that are members of the political entity. This is what is meant by "bounded rationality" in the title of this chapter. Reason, when oriented to achieving goods of any kind, is practical—and as practical, is always limited or bounded in a scope defined or indicated by the nature of that good.

There is, therefore, an accordion effect when one considers the various levels of common goods in which anyone is involved. For the sake of illustration, I reflect my own situation and experience in elaborating the following set of questions:

1. What is the common good of Campion Hall as a hall of the University of Oxford?
2. What is the common good of the Faculty of Theology and Religion?

3. What is the common good of the University of Oxford?
4. What is the common good of the British higher education system?
5. What is the common good of the United Kingdom?

And so on.

Wherever people cooperate—and they do at all these levels—they cooperate for a good in common. Especially in education, academia, teaching, and research, those cooperating will put some effort into specifying their purpose—that for the sake of which they build and operate the relevant institutions and gather the communities of teachers and students, researchers and administrators, benefactors and beneficiaries, patrons, and clients. They will publish mission statements, record their histories, and highlight their values revealed in continuity with the past. But no matter how well the formulations are fashioned, there will always be the question of whether the espoused values are coincident with the operative values. Truth might be espoused as a key value, but one might find oneself or one's colleagues economical with the truth when the interests of benefactors or civil and ecclesiastical authorities are jeopardized. Besides, the implication of a neat nesting of the levels listed above may be deceptive, as when the values espoused by the theological faculty are found to be disruptive of the university's growth plans based on a willingness to accept funding from sponsors regardless of their political or ethical credentials.

The One and the Many "Common Goods"

The second set of questions may seek the one among the many, the common factor that makes it meaningful to apply the term so widely. I return to Aristotle for the common root of the many usages: as all action is for some good, whoever acts, acts for some good; whoever cooperates, acts for a good in common, a common good. Good is what is the end of action, what is desired.[30] "Common" is applicable either when the good is the end of cooperation or when the benefits are shared, or both. Analogy illustrates how this can be applied in so many ways, but meaningfully, without always ending in contradiction or equivocation. The previous discussion of analogy highlights the danger of seeking a central case to ground analogical predication.[31] But identifying the relationship between action in common and the common good is not specifying a core instance. Rather, the act-end relation can range over the whole spectrum, from God's act in creation along with the good of created reality to the ordering of affairs in a golf club along with the good of golfers and their sport.

It may be useful to take some examples clarifying cases where "common good" is not appropriately used. Two similar terms are often identified as common goods, but in some cases mistakenly. The related terms are "commons" and "public goods."

The term "commons" has become familiar through its inclusion in the expression "the tragedy of the commons."[32] There are natural commons and human-made commons. Natural commons include a climate, the atmosphere, the seas and oceans, and, with qualification, natural resources. There are agricultural commons that give us the term, such as Port Meadow in Oxford, shared grazing land in the river's flood plain. Other examples of human-made commons are the conditions of war or peace, or of health risk due to infections or pandemics.

Commons can be good or bad. Goodness and badness I specify in terms of fostering or impeding human life and human activity. The COVID-19 pandemic situation is a commons, but definitely a bad one, since it poses a threat to human life and places unwelcome limitations on human activity. The climate in any place is also a commons; some climates are inhospitable to human life, such as those at the North and South poles and in some deserts. Given the interconnectedness of various climates, changes in conditions in any one situation impact inevitably on others. While cultural adaptation of some kind is required for human existence in every physical environment, there are some environments where conditions are so extreme that human life and activity cannot be conducted there without major cultural adaptation. A good commons is not ipso facto a common good, since the latter term, borrowed from Aristotelian practical philosophy, indicates that the good in question is an object of joint attention and cooperation. A commons becomes a common good when it is the object of human attention, valuing and leading to care, maintenance, or repair. A health environment without smallpox is a commons that has been the product of large-scale human cooperation. The project to eliminate malaria attempts to realize a similar commons. It is understandable when, in conversation focused on beneficial commons such as the temperate climate of northwestern Europe, the assumption is made that the climate everywhere is a common good, but many climates are not beneficial for human life and society. The climate, simply, is not a common good. Any climate is a commons; some climates are good or beneficial commons, and those become common goods when they are the focus of human valuing leading to action to protect, sustain, or repair.

A related notion is that of public goods. The meaning of the term "public good" has changed over time as the categories of economics have entered the shared vocabulary and come to dominate public discourse. For example, citing again Thomas Gilby's commentary on Aquinas as an example, the term "public good" was formerly used to identify the appropriate concern of political leaders: "The political common good is sometimes called the public good, and is contrasted with a private good: the terms come from the Roman jurists."[33] In contemporary twenty-first-century usage, the terms taken from economics predominate, and many people schooled in economics assume that when we speak about common goods we are really talking about public goods, not as Gilby does but as economists do. Relying on how costs and benefits are distributed in the production of goods, the discipline of economics distinguishes public, private, and club goods, and also recognizes commons—what economists used to call "free goods." These categories of goods are constructed in economic terms, considering the cost of providing the goods and their allocation to beneficiaries. Natural commons used to be considered free goods, since no costs were borne in their production and they are freely available to all. However, pollution of the atmosphere has made it necessary to focus on breathable clean air, and that is not achievable without cost. Clean air becomes a common good as people collaborate to achieve it. The costs of doing so mean it is not a free good but must be paid for.

Another economic category, then, is relevant. Public goods are said to be nonexcludable and nonrivalrous. Familiar examples are street lighting, traffic lights, or national security. Once they are in place, no one can be excluded from enjoying them—hence nonexcludable—and the addition of extra beneficiaries does not diminish the share of those already enjoying the goods, hence nonrivalrous. At the other end of the spectrum are private goods, which are both excludable and rivalrous. My dinner is an example: if I eat it, it is not available to anyone else, so it is excludable, but if I offer to share it, then there is less for me; in this sense it is rivalrous. Between public and private goods on the spectrum are club goods, goods shared only among members of the club and so excludable of nonmembers, but which up to a point of saturation are not rivalrous, such as a golf course enjoyed by members of a golf club. Technology can change the economic nature of some goods, as when it became possible to replace free-to-air television broadcasting with a pay-as-you-watch regime. Famously, public goods exhibit what is known as market failure, since, being nonexcludable, they cannot be provided by the market. No entrepreneur will undertake the costs of provision (e.g., street lighting) where there is no possibility of recouping the investment: once the good is in place, no one can be excluded from enjoying it.[34]

In contrast to the economic categories of public and private goods, the language of common goods comes from Aristotelian practical philosophy, where the relationship between cost bearers and beneficiaries is not the focus. All kinds of goods from the economic categories of public, club, or private could be the intended goods of cooperation and so be common goods in Aristotle's sense. For the sake of completeness, we should note "collective goods" as another relevant category; these could also be common goods in the sense I defend. Seumas Miller builds his collective ends theory for the analysis of the ethics of institutions on the concept of collective goods. They have three properties: They are produced "by means of the *joint activity* of members of organizations"—for example, schools or police services. The goods "are *available to the whole community*"—for example, education or security. Finally, they *ought* to be produced for the whole community "because they are desirable (as opposed to merely desired) and such that the members of the community have an *(institutional) joint moral right* to them."[35] Evidently collective goods can be spoken of as common goods, but not all common goods are collective goods. They are limited by being products of cooperation in an institution or organization, and by their prescription as objects of moral rights.

Some authors limit the category of common good unnecessarily and claim Aristotle's authority for doing so. In considering public health provision as a common good, for instance, we can read the following: "Something qualifies as a common good if it serves the interests of all in a given community [universality], serves those interests in a uniform way for each person [uniformity], and does so in a non-rivalrous manner, i.e. the serving of anyone's interests is not at the expense of serving any other's [nonrivalrousness]."[36] Such an understanding of common good is intelligible, but I object to the restriction of the term "common good" to such cases of public goods. It is perfectly consistent with Aristotle's use that people would cooperate to provide private goods for themselves, or even club goods. The golf course is a common good of the golf club members. Private dwellings are the common goods of cooperation of a housing cooperative. Collective goods are the common goods of the organizations that produce them and the beneficiaries that enjoy them.

A similar restriction is evident in Rawls's definition of the term "common good" in *A Theory of Justice*. In a section devoted to possible constitutional restrictions on participation in political life, he refers to the common good in a way that is echoed in later writings. Government, he writes, "is assumed to aim at the common good, that is, at maintaining conditions and achieving objectives that are similarly to everyone's advantage."[37] Later, in passing, he offers a definition of what he means by the term: "The common good I think of as certain general conditions that are in an appropriate sense equally to everyone's advantage."[38] These formulations appear to echo the Vatican Council's understanding of the common good as a set of conditions for the flourishing of persons and their communities. Rawls's version adds the requirement that a condition be "equally to everyone's advantage." There may be such cases, but it seems too restrictive if Rawls's definition is used to exclude other meanings. The common good of a family, for instance, is not "equally to every member's advantage." Aristotle would qualify such a use of "equally" to specify it as meaning "proportionately." It would be more correct to formulate it as follows: "Among the common goods aimed at by government will be certain general conditions that are to everyone's advantage." Examples would include important social conditions such as the rule of law. But many actions undertaken by government or its agencies—rescuing the banks in 2008, for instance—are not and cannot be *equally* to everyone's advantage. Certainly, failure of the banks would have disadvantaged everyone, but some more than others, such as depositors or shareholders. Securing the conditions for the good functioning of markets may require actions that inevitably benefit some groups more than others, and such beneficiaries can have a vested interest in ensuring that the intervention is undertaken. Licensing and patenting can be appropriate state action in some circumstances to secure public goods, but such interventions have negative consequences as well as benefits. They inevitably exclude some from participation and privilege those who can access the patents or licenses. The beneficiaries mobilize to ensure that their benefits are not taken from them. Tension between traditional licensed taxis and the new competitors Uber and Lyft facilitated by new technology exemplifies the difficulties that arise with government action.

Common Goods and Normativity

The final set of questions is about normativity. Does invoking common good entail a prescription—something that ought to be pursued, something that should be done? Prescriptive normativity is expressed with terms like "ought," "should," "duty," "obligation." What role, if any, has prescription in talk of common goods? Such questions arise inevitably in an intellectual culture in which rules and norms dominate morality and moral theory is polarized between utilitarianism and deontology as alternate ways of justifying rules. Utilitarianism offers an account of obligatory action and binding rules as those that achieve the most good on balance. The estimation of the good at stake is made in terms of a basic calculus of utility (or economic costs and benefits, or preference satisfaction, in later versions). Opposed to such a utility-based account of right action is that offered by deontology, frequently appealing to Kant. The right action is that which ought to be done simply because it is right, according to law, and not with regard to its consequences. Kant offered his tests for determining the right actions—namely, those in accordance with universal law—to be done out of respect for the law. Respect for the law, for what is right, imbues the sense of duty, the obligation, what ought to be done, and this normative emphasis is Kant's lasting legacy for modern consciousness. Given this typical polarization between utilitarianism and deontology, talk of the common good is usually placed at the "most good" pole, and the obligation to do the right thing is invoked as the standard counterargument.

The polarization in moral theory, focused on answering the question of how an action or a norm or law could be justified as obligatory, is a modern phenomenon. Equally modern is the tendency to subordinate the good to the right, with the result that questions about what is good are neglected. Aquinas could distinguish between affirming the good and commanding the good. He recognizes elements of normativity in the notion of command, from the will of the ruler, as well as from the will of the responsible agent. In his question about whether the lawgiver himself is subject to the law, he draws on his earlier distinction between the two forces of law—the directive force and the coercive force. The latter is involved in the enforcement of law, including prosecution and punishment. The lawgiver, who exercises the coercive force, does not coerce himself or herself and so is not subject to the law, in that sense. But the directive force of the law is its intelligibility in relation to common goods, and this reasonableness is binding on the lawgiver as much as on all others. However, not all are equally well-positioned to understand the point of the law, and Aquinas describes some people as wicked or immature, unable to see the connection between the particular prohibited or commanded action and the good in common, and needing, therefore, the additional motivation of fear of punishment.[39] Insofar as we have access to goods, and to goods in common, they have their own attractiveness that can motivate action in their pursuit. Corresponding to those various types of goods are what Aquinas calls *inclinations* in people. The desire to live, to partner and reproduce, to bond in society and to know what is good—these are given, and it is superfluous to command people to live, to be healthy, to mate, to seek knowledge. They have libido, drive, enough to command themselves to act in pursuit of what they desire. They may be helped by being informed about what is not conducive to health, what jeopardizes social well-being, what undermines social trust. In his section on the natural law, Aquinas mentions but hardly spells out these inclinations corresponding to the constituents of human nature, as substance, as animal, and as rational.[40]

One point relevant to the present question is how to interpret what Aquinas identifies as the first principle of practical reason: *Bonum est faciendum et prosequendum, et malum vitandum*. Some have translated this as a command: "Do good, avoid evil." Others see it as elaborating what is meant by the notions of good and evil. Preceding this, Aquinas explained the meaning of good, "namely that it is what all things seek after." The Dominican translation of the first precept is "That good is to be sought and done, evil to be avoided."[41] Accordingly, the normative power of the good in a positive sense is the attractiveness of the goods, the ends to which people as individuals and as communities are drawn. Only the directive force of the law is relevant to those who grasp what is at stake. On the other hand, the coercive force of the law is needed in the case of those who do not recognize the common good for which the law is a reasonable directive. Aquinas writes, "Thus virtuous and upright [persons] are not bound by law, but only wicked [persons]. What is constrained and forced is contrary to one's own will. The will of good [persons] harmonizes with the law, whereas the will of wicked [persons] clashes with it, and in this sense only the wicked are subject to law, not the just."[42] The need to prohibit some vicious actions is because of the threat they pose to social existence. Aquinas mentions what cannot be tolerated. He also sees the link between these necessary prohibitions and the prohibitions of the Decalogue. What is necessary and helpful is the negative injunction to avoid evil, to desist from harm, and to take precautions against unwanted consequences of our actions. We will return to the distinction between evaluation and prescription in chapter 8.

CONCLUSION

Using the image of the accordion, with the dynamic of expansion and contraction, we can illustrate the analogical use of the notion of common good. Sometimes it refers to the concrete good ambitioned by a number of people who act together to attain their goal—for instance, a couple of fisherfolk working a net. Sometimes it refers to the purpose of a complex form of cooperation, as the end of a state securing peace, order, and prosperity. Whenever the term is used, therefore, it is important to reflect on which extent of cooperation is intended, how wide or narrow the focus is. In a theological context, the term can refer to God as the final cause of all that is, Goodness itself in whom all created good participates. This is the most unrestricted horizon possible. In a political context, the term can refer to that which corresponds to the appropriate instruments of a state with its laws—namely, the total set of conditions and means that facilitate individuals and groups in pursuing their fulfillment. More extensively, again, the term can embrace, in addition, the elements of their fulfillment that participants in civil society and its organizations pursue. Families; networks of friends; clubs and societies; and cultural, educational, and religious bodies all have their goods in view, which transcend what the organs of the state can achieve. The common good of society is more extensive than the common good of the state, even though in both cases it is impossible to specify in precise detail the content of the common good.

NOTES

1. I rely primarily on the texts from the *Summa Theologiae*, vol. 28, trans. Thomas Gilby, OP (London: Blackfriars, in conjunction with Eyre and Spottiswoode, 1966), pt. 1–2, questions 90–97, dealing with law. The dangers of such a narrow focus on a limited number of texts when reading Aquinas are noted in the chapter.
2. "Et sic ex quatuor praedictis potest colligi definitio legis, quae nihil est aliud quam quaedam rationis ordinatio ad bonum commune, ab eo qui curam communitatis habet, promulgata." Aquinas, *Summa*, pt. 1–2, q. 90, a. 4. The gendered language in translations of Aquinas is explained by the date of the translation.
3. Brian Tierney, *Liberty and Law: The Idea of Permissive Natural Law, 1100–1800* (Washington, DC: Catholic University of America Press, 2014), 83, and note 55.
4. Aquinas, *Summa*, pt. 1–2, q. 90, a. 1, ad. 3.
5. Augustine, *City of God*, ed. D. Knowles, trans. H. Bettensen (Harmondsworth, UK: Penguin, 1972), bk. 4, c. 4.
6. Aquinas, *Summa*, pt. 1–2, q. 90, a. 2.
7. Aquinas, pt. 1–2, q. 90, a. 2:

    > Again, since the subordination of part to whole is that of incomplete to rounded-off reality, and since a human individual . . . is part of the full life of the community, it must needs be that law properly speaking deals with this subordination to a common happiness. Thus Aristotle, having explained what he means by 'legal,' mentions the happiness of the body politic when he says in the *Ethics* that *we call those acts legally just that tend to produce and preserve happiness and its components for the political community*, the perfect community, according to the *Politics*, being the State.

8. Aquinas, pt. 1–2, q. 91, a. 1, ad. 2.
9. Aquinas, pt. 1–2, q. 95, a. 2.
10. Aquinas, pt. 1–2, q. 96, a. 4.
11. Aquinas, pt. 1–2, q. 96, a. 3.
12. Aquinas, pt. 1–2, q. 96, a. 2.
13. Aquinas, pt. 1–2, q. 96, a. 2. The original formulation in the translation is adjusted to avoid gender bias.
14. John Stuart Mill, *Utilitarianism, On Liberty and Considerations on Representative Government*, ed. H. B. Acton (London: Dent, 1972), 78, emphasis added. The nineteenth-century context of his writing explains Mill's use of gendered language.
15. Aquinas, *Summa*, pt. 1–2, q. 96, a. 3.
16. Aquinas, pt. 1–2, q. 96, a. 4.
17. David Burrell, *Analogy and Philosophical Language*, with an introduction by Stephen Mulhall (Eugene, OR: Wipf and Stock, 2016), 23.

18. David Burrell, *Aquinas: God and Action* (London: Routledge, 1979), 56.
19. Bernard Lonergan, *Method in Theology*, 2nd ed. (London: Darton, Longman & Todd, 1973), 346.
20. Bernard Lonergan, *Verbum: Word and Idea in Aquinas*, ed. David Burrell (Notre Dame, IN: University of Notre Dame Press, 1967), 207.
21. Lonergan, 206.
22. Thomas Gilby, "Law and Dominion in Theology (1a2ae, 90, 1–4)," Appendix 1 in Aquinas, *Summa Theologiae*, vol. 28, 157.
23. Aquinas, *Summa*, pt. 1–2, Preface to p. 90, Gilby's commentary note c, 3.
24. Aquinas, pt. 1–2, q. 91, Gilby's commentary note a, 18–19.
25. Thomas Gilby, "The Theological Classification of Law (1a2ae, 90, 1–3)," Appendix 2 in Aquinas, *Summa*, 162.
26. J. Budziszewski, *Commentary on Thomas Aquinas's Treatise on Law* (Cambridge: Cambridge University Press, 2014), 57.
27. Budziszewski, 59.
28. Budziszewski, 61.
29. Thomas Gilby, "Common and Public Good (1a2ae, 90, 2)," Appendix 4 in Aquinas, *Summa*, 172.
30. In other publications I have engaged with and rejected Hume's anti-realist interpretation of "good" as what is desired. See Patrick Riordan, *A Grammar of the Common Good* (London: Continuum, 2008), 17–18, and *Global Ethics and Global Common Goods* (London: Bloomsbury, 2015), 34–35.
31. Burrell, *Analogy*, 30.
32. Garrett Hardin, "The Tragedy of the Commons," *Science* 162 (1968).
33. Gilby, "Common and Public Good," 173.
34. Richard A. Epstein, *Principles for a Free Society: Reconciling Individual Liberty with the Common Good* (Reading, MA: Perseus, 1998), 320.
35. Seumas Miller, *The Moral Foundations of Social Institutions: A Philosophical Study* (Cambridge: Cambridge University Press, 2010), 4. Emphasis (italics) in the original.
36. John Tasioulas and Effy Vayena, "Just Global Health: Integrating Human Rights and Common Goods," in *The Oxford Handbook of Global Justice*, ed. Thom Brooks (Oxford: Oxford University Press, 2020), 153.
37. John Rawls, *A Theory of Justice*, rev. ed. (Cambridge, MA: Belknap Press, 1999), 205.
38. Rawls, 217.
39. Aquinas, *Summa*, pt. 1–2, q. 94, a. 5.
40. Aquinas, pt. 1–2, q. 94, a. 2.
41. Aquinas, pt. 1–2, q. 94, a. 2.
42. Aquinas, pt. 1–2, q. 94, a. 5. The original translation is adjusted to avoid gender bias.

CHAPTER 5

IS LIBERALISM THE ENEMY?

Among Catholic or religious voices today, one must search hard to find arguments in favor of liberal politics and forms of government that prioritize the freedoms of persons. There are many that can provide a critical review of our contemporary situation, and that lay the blame squarely at the feet of what they label "liberalism." Patrick Deneen's *Why Liberalism Failed* is a notable example; Deneen's work has been endorsed by the legal scholar Adrian Vermeule.[1] Another example is Mark T. Mitchell's book, *The Limits of Liberalism: Tradition, Individualism, and the Crisis of Freedom*. Mitchell highlights the denigration of tradition that is associated with liberalism, a point also made repeatedly and convincingly by Vermeule. Tradition becomes relegated because of liberalism's promotion of the "autonomous self—independent and free from any obligations that have not been expressly chosen."[2] Everything is open to choice: neither nature nor God constrains the freedom to choose. A favorite example of the absolutization of choice is the opinion of US Supreme Court Justice Kennedy, delivered in 1992: "At the heart of liberty is the right to define one's own concept of existence, of meaning, of the universe, and of the mystery of human life."[3] Even one's conception of the good might be chosen, it is alleged, despite the obvious difficulty in seeing how such a choice could be reasonable if not made in terms of an already embraced standard of what might be satisfactory—that is, good. Theologian William Cavanaugh has added his voice to this analysis of the sovereignty of choice, highlighting how the consuming individual has become identified with the free individual.[4] Another recent publication offering a theological critique of liberalism is *Send Lazarus: Catholicism and the Crises of Neoliberalism* by Matthew Eggemeier and Peter Fritz.[5] It offers a similar reading of modern experience in which the logic of the market appears to dominate all relationships but the appearance of freedom of choice turns out to be illusory, since the needs of capital dominate.

IS LIBERALISM THE ENEMY?

With so many critical voices making a coherent case against liberalism, the question in the title of this chapter must arise: Is liberalism the enemy? When we attempt to present a view of the common good as rooted in the Catholic intellectual tradition, when we seek to outline a vision of social, economic, and political existence commensurate with the dignity of the human person and their communal nature, must we inevitably target liberalism and liberal regimes as the opponent? I dare to answer no to both questions. To explain my answer, I need to take a few steps back and clarify the task with some further questions: Is the identification of liberalism as opponent a new experience in Catholic intellectual history? What is meant by liberalism? Is it a doctrine or a regime, or both? Is there an alternative to liberalism envisaged by the critics that will not itself succumb to the identified failures? Given the theological interest, how should we evaluate the church's present position on liberalism? These questions structure the material of this and subsequent chapters.

Compare the following two passages:

> Almost all of the promises that were made by the proponents of liberalism have not come to fruition. These promises range from limited but effective government to rule of law, an independent judiciary, responsive public officials, and free and fair elections. After being conceived as a political philosophy some 500 years ago, and put into effect at the birth of the United States nearly 250 years later, liberalism appears to have failed—not because it fell short, but because it was true to itself. In practice, liberalism promotes gross inequality, enforces uniformity and homogeneity, fosters material and spiritual degradation, and undermines freedom. Its vision of human liberty seems increasingly to be a taunt rather than a promise.[6]

This is from Patrick Deneen's 2018 book *Why Liberalism Failed*. Compare his indictment of liberalism with the following:

> During the 17th and 18th centuries practically all the nations of Europe and America . . . fell under the influence of Liberalism—meaning "the political and social doctrine which repudiates all divine authority in public life."
>
> "The will of the majority" is viewed as "the ultimate source of authority."

"The 'rights of Man,' often minus his responsibilities, became the measuring rod. The claims of justice, charity and patriotism, which are the bonds of social life, may be over-ruled by the wish of a majority, however temporary or fickle."

A by-product is economic liberalism, which opened the door to unbridled capitalism and the consequent exploitation of the working population and the growing power of financiers in the function of government. A further development was the prevailing materialism, the fostering of the craving for pleasure and for wealth, and often a reckless mismanagement, waste and misappropriation of the public funds, that resulted in ruinous taxation or the imposition of severe cutbacks on the people.[7]

The similarity of these two texts is remarkable, but ninety years separate them. The author of the second text, an Irish Jesuit, Fr. Edward Cahill, SJ, was a great admirer of Pope Pius XI, and echoed his indictment of liberalism and his fear of unbridled capitalism. The quoted text is from a pamphlet published by Cahill in 1928 entitled *Ireland and the Kingship of Christ*. He was a man of his time, writing in the twenties and thirties of the twentieth century. He founded a movement of Catholic action with a view to influencing the quality of public, cultural, and economic life being shaped in the newly independent country of Ireland. This movement was given the name *An Ríoghacht*, meaning "The Kingship," the kingship mentioned in the pamphlet's title. Cahill was convinced that Catholic thought provided a distinctive sociology that could be the basis of political life. He produced a book in 1932 with the revealing title *Framework for a Christian State*.[8] This brought together the ideas that he had published in various religious journals in the years between 1924 and 1930, and that he had presented to the membership of his Catholic lay movement. Friendly with Eamon de Valera, the Irish *Taoiseach* (prime minister), he sent his *Framework* book to him and engaged in extended correspondence with him during those years of the 1930s when de Valera was drafting a new constitution for the country, which was eventually adopted in 1937.

Cahill's efforts to influence de Valera were not very successful. The *Taoiseach* himself, in advocating support of the new constitution by praising it as Christian Democratic, pointed to its explicit defense of the freedom of will and of conscience. In December 1937, he announced on radio that "the chief significance of the new constitution" was "that it [bore] on its face, from the first words of the preamble to the dedication at its close, the character of the public law of a great Christian democracy."[9] By invoking this label of Christian Democracy, de Valera was associating his constitution with ideas gaining currency in Europe, associated in particular with the thought of Marc Sangnier, a French Catholic politician with whom de Valera had collaborated. For a document produced in the later years of the 1930s in Europe, where Germany and Italy were subject to authoritarian forms of rule, and Catholic countries such as Spain and Portugal were also embracing dictatorships with strong religious affiliations, the 1937 Irish Constitution is remarkable. It guarantees the state's respect for all religious communities, explicitly including the Jews, while acknowledging the "special position" of the Catholic church as the church of the great majority of its citizens. This clause respecting religious liberty was removed in a later referendum in 1973, as a gesture of conciliation with the Unionists of Northern Ireland, who, it was thought, were offended by the special position accorded the Catholic church. However, the constitution was not as Catholic as some, including Cardinal Pacelli (later Pope Pius XII), the Vatican's secretary of state, would have wished. Invited to comment on the constitution, he declined to give his approval, since the constitution did not acknowledge the Catholic church as the one true church of Christ. But the cardinal also promised not to obstruct its adoption. Fr. Cahill probably shared the cardinal's preference and must have been disappointed by the eventual text of the constitution. Christian Democratic, perhaps, but certainly not the kingship of Christ in a Christian state.

Pope Pius XI was outspoken in his condemnation of liberalism. This included the political version of liberalism that Cahill also rejected, with its connection to unbridled capitalism. One should not try to water down the extent of his critique of political and economic liberalism in *Quadragesimo anno*, 1931, celebrating forty years since the publication of Pope Leo XIII's *Rerum novarum*. Liberalism for Pius XI was closely linked to "modernism," and that was seen as a grave threat to the identity and mission of the Catholic church. Modernism's celebration of freedom threatened to undermine authority, as rooted in an objective order. Cahill's text, cited earlier, summarizes the pope's anxieties, that the will of the majority becomes the ultimate source of authority, that the "rights of man" become the moral standard, ignoring responsibilities. The supposed duty of the state to safeguard religion and morality, to suppress public incentives to vice, is denied in the name of freedom. In the economic sphere the desired freedom on the one hand encourages materialism, the craving for pleasure and wealth, and on the other hand permits the exploitation of workers. My interest is primarily in the political, social, and economic connotations of liberalism, but in Pius XI's mind these could not be separated from the theological problems he saw arising from the adoption of new freedoms by Catholic theologians as they investigated the tradition with the aid of updated methods in hermeneutics and the human sciences.[10] While we concentrate here on the political, the theological context should not be forgotten.

A recent book presenting a personal appropriation and discussion of Catholic social teaching (CST) reflects the negative evaluation of "liberalism" presented here, but acknowledges the ambivalences. Edward Hadas's *Counsels of Imperfection: Thinking through Catholic Social Teaching* chooses to follow the usage of the term "liberal" as he finds it in early papal documents, and admits that it is tinged with the expectation of being anti-Catholic: "They have used it to express both specific objectionable beliefs and the general wrong-headed and anti-Catholic spirit of the modern world."[11] Hadas returns to the discussion of the idea of liberty and liberalism in a section dealing with subsidiarity in relation to the economy. Subsidiarity is one of the key principles of CST, and it articulates the duty of higher instances to be of assistance to, but not to replace, lower instances in a hierarchy in the performance of their functions. Accordingly, if a family can provide for the educational needs of its children, the state authorities (local or national) should provide assistance but should not take over the function the family is able to provide for itself. Hadas argues that the modern state, whether of Hegelian inspiration or liberal ancestry, cannot avoid violating this principle of subsidiarity, and that the modern state must find itself threatened by any who uphold the principle.

> The popes have understood this well. Pius XI looked back at the budding 19th century culture of "liberalistic individualism, which subordinates society to the selfish use of the individual" (1937: 29) and saw that it was fatally flawed. Its godlessness left people open to the lure of the "autocratic abuse of State power" (ibid, 32), first in "atheistic communism" (ibid, 3) and subsequently in what one of his successors would call the liberal societies' "burdensome system of bureaucratic control which dries up the wellsprings of initiative and creativity" (1991: 25).[12]

At the Second Vatican Council in the 1960s, the church revisited its condemnatory stance against modernity and its values of freedom, and embraced religious liberty and individual rights. With its Declaration on Religious Liberty, *Dignitatis humanae* (1965), the council affirmed its commitment to upholding persons' rights to live according to their conscience and, on the other hand, its commitment never to rely on the exercise of the state's coercive power to ensure conformity to the truth.[13] This was an express move from the shorthand statement that *error has no rights* to a clear acknowledgment that *persons have rights, even when they are mistaken or misguided in their chosen affiliation*. In the context of the previous papal condemnations of the assertions of the centrality of human freedom, this development in the church's position did not mean an abandonment of the importance of truth, nor did it mean an option for arbitrariness, relativism, or subjectivism to supplant grasp of the real. Instead, it represented a moment of growth in appreciation of the dignity of the human person and their essential constitution as a creature drawn toward eternal mystery. Pope Benedict would eventually expand on this appreciation, as elaborated later in this chapter.

HOW TO EXPLAIN THE CHANGE?

How did this change in the thinking of the church's leadership come about? The concern of the theologians of the modernist period had not gone away, despite their being silenced. How the faith could be made intelligible and attractive in the context of modernity remained an issue for those engaged with people and communities in the circumstances of the mid-twentieth century. In due course, the church under the leadership of Pope John XXIII, and after him Pope Paul VI, accepted the validity of these questions and attempted to address them. The exigency of the questions drove the renewal of the thinking of the church. But the changing historical context also provided an impetus to change.

How was it possible for the church to change its stance from opposition to adoption of several of modernity's key notions? How could Catholics who once proclaimed the obligation of a political community to subject itself to the law of Christ adjust their stance to an acceptance of the principle of church-state separation and the effective exclusion of clerical authorities from civil power? One element in the explanation is the recognition of the church's more positive experience of liberalism in the anglophone world, especially in the United States, as articulated by American Jesuit priest John Courtney Murray.[14] The European experience of liberalism had been different, as in France, Spain, and Italy, where liberal parties were expressly antichurch. James Chappel, in his 2018 book *Catholic Modern: The Challenge of Totalitarianism and the Remaking of the Church*, notes the extent to which the church embraced modernity: "Catholic thinkers and leaders take for granted that they are living in a religiously plural world, and that their task is to collaborate with others in the name of the common good."[15] Catholics, he writes, do not seek church-state fusion, they do not call for an overturning of the secular order nor pursue a reinstatement of the church as "the sole guardian of public and private morality." As noted in chapter 3, there are Catholic voices in contemporary movements that are now making such calls. One such movement is "integralism," with a project of subordinating civil and secular authority to ecclesiastical authority.[16] But church leadership in general adheres to the direction signaled by the Second Vatican Council.

Chappel explores how Catholics came "to embrace religious pluralism, human rights, and the secular state as positive goods—and not only as brute facts to be grudgingly accepted."[17] He surveys some European experiences from the First World War to the 1960s, focusing on France, Germany, and Austria. He investigates lay Catholic figures and civil society organizations rather than the magisterium or clerical-led political stances. He reveals a complex and richly textured history, and so provides a helpful counterpoint to the simplistic narratives of secularizing liberalism on one side and compromise, betrayal, or failure on the side of the church.

The notion of "secular modernity" today is most probably associated with liberal democracy and market liberalism. But for Christians of the 1930s, secular modernity appeared in the guise of a choice between Fascism and Communism. (Socialism was not always distinguished from Communism but was seen as a stage on the way toward Communism.) Edward Cahill in Ireland was in step with coreligionists on the continent of Europe in dismissing liberalism as a failure. Liberalism belonged to the past. Politically, it was seen to have failed in the Weimar Republic; economically, it was seen to have failed in the Great Depression, hyperinflation, and widespread unemployment of productive capacities. The Great Depression and the threat of Communism in the 1930s obliged Catholics in public life to find a position other than a blanket rejection of modernity. While the church's anti-modernism from the nineteenth century seemed plausible following the horrors of the First World War, an event interpreted as the direct outcome of liberal modernity, persistence in the rejection of modernity was not viable. If liberal democracy had no future, as was commonly assumed, Catholics would have to deal with a form of rule characterized by either Fascism or Communism. As Chappel puts it, they moved from framing their question as "How can we overcome the secular state?" to "How can we shape secular modernity to suit our specifications?"[18] In this latter framing of the question, it was commonly assumed that liberal democracy (as one possible model of secular modernity) had no future, and that the church would be faced with a choice between Fascism or Socialism. These appeared as the only options for modern societies. Chappel documents how lay Catholic leaders and politicians in Europe sought to position themselves in this situation, how they defined for themselves how to be Catholic and remain faithful amid social and political life. Catholics were inclined in both directions, but common to both paths was an acceptance of modernity. They engaged in public debate, principally in publications, largely about which of the alternatives, Socialism/Communism or Fascism, posed the greater threat.

Chappel's basic argument is that the experience of totalitarianism in the twentieth century challenged the church to review its stance in relation to the political in the broadest sense of rule. The Fascist, extreme nationalist, and Soviet Communist forms of totalitarianism provoked some Catholic lay intellectuals into revising their attitude to politics. He argues that two forms of Catholic modernism evolved in this context, each of them determined by its preferred opponent. Some Catholic thinkers were so opposed to the threat of atheistic Communism that they saw some benefit in what Fascist movements could offer and were particularly sympathetic to the authoritarian stance exhibited in those movements. This strand Chappel labels Paternal Catholic Modernism, and it is characterized by figures and movements such as George Moenius and neomedievalism, or Waldemar Gurian and ultramodern Catholicism. These thinkers aspired to recovery of a medievalist integration of church and secular life. On the other side were Catholic thinkers who could see some good in the ideas of Karl Marx and were prepared to collaborate with others, including Socialists, in working for a more fraternal and solidaristic society. Their preferred enemy was Fascism, emphasizing its threat to human rights and dignity. This strand he calls Fraternal Catholic Modernity, and its principal exemplars were figures like Charles Maurras and Jacques Maritain. These are not self-applied labels adapted by schools of thought, but instead labels to distinguish two different styles of Catholic adjustment to modernity. There was considerable fluidity, and individual thinkers fluctuated in their thought. What made them both forms of *modernism* was their acceptance that the state itself would not be confessional, that public matters such as legislation and the economy would be beyond the control of religious authorities, and that religious freedom would be protected. Chappel writes, "If secular modernity is a state-sanctioned condition of religious freedom, religious modernism can be understood as the set of tactics that religious communities use to conceptualize, mobilize within, and shape that modern settlement."[19] He qualifies the notion of the "privatization" of religion, stressing the departure from certain public roles but insisting that it enabled new forms of public intervention.

Nostalgia for a medieval past along with a sympathy for authority led many Catholics to favor Fascism as an ally against atheistic Communism. Pope Pius XI was deemed to take this line, and in support it is remarked that his sweeping condemnation of Communism in the encyclical letter *Divini redemptoris* in 1937 was not matched by a condemnation of Nazism as such in his letter *Mit brennender Sorge* of the same year, which complained of Nazi excesses and violations of church privileges.[20] Many Catholics continued to long for "a monarchist restoration, church-state alliance, and the return of monoconfessional civilization."[21]

Chappel documents how Pius XI's 1937 encyclical marked a significant development in his own position, and its language is in stark contrast to that employed in 1922, in *Ubi arcano Dei consilio*, his reflection on the Great War and its consequences. The earlier encyclical was a traditional one, calling on states to recognize publicly that their power derived from God and to accept that only the church was "able to set both public and private life on the road to righteousness."[22] In 1922, about 80 percent of the invocations of rights in the letter were ascribed to institutions or to God, not to individuals. In his anti-Communist encyclical *Divini redemptoris*, fifteen years later, about 80 percent of the invocations of rights referred to the individual as their bearer. The later encyclical, meanwhile, said nothing at all about the state's duty to recognize God as the source of its authority.[23]

There was a significant change in tone and content in Catholic thought, both papal and lay, with regard to the political aspects of modernity. From a condemnation of liberalism, with its emphasis on freedoms, individuals' rights, and limitations of authority, we find a more nuanced acknowledgment of these goods. Chappel is careful in formulating his claims. Especially with Paternal Catholic Modernism, the change was toward a modern version of a conservative vision: "Many Catholic political actors and theorists continued to support racist legislation and the suppression of civil liberties. They defended their politics, though, in a new way, with little recourse to natural law or the medieval model. Instead, they mobilized a vaguely articulated notion of Western culture to claim that strong leadership was necessary to protect the rights and dignities of European citizens from Bolshevik barbarians at the gates."[24]

Despite the preferences of various Catholic politicians and intellectuals, the official church position asserted by Pius XI in his encyclical *Dilectissima nobis* (1933) remained constant. In that 1933 letter he addressed the situation of the church in Republican Spain, and reaffirmed that the church did not support any particular political ideology: "Universally known is the fact that the Catholic Church is never bound to one form of government more than to another.... She does not find any difficulty in adapting herself to various civil institutions, be they monarchic or republican, aristocratic or democratic."[25] In writing this he must have been aware of how his predecessors in the nineteenth century would have given a very different impression—namely, one of preferring monarchy to democracy. But perhaps he felt supported by Augustine's assertion of a similar principle in *The City of God*:

While this Heavenly City, therefore, is on pilgrimage in this world, she calls out citizens from all nations and so collects a society of aliens, speaking all languages. She takes no account of any difference in customs, laws, and institutions, by which earthly peace is achieved and preserved—not that she annuls or abolishes any of those, rather, she maintains them and follows them (for whatever divergences there are among the diverse nations, those institutions have one single aim—earthly peace), provided that no hindrance is presented thereby to the religion which teaches that the one supreme and true God is to be worshipped.[26]

VATICAN II, POPE JOHN PAUL II, AND POPE BENEDICT XVI ON LIBERALISM

Given the principle enunciated by Pope Pius XI, it would be surprising to find an official endorsement by the Catholic church of liberal democracy as the preferred form of government, much less its requirement as Catholic teaching. And yet, with the Second Vatican Council's strong affirmation of religious liberty and its grounds in the dignity of the human person, we can inquire which forms of state and government are compatible with this central value of human dignity and fundamental liberties. This, I suggest, is a central question: If the dignity of the human person is fundamental to political life, which political ideology is compatible with it and likely to serve it best? This is not merely a question about a preferred doctrine; it also has practical relevance. Of the different ideologies characterizing governments in power or parties likely to come to power, which ideology is at least partly compatible with the church's understanding of human dignity linked to the political common good? While the church since the Second Vatican Council has nowhere endorsed any one political philosophy, signs of approval for liberal democracy can be noted in official statements as well as in the words and actions of Pope Benedict XVI discussed later in this chapter. This stance is shared by other Christians facing the challenge of combining Christian fidelity with political engagement. Jonathan Chaplin, for instance, concludes that "Christian political thought robustly affirms democracy," understanding democracy as a "vigorous, participatory search by people and state for public justice," a term he sees as equivalent to the common good.[27]

The pastoral constitution *Gaudium et spes* observes that a growing awareness of human dignity throughout the world has led to "attempts to bring about a politico-juridical order which will give better protection to the rights of the person in public life. These include the right freely to meet and form associations, the right to express one's own opinion and to profess one's religion both publicly and privately. The protection of the rights of a person is indeed a necessary condition so that citizens, individually or collectively, can take an active part in the life and government of the state."[28] Criticism is directed at political systems that deny religious liberty, or that permit the use of power to favor the interests of some in preference to the common good. The service of the common good is said to be the purpose of the political community, but the form of "the political regime and the appointment of rulers are left to the free will of citizens."[29] Having located the priority of human persons' dignity and the free choice of citizens as determinant of state form, the pastoral constitution considers the relationship between church and state. Three points are made: The first point is a distinction between the two, and between what persons do as citizens and what they do as members of the church. The second point affirms a clear separation between church and state. In making this point, the role of the church is said to be both "a sign and a safeguard of the transcendent character of the human person."[30] The dignity of the human person is the bond between church and state, since, in a third point, the constitution affirms that while "the church and the political community in their own fields are autonomous and independent from each other," both "are devoted to the personal and social vocation of the same persons. The more that both foster sounder cooperation between themselves with due consideration for the circumstances of time and place, the more effective will their service be exercised for the good of all."[31]

These passages underline the importance of the complexity of the notion of common good. It can refer both to ultimate end, mentioned in the text as "eternal vocation," and the means and conditions for achieving this fulfillment, both individual and communal—listed here as "the temporal order," the means proper to the city in history, respecting the "political freedom and responsibility of citizens." The church commits to contributing to the latter but promises not to interfere, except as it deems it necessary to "pass moral judgment in those matters which regard public order when the fundamental rights of a person or the salvation of souls require it." Presenting itself at the beginning of this passage as "a sign and safeguard of the transcendent character of the human person," the church commits to standing up for persons when their rights are being violated.[32]

The highest value at stake in politics is said to be the dignity of the human person. This dignity is spoken of as transcendent. In the earlier chapter of the pastoral constitution, it is explained in terms of the divine image, underlining that there is something wondrous and mysterious about persons. The dignity of human intellect in the orientation to truth, of human freedom in the orientation to what is good, and the dignity of conscience are presented as key elements of human dignity.[33] The notion of human freedom invoked here is far from the autonomy that denies any constraints except those freely adopted.

The extent of this transformation in the political thought of the church should not be underestimated. It illustrates the fact that the church's social thought is not only teaching or doctrine, but is at the same time a learning. The church in its history has a mission from Christ to teach and sanctify. But its history is also a process of discovery and learning. This reality was exemplified in the Christological councils as the believing community strove to find the right language in which to speak of the Incarnate Word of God and the relations of the persons of the blessed Trinity. Other elements of the Christian mystery were also clarified in conciliar pronouncements on the sacramental life of the church, its authority, and its mission. In the domain of social ethics, the church's learning has been part of the general learning of humankind, as challenges arising from social change, political revolution, technological development, scientific culture, and mass education have provoked adjustment and adaptation. Humanity has been challenged to reject an uncritical acceptance of tradition, whether in the domains of culture, science, or social and political life. Economic change linked to the dynamics of market expansion and globalization has also brought distant cultures and worldviews into closer proximity. The arrival of the global village has shattered the self-sufficiency of local cultures. Humanity has been struggling to adapt, to learn, and the church's own process of adaptation has also required an openness to discovery. In relation to the dynamic of discovery represented by the documents of the Second Vatican Council and later popes, a large part of the dynamism of that process came from lay Catholics who struggled to make sense of their faith amid the modern world. Chappel's study cited earlier documents how the engagement of lay Catholics contributed to the development of the church's teaching.

DAVID WALSH:
THE "OTHER" BENEDICT OPTION

Professor David Walsh, a lay Catholic and professor of politics at the Catholic University of America, has written extensively on the topic of the human person, but more significantly for our purposes here, he has stressed the enormous intellectual contribution of Pope Benedict's papacy. Benedict took forward his predecessor John Paul the Second's interest in the "acting subject," the person as moral agent, and elaborated the dignity of the person as the mysterious reality at the heart of cultural and political life. The thrust of Walsh's recent books is to establish the link between what has been proclaimed by Pope Benedict and by Catholic teaching since the Second Vatican Council on the one hand, and the emergent tradition of liberal political philosophy on the other. In his 1997 book, *The Growth of the Liberal Soul*, Walsh observes that the Catholic church, in the Second Vatican Council, "emphatically sided with the liberal freedom of religion as taking precedence over all authoritarian arrangements and thus sided with the liberal primacy of emphasis on individual self-determination as the sine qua non for the reception of all truth."[34] Note here how freedom and truth are paired.

Walsh takes this theme forward in his later books, and in his most recent one he links his analysis of the liberal highlighting of the self-responsible liberty of the human person with what Pope Benedict made a keynote of his pontificate.[35] Walsh interprets the papacy of Benedict XVI in terms of this transcendent dignity of the person. He sees it at the heart of the movement of new evangelization initiated by the pope. Benedict strove for a new encounter between the church and the world, convinced that "the church must meet the modern world where it is, and at the same time open itself to the vulnerability of rejection."[36] Walsh believes that the intellectual achievement of Benedict's papacy has scarcely been noticed, a working out of what the more personalist emphasis begun by Pope John Paul II would mean for "the way Christianity understands itself in the heart of the secular world. The church would change the world, neither by separating from it nor submitting to it, but by revealing the eschatological secret buried within it."[37]

The encounter between the then Cardinal Joseph Ratzinger and German philosopher and sociologist Jürgen Habermas was significant for understanding Benedict's undertaking. They agreed that the secular world, which must be understood in its own terms, has difficulty in finding the spiritual resources for its own survival. To identify and formulate those resources was the challenge accepted by Joseph Ratzinger.

As Pope Benedict, Ratzinger always spoke up for religious liberty, seeing it as a gateway into the whole regime of rights. In the case of religious liberty, the human rights discourse expresses more than it is able to say. Benedict of course wanted to protect believers from persecution, but also wanted to establish the primacy of religious liberty within the order of rights.[38] Accommodating this right to freedom of religion is acknowledging the transcendent destiny of the human person, the sought-for spiritual resource for the secular world.

Benedict's Own Words

Freedom, properly understood, is a constant theme in Pope Benedict's writing and speaking. He used his public speeches before audiences of diplomats and politicians to reinforce his message of the centrality of religious liberty. It is noticeable how his stance was very much in contrast with the stance of those who saw in liberalism and contemporary democratic regimes in pluralist societies only enemies of the common good. The following five points reinforce what I understand to be the position of the Catholic church as expressed by Pope Benedict, a position that is misrepresented by some who claim to speak for the church. These points are based on Benedict's addresses to the General Assembly of the United Nations in New York in 2008, to assembled parliamentarians and diplomats in Westminster Hall, London, in 2010, and to the houses of the German parliament, the *Bundestag* and *Bundesrat* in Berlin, 2011.[39]

1. Complexity and Ambiguity of "Common Good"

Pope Benedict acknowledged the ambiguity in the notion of the common good, as referring both to ultimate ends of human individual and communal life and to the means and conditions for achieving those ultimate ends.

When addressing the United Nations General Assembly in New York on April 18, 2008, Benedict noted the distinction between levels of common good. The goods pursued by the United Nations, he said, expressed in its founding principles—"the desire for peace, the quest for justice, respect for the dignity of the person, humanitarian cooperation and assistance"—were said to represent a fundamental part of the common good, but they did "not coincide with the total common good of the human family." Benedict saw the connection between the rules and structures of international relations as "intrinsically ordered to promote the common good, and therefore to safeguard human freedom." The occasion of his speech was the celebration of the sixtieth anniversary in 2008 of the Universal Declaration of Human Rights (UDHR). He stressed that the securing of human rights was a core element of the common good and a critical instrument for achieving the end of human flourishing. He repeated this link between rights and common good, not presenting the latter as an extrinsic consequence of the application of means, but instead indicating that the common good was realized as rights were secured.

2. Recognition of Partner Assemblies

Pope Benedict XVI recognized the assemblies that he addressed as partners with the Catholic church in serving the interests of human persons in their various nationalities and societies.

In 2008 Benedict addressed the General Assembly with the marked self-assurance that he was entitled to be present as representing the church that was partner with states and with the United Nations. He asserted that "the Holy See ha[d] always had a place at the assemblies of the Nations, thereby manifesting its specific character as an actor in the international domain." Collaborating in making international law, he said, the Vatican saw itself also as addressed by that law and acting in conformity with it. He explained the purpose of his presence as demonstrating "the willingness of the Catholic Church to offer her proper contribution to building international relations in a way that allows every person and every people to feel they can make a difference."

Before British parliamentarians and diplomats in London in 2010, he highlighted the parallels between the common law tradition and its respect for human freedom, and the tradition of CST, which upholds the same values but in a different language, expressing an "overriding concern to safeguard the unique dignity of every human person, created in the image and likeness of God."

3. Promotion of Human Rights, Including Religious Liberty

In highlighting the interests of persons, Pope Benedict concentrated on the promotion and protection of human rights and paid particular attention to the right to religious liberty.

The narrative of the production of the UDHR is similar to that told in the Vatican Council's *Gaudium et spes*. It is about the discovery of the importance and centrality of the human person, and the relativization of political structures and institutions to serving the good of persons. No doubt few of the attendees at the assembly would have spontaneously told the story this way, but this was the pope's perspective, consistent with that of the Second Vatican Council. The declaration, he said, was "the outcome of a convergence of different religious and cultural traditions, all of them motivated by the common desire to place the human person at the heart of institutions, laws and the workings of society, and to consider the human person essential for the world of culture, religion and science." Throughout, he repeated the emphasis on the dignity of persons, for which the institutional arrangements upholding human rights are safeguards. He countered the invocation of radical cultural pluralism to insist that human persons everywhere were endowed with dignity. This was not just a Western value, for the protection of Western citizens. Pope Benedict always gave special attention to religious liberty since the neglect of this dimension of the human person is a denial of human dignity.

Speaking in Westminster Hall in 2010, Benedict praised the British parliamentary tradition for the values it upheld and the influence it had had throughout the world in communicating those values. He maintained that "Britain ha[d] emerged as a pluralist democracy which place[d] great value on freedom of speech, freedom of political affiliation and respect for the rule of law, with a strong sense of the individual's rights and duties, and of the equality of all citizens before the law." He stressed the agreement of CST with this approach, sharing an overriding concern to safeguard the unique dignity of every human person, created in the image and likeness of God. The correspondent duty of civil authority to serve the common good in which the protection of the dignity of human persons is paramount was equally emphasized.

The following year in Berlin, before the two houses of the German federal parliament, Benedict reprised his core theme in the context of the discussion of the nature and purpose of law and the difficulty in determining what is just. He recalled the achievement of the German Basic Law of 1949 in committing the nation to "inviolable and inalienable human rights as the foundation of every human community, and of peace and justice in the world," as formulated by the German constitution. But to implement that vision, he said, it was not enough to appeal to the democratic principle:

> For most of the matters that need to be regulated by law, the support of the majority can serve as a sufficient criterion. Yet it is evident that for the fundamental issues of law, in which the dignity of [the human person][40] and of humanity is at stake, the majority principle is not enough: everyone in a position of responsibility must personally seek out the criteria to be followed when framing laws.

For Benedict, human dignity was at stake; it was the value to be served. The modern politician, no less than Solomon, requires wisdom.

4. The Ethical Grounds of Rights

Pope Benedict always raised the question of the ethical grounding of the demands of human rights and noted the limitation of a purely legal process in their promotion. The social and philosophical explorations needed to pursue an adequate grounding, he believed, were an opportunity for an engagement between reason and faith. He denied the possibility that faith could replace reason, or that the grounding of rights could be solely located in an act of faith.

Relying on the UDHR as the authoritative statement, Benedict did not have to argue in defense of it. But he did not shy away from making his usual points, consistent with the council, about the "common origin of the person, who remains the high point of God's creative design for the world and for history." He appealed to human nature, without mentioning it, by referring to the law written on the human heart, and common to all cultures. What was this law, he asked, if not the Golden Rule: "Do not do to others what you would not wish done to you!" The recognition of the transcendent value of every person, he said, could ground "a commitment to resist violence, terrorism and war, and to promote justice and peace."

More than in New York in 2008, in London in 2010 Benedict highlighted the question of the ethical foundation of politics: "Where is the ethical foundation for political choices to be found? The Catholic tradition maintains that the objective norms governing right action are accessible to reason, prescinding from the content of revelation." He proceeded to discuss the contribution of religion to this search for ethical foundations, insisting that religion could not offer norms not otherwise available to nonbelievers, nor did it claim to have unique solutions to serious problems. This perspective implies that the church's invocation of the common good in relation to public issues is not an appeal to a norm not otherwise knowable, nor is it a claim that some solution is derivable from church teaching on the common good.

Benedict spoke of the "corrective" role of religion, admitting that it was not always welcome because of sectarianism and fundamentalism, distorted forms of religion that are themselves sources of social problems. But these distortions point to religion's need for the corrective influence of reason. He spoke of a two-way process. Many will spontaneously agree that religion needs the help of reason but may not admit so quickly that there is a reciprocal need on the part of secular rationality. Benedict gave examples of how human reason can be distorted, instrumentalized by ideology, or captured by partial interest: "Such misuse of reason, after all, was what gave rise to the slave trade in the first place and to many other social evils, not least the totalitarian ideologies of the twentieth century." Reason can benefit from the corrective influence of religious faith. For Benedict, these two worlds—the world of secular rationality and the world of religious belief—needed one another and should not be afraid to enter into a profound and ongoing dialogue, for the good of our civilization.

In Berlin in 2011, Benedict raised a similar concern focused on the rational grounds of law. Recalling German history when law ceased to be an instrument of justice, Benedict asked how reason could avoid being hijacked or distorted. This time he did not invoke the corrective function of faith but appealed for reason to overcome the narrow confines in which it could be constrained. "How can reason rediscover its true greatness, without being sidetracked into irrationality? How can nature reassert itself in its true depth, with all its demands, with all its directives?" he asked. In his answer he pointed to the emergence of the environmental movement and the way it challenged a purely exploitative attitude to nature. Benedict endorsed its rejection of a purely positivist rationality, and encouraged a more comprehensive openness to reality, including the human reality.

5. Critique of Failure

Pope Benedict, like his predecessors in the twentieth century, used his platforms to point to the failures, weaknesses, and excesses of the institutions he addressed. But unlike the earlier popes who condemned modernism and liberalism, his critique was couched in an attitude of willingness to cooperate and facilitate the improvement of those institutions.

Was there a veiled criticism in the remarks made to the United Nations that the right to religious liberty should never be curtailed, implying that sometimes it is, either in excessively secular, anticlerical, or theocratic countries? "It should never be necessary," he said, "to deny God in order to enjoy one's rights. The rights associated with religion are all the more in need of protection if they are considered to clash with a prevailing secular ideology or with majority religious positions of an exclusive nature." There was perhaps another veiled criticism when he considered the problems associated with the proliferation of rights. With national legislatures responsible for establishing rights, the danger remains that in some cases regimes are sustained that undermine the dignity and rights of persons. Here, obviously, he was caught in the tension between an aspirational moral vision of rights and the practical implementation in the hands of those who hold power to make law.[41]

Criticisms voiced in London and Berlin were veiled and indirect. In London, Benedict recalled the horrors of the slave trade, and in Berlin he recalled German history and the way in which law and power had become instruments of injustice, harming persons and societies. This honesty underlined his message about the need for courage and vigilance on the part of the various assemblies.

Liberalism as Ally, Not Enemy

Pope Benedict engaged with liberalism, not by treating it as an enemy but by dialoging with it and challenging its understanding of human liberty and the prospects it offers of human fulfillment. He endorsed the centrality of freedom but rejected the understanding of liberty as unconstrained choice. An absolute autonomy without regard for human nature or a moral order, or without the prospect of transcendence, is inconsistent with human experience. These perspectives require reflection and understanding and correspond to the other great human capacity for knowledge and truth. The concern for freedom must be complemented with the respect for truth. In making this point, whether speaking to parliaments or writing to a wider audience, Benedict did not appeal to any revelation or aspect of Catholic doctrine but to the ordinary experience of humankind as reflected in literature and in philosophy.

When Martha Nussbaum recounts the history of respect for freedom of conscience, she underlines this dimension of the demand that conscience be allowed freedom to pursue the truth in any field. Freedom is demanded by beings who have the capacity to raise and pursue profound questions about humankind and life's purpose. This was the claim raised by Charles Williams, who resisted the tyranny of the Puritan settlers in New England to create the colony of Rhode Island, built on the principle of religious liberty. Nussbaum identifies the same concern in the writings of Jacques Maritain and quotes him with approval.[42]

John Stuart Mill's advocacy on behalf of liberty was also closely linked with the need for freedom to pursue the truth. Open examination and debate would not be possible if participants were not free to raise questions and express their opinions, and without such questioning and challenge, superstition and ignorance would never be overturned. Benedict, both as Ratzinger the theologian and as pope, challenged liberals to be more faithful to the inspiration behind Mill's defense of liberty. The neglect of the search for understanding and knowledge and the exclusive promotion of freedom understood as unconstrained autonomy has led to the loss of common ground and a shared intellectual culture for addressing issues of social conflict.[43]

Benedict embraced the respect for liberty and reinforced its importance for authentic human existence. That is why he highlighted the central right to religious liberty, because of the openness to discovery of ultimate grounds and ultimate ends. He appealed to no religious doctrine in making this case, only to the capacity of the human to raise the questions and the capacity freely to shape one's life around what is discovered. The acknowledgment of the right to religious liberty is the acknowledgment of the human capacity to wonder and inquire beyond the limits of the immediate. What transcends our limits is heuristic, naming something we seek but which can only be known inchoately.

CONCLUSION

This brief review of the present public stance of the church in relation to religious liberty, the transcendent dignity of the human person, the relativization of the purpose of politics to serving the common good understood in terms of human rights and dignity should serve as a corrective to those views that attempt to claim the banner of common good for the rejection of liberalism. Liberalism as a doctrine for government predicated on the centrality of human freedom is not the enemy of the common good.

Following on the Second Vatican Council's strong affirmation of religious liberty and its grounds in the dignity of the human person, we can inquire which forms of state and government are compatible with this central value of human dignity and fundamental liberties. This, I suggest, is the key question today: If the dignity of the human person is fundamental to political life, which political ideology, which -ism, is compatible with it and likely to serve it best?

Perhaps, therefore, the announcement of the failure of liberalism in the twenty-first century will prove to be as premature as that voiced a century earlier. And if the Benedict Option advocates a monastic-style withdrawal from the world, Pope Benedict's work advocates a spirited engagement with the world, celebrating its recognition of human dignity and the importance of human freedom but pointing beyond to that unlimited horizon of truth and goodness to which it is open. This other option may prove to be a fruitful Christian stance. As shown earlier, Walsh formulates this principle as follows: "The church hopes to change the world, neither by separating from it nor submitting to it, but by revealing the eschatological secret buried within it."[44]

NOTES

1. Adrian Vermeule, "Integration from Within," review of *Why Liberalism Failed*, by Patrick Deneen, *American Affairs* 2, no. 1 (Spring 2018), https://americanaffairsjournal.org/2018/02/integration-from-within/.
2. Mark T. Mitchell, *The Limits of Liberalism: Tradition, Individualism, and the Crisis of Freedom* (Notre Dame, IN: University of Notre Dame Press, 2019), 1.
3. *Planned Parenthood of Southeastern PA v. Casey* (1992), http://caselaw.findlaw.com/us-supreme-court/505/833.html, cited in Mitchell, 8.
4. William T. Cavanaugh, "The Church's Place in a Consumer Society: The Hegemony of Optionality," in *The Church in Pluralist Society: Social and Political Roles*, ed. Cornelius J. Casey and Fáinche Ryan (Notre Dame, IN: University of Notre Dame Press, 2019).
5. Matthew T. Eggemeier and Peter Joseph Fritz, *Send Lazarus: Catholicism and the Crises of Neoliberalism* (New York: Fordham University Press, 2020).
6. Patrick Deneen, *Why Liberalism Failed* (New Haven, CT: Yale University Press, 2018).
7. This text is a composite of passages from a pamphlet by Edward Cahill, *Ireland and the Kingship of Christ* (Dublin: Irish Messenger, 1928). The quotation marks signify text taken from papal documents.
8. Edward Cahill, *Framework for a Christian State* (Dublin: Gill, 1932).
9. Cited in Owen McGee, *A History of Ireland in International Relations* (Newbridge, Ireland: Irish Academic Press, 2020), 106.

10. Karl Rahner and Herbert Vorgrimler, "Modernism," in *Dictionary of Theology*, rev. ed. (New York: Crossroad, 1981).
11. Edward Hadas, *Counsels of Imperfection: Thinking through Catholic Social Teaching* (Washington, DC: Catholic University of America Press, 2021), 28.
12. Hadas, 86.
13. Second Vatican Council. *Dignitatis humanae*, "Declaration on Religious Freedom," §§10, 12, 13, 1965, https://www.vatican.va/archive/hist_councils/ii_vatican_council/documents/vat-ii_decl_19651207_dignitatis-humanae_en.html.
14. John T. Noonan Jr., *The Lustre of Our Country: The American Experience of Religious Freedom* (Berkeley: University of California Press, 1998), 353, quoted in Leslie Griffin, "Commentary on *Dignitatis humanae* (Declaration on Religious Liberty)," in *Modern Catholic Social Teaching: Commentaries and Interpretations*, ed. Kenneth R. Himes, OFM, et al. (Washington, DC: Georgetown University Press, 2005), 250.
15. James Chappel, *Catholic Modern: The Challenge of Totalitarianism and the Remaking of the Church* (Cambridge, MA: Harvard University Press, 2018), 1.
16. Thomas Crean and Alan Fimister, *Integralism: A Manual of Political Philosophy* (Neunkirchen-Seelscheid, Ger.: Editiones Scholasticae, 2020).
17. Chappel, *Catholic Modern*, 3.
18. Chappel, 12.
19. Chappel, 5.
20. Chappel, 63.
21. Chappel, 93.
22. Chappel, 94, citing Pope Pius XI, *Ubi arcano Dei consilio* §43, https://www.vatican.va/content/pius-xi/en/encyclicals/documents/hf_p-xi_enc_19221223_ubi-arcano-dei-consilio.html.
23. Chappel, *Catholic Modern*, 94.
24. Chappel, 95.
25. Pope Pius XI, *Dilectissima nobis*, "On Oppression of the Church in Spain," §3, 1933, https://www.vatican.va/content/pius-xi/en/encyclicals/documents/hf_p-xi_enc_03061933_dilectissima-nobis.html.
26. Augustine, *City of God*, ed. D. Knowles, trans. H. Bettensen (Harmondsworth, UK: Penguin, 1972), bk. 19, c. 17.
27. Jonathan Chaplin, *Faith in Democracy: Framing a Politics of Deep Diversity* (London: SCM Press, 2021), 221.
28. Second Vatican Council, *Gaudium et spes*, §73, Pastoral Constitution on the Church Today, 1965, https://www.vatican.va/archive/hist_councils/ii_vatican_council/documents/vat-ii_cons_19651207_gaudium-et-spes_en.html.
29. Second Vatican Council, §74.
30. Second Vatican Council, §76.
31. Second Vatican Council, §76.
32. Second Vatican Council, §76.
33. Second Vatican Council, §§12, 14–17.
34. David Walsh, *The Growth of the Liberal Soul* (Columbia: University of Missouri Press, 1997), 243.
35. David Walsh, *The Priority of the Person: Political, Philosophical, and Historical Discoveries* (Notre Dame, IN: University of Notre Dame Press, 2020).
36. Walsh, 270.

37. Walsh, 270.
38. Walsh, 272.
39. The quoted material in this section is taken from Pope Benedict XVI, "Address to the United Nations," New York, 2008, https://www.vatican.va/content/benedict-xvi/en/speeches/2008/april/documents/hf_ben-xvi_spe_20080418_un-visit.html; "Address to Representatives of British Society," Westminster, 2010, https://www.vatican.va/content/benedict-xvi/en/speeches/2010/september/documents/hf_ben-xvi_spe_20100917_societa-civile.html; "Address to the German Federal Parliament," Berlin, 2011. https://www.vatican.va/content/benedict-xvi/en/speeches/2011/september/documents/hf_ben-xvi_spe_20110922_reichstag-berlin.html.
40. The original formulation is adjusted to avoid gender bias.
41. Mary Ann Glendon, "Justice and Human Rights: Reflections on the Address of Pope Benedict to the UN," *European Journal of International Law* 19, no. 5 (2008): 926, identifies nine dilemmas that beset the human rights project as highlighted by Benedict in his speech.
42. Martha Nussbaum, *Liberty of Conscience: In Defense of America's Tradition of Religious Equality* (New York: Basic Books, 2008), 23, 333.
43. John Stuart Mill, *Utilitarianism, On Liberty and Considerations on Representative Government*, ed. H. B. Acton (London: Dent, 1972), 80–83.
44. Walsh, *Priority*, 270.

CHAPTER 6

THE ROLE OF CONFLICT IN A POLITICAL ACCOUNT OF COMMON GOODS

"The question about our world is not really why so much violence, but why so little? Why are we not always at each other's throats?"¹ This question was formulated by the French scholar of literature, René Girard, famous for his mimetic theory of desire and the analysis of the scapegoating mechanism, as the political question par excellence. He raised it when delivering a D'Arcy Lecture at Oxford in 1997 on the topic "Victims, Violence, and Christianity." While recognizing the power of Girard's question, I would like to reformulate it in more positive terms: How do we succeed (when on rare occasions we actually do succeed) in managing our conflicts such that they do not erupt in violence? How do we institutionalize the peaceful handling of conflict in such a way that it becomes self-reinforcing in a virtuous circle?

In his lecture, Girard, who has his own analysis of the sources of conflict in mimetic desire, finds echoes of his description of the problem in the account of the origins of conflict given by the English political philosopher Thomas Hobbes. But when it comes to proposing a solution, Hobbes is not convincing, according to Girard: "You must have a master, Hobbes says, and this master human beings choose together among themselves in a friendly and amicable way. In order to stop their fighting, they must get together and form a government. But they do it at the very moment when they should be incapable of doing it, when the crisis is most intense, when the violence should run to extremes."²

Girard's question begins with the reality of conflict and inquires how we humans have managed conflict so that we can learn from our experience. As noted in chapter 2, where Aristotle presupposes harmony and agreement about the good life, modern political philosophy presupposes conflict. This impinges on how we are to understand the common goods of political life. I propose that we understand politics in terms of managing conflict. We should acknowledge the achievement of human cultures that have learned and continue to learn to be political in the sense of managing conflict without violence. With such an understanding, we do not discount the reality and pervasiveness of conflict, conflict that at any time could erupt into violence and have us "at each other's throats," as Girard formulates it. Hence my reformulation of the question. What is it that humankind has learned from experience about the management of conflict, and how can we reinforce and continue this learning? A further question concerns the Catholic church and whether it has been able to appropriate this learning in its reflections on social and political existence.

On this point, as elsewhere in this book, my inspiration is Aristotle, and the reception of Aristotle with interpretations of his thought. Earlier chapters explore the distinctive Aristotelian approach to political affairs and the contrast with modern approaches. Here, the immediate focus is on how politics, and the role of conflict in politics, are to be understood. In pursuing these questions, I develop some of the ideas from chapter 2, in which I defend the relevance of Aristotle to the analysis of contemporary political reality.

WHAT IS POLITICS?

To this short, blunt question I offer a succinct summary answer that requires further elaboration: politics is one way of managing social conflict. In taking this line I follow Bernard Crick's *In Defence of Politics*, which revises Aristotle's approach.[3] Politics is by no means the only way of dealing with conflict, and it may not even appear to be the most effective way. Conflict arises because the goals pursued by different people are mutually frustrating or incompatible. Conflict is socially significant when the number of people involved is large, typically when the goals pursued by different groups or classes or parties are mutually incompatible. At the beginning of the twentieth century, an Irish republic encompassing the whole island was incompatible with the continuation of Ireland within the United Kingdom; a united Ireland is incompatible with the continued existence of Northern Ireland; Brexit is incompatible with a customs union. Conflict can be managed by one group or party succeeding in imposing its will on the other group(s) through coercion. This can occur through the actual use or the threat of violence. It is helpful to clarify some terms at this point. Violence is the destruction or harming of human persons or their goods. Force is the use or threat of violence. Coercion is the effect of force. However, experience shows that coercion through the use or threat of violence is not an enduring or stable way to manage conflict.[4] As previously noted, I understand conflict in terms of incompatible *goals*: people want different things that cannot both be achieved, such as nationalization or privatization of some industry. Conflict is to be distinguished from disagreement, incompatible *propositions*, where people hold beliefs that are opposed. Disagreement does not always entail conflict; conflict always presupposes some disagreement.

The management of conflict is political when it renounces a primary reliance on coercion and attempts to achieve conciliation through negotiation, argument, and persuasion. The standard case is where the management of conflict occurs within a territory that enjoys a form of rule. Normally, today, we speak of a territory with its own form of rule as a state, or perhaps a sovereign state or even a nation-state.[5] While many wish to speak of politics in the context of international relations, the global form of conflict management lacks a sovereign authority, and while there may be impressive achievements in international law, there are not the equivalent structures of legislature, judiciary, and executive powers of implementation. What is available depends on the voluntary self-binding of states in treaties.[6]

The key to a philosophical understanding of politics is not primarily the form of the state institutions but the reliance on talking and persuasion to achieve some accommodation between conflicted parties. The common use of the English word "politics" is of the way in which interest groups compete for power within a state so as to pursue their interests as effectively as possible. The struggle for power is the core of this common usage of "politics": the contest between Republicans and Democrats in the United States, between Conservative and Labour parties in the UK. Accordingly, the conflict element is carried over in the colloquial usage, but the reliance on nonviolent means for managing conflict is not incorporated in the usual definition. For the purposes of analysis and argument, it is important to have some way of distinguishing between the handling of conflict that relies on talking or negotiation and the handling of conflict that relies on force. I attempt to maintain this distinction by stressing that only some forms of state rule are political. There are many forms of rule that (a) deny the reality and inevitability of conflict and/or (b) attempt to eliminate or resolve conflict by force. Of course, the importance of the distinction does not entail that there can be a complete separation of these elements. Max Weber rightly emphasizes that a state must claim a monopoly on the justified use of coercive force within its territory.[7] It is important to note, however, that Weber's emphasis is not on the use of force but on having a monopoly on the justified use of force. Even a state that always succeeded in handling conflict by negotiation and never had to use force would still have to claim monopoly of legitimate use of force. And this claim would on occasion be invoked in practice when individuals or groups within the state attempted to achieve their interests by violence at the expense of others or the good of all (the common good). Weber's definition picks out an unavoidable feature of a state but does not claim to be exhaustive in its explanation of the state.

In claiming Aristotle's ancestry for some key ideas, here I must take care not to misrepresent him. Zoli Filotas warns against this danger. He points to the phenomenon that scholars on both sides of the polarization between liberalism and communitarianism invoke Aristotle's patronage. He writes, "One of the reasons Aristotle scholars sometimes exaggerate his continuities with liberalism is to answer another influential group of people who distort him by exaggerating his disagreements with it, for example, by treating him as the father of an anti-liberal communitarianism."[8] Filotas interprets Aristotle as offering an account of a plurality of rule, as the subtitle of his book indicates. On this reading of Aristotle, in all forms of rule there is some hierarchy whereby someone in the cooperation provides to the other or others the end that is the telos of their collaboration. Ruling involves providing people with purposes, but that is not to be understood as commanding them or influencing them with threats or bribes. It involves speech and argument. The similarity to Aquinas's intellectualist understanding of law as discussed in chapter 4 should be evident: law is not primarily a command, but a reasonable directive pointing out what is conducive to the common good, the end or telos of the cooperating community. There is a consistency here in the emphasis on reasons and ends. Something more is at stake, however. Aristotle qualifies a form of rule as political where those people in the relationship of ruler and ruled are more or less equal, and they rotate the role of ruler. For Aristotle, when free people form relationships with their equals, they ought to take turns ruling and being ruled, and that means they rule "politically." Filotas concludes, "The clear implication is that political rule is one kind of rule among many and that even virtue friends must, when they act together, somehow negotiate the dynamics of ruling and being ruled."[9] Among equals, therefore, the role of ruler is not occupied permanently. Even in the case of a master's rule of slaves, Filotas finds Aristotle recommending the use of reason as "the most efficacious tool for controlling their souls."[10] Accordingly, a simple distinction between rule over free citizens and rule over slaves would not account for what Aristotle would consider the common element in forms of rule—namely, the use of reason to determine and provide ends or purposes for the persons ruled. This key notion grounds Filotas's critique of some modern versions attributed to Aristotle. A presupposition of those versions is that "there is one good or legitimate sort of rule that manages to avoid wronging its subjects—for example, by securing their consent, by using procedural mechanisms to protect everyone's rights, or by eliminating oppression and exploitation."[11]

My concept of politics shares Aristotle's fundamental conviction that the provision of the ends and purposes of cooperation by reasoning is central to rule over people. The difference with Aristotle's account is due to an accommodation to the conditions of modern states in which there may well be rotation of some offices with periodic elections. But this is to be understood as a way of managing the conflict over the allocation of power rather than an adjustment to the equality of rulers and ruled. Managing conflict with reasons is key to politics, and this idea is acknowledged to be Aristotelian. Those who are ruled thereby have reasons to cooperate willingly, since their rights are respected and the procedures are transparent, and so neither exploitative nor oppressive. Such benefits are typically welcomed by liberals.

Introduction of Terms

The political management of conflict will usually involve compromise. Not every party to a conflict can achieve the realization of all its goals—otherwise there would not have been a conflict in the first place. This is one reason to speak of managing and handling instead of resolving conflict. Conflict persists, but the achievement of politics is that the conflict is conducted by talking rather than with the use of force. Where a society has learned to rely on law in handling conflicts, it can appreciate the institutionalization and standardization of argument and reason as a professionalized instance of talking. Similarly with parliamentary forms. Only where there is a willingness on all sides to forego some of their objectives can political accommodation be reached. It is not surprising if weaker parties are prepared to compromise: the willingness of an economically and militarily stronger party to enter into a compromise for the sake of a peaceful settlement is not to be presupposed. Of course, the practice of politics requires considerable skill, and a culture committed to managing its conflicts by political means will devote resources to cultivating those skills. Beyond skills are virtues: qualities of moral character whereby even the stronger, more powerful personalities constrain their desire to win and get their own way in the name of fairness, justice, and the value of politics itself. This requires commitment. I will return to these topics in the final chapter.

Goals or Ideals

Conflict is understood in terms of incompatible goals. Goals are to be distinguished from ideals and values. A goal is a state of affairs which one hopes to bring about (e.g., free basic education for all children). The state of affairs is capable of being described in all relevant features. By contrast, ideals or values such as justice, peace, or compassion can be invoked to make sense of, for example, one's motivation for wanting to bring about the quality of education envisaged. Of themselves, the ideals or values are not capable of such precise description, as is the case with goals. It should be noted here that these terms, such as "justice" or "compassion," can also name virtues of persons or groups, corresponding to the values as ideals.

Notoriously, people on opposite sides of a conflict can claim justice or peace or similar values to make sense of their position. Litigants who resort to courts hope to get justice, but until the court has decided the issue, parties in dispute presume that justice in the case lies with them. The point here is not to affirm that courts always succeed in doing justice; there are too many examples of blatant miscarriages of justice to make that case. Instead, the point is that many who invoke justice are not in agreement on what arrangements they judge as just: the appeal to justice alone does not provide common ground. Conflict is not resolved simply by parties in dispute espousing values and ideals such as justice or even care for our common home. The language of values and ideals is aspirational, and it is not necessarily helpful for managing conflict. In fact, it can hinder the political dealing with conflict because an apparent agreement at the level of ideals may obscure the real differences of interests in what is proposed. For example, those who advocate the nationalization of the banks are opposed by free market proponents, but both sides make their case in terms of what is conducive to the good of the economy and the common good. Reference to the values of the public welfare or the common good does not decide the issue in favor of one or another goal. A different impression is given when the "common good" is deemed sufficiently specific to delineate an alternative to the object of criticism, such as Sandel's writing of the common good as if it were an alternative to meritocracy, or Mark Carney's wishing to restore values to public discourse.[12] I endorse the commitment to common goods and the need to espouse values, but the hard work remains of working out what goals we can agree on to implement our values. These authors will be discussed more fully in chapter 9. The point here is to illustrate the use of value terms as vague and ambiguous.

There are some advantages in using ambiguous language as we attempt to manage conflicts. Capitalists and Communists were able to sign up to the Universal Declaration's right to work: capitalists understood it as a liberty, the freedom to pursue a career and enter into employment without interference by the state, and so imposing a negative duty on the state not to interfere; Soviet Communists understood it as a claim-right with a corresponding positive duty for the state to be employer of last resort, guaranteeing everyone a job. Ambiguities facilitate the management of conflict but illustrate how they do not resolve it: the conflict is postponed or moved to a different level.

Goals and Means: Practical and Technical

The distinction between means and goals is also relevant, and it allows a further distinction between the technical and the practical. The practical has to do with goals while the technical concentrates on means. Many of those who hold power in public office often prefer to see politics as a technical matter. Candidates present themselves to electorates as technicians, with the necessary competence to implement the measures which are means to the assumed goals: "Get Brexit Done!" "Make America Great Again!"[13] The goals are assumed to be agreed and are typically presented in noncontroversial language: full employment, social welfare, education, health care, security. However, the assumption of agreement glosses over the real conflicts between incompatible goals, so the language of ideals and values short-circuits the process. Since all are assumed to want justice, peace, and prosperity, it appears that the only issue remaining is to decide on the means to be adopted to bring them about. And that issue reverts to the question of which professionals are most skilled in the selection and operation of means and so best placed to deliver the desired goals.

Some of those who theorize about politics reinforce this view that it is ultimately not a practical matter, about divergent goals, but a technical matter, about implementing the right means. Plato's vision of the philosopher king is one example, giving priority to the mastery of the knowledge whereby the city could be guided to good order, without allowing for the possibility that there might be validly diverging views about what would constitute good order. Machiavelli in *The Prince* also concentrated on the question of means, assuming the goals of the prince were given. Curiously, nationalists, republicans, and socialists also tend to deny the practical nature of politics. While they provide an analysis to explain the occurrence of conflict (incompatible goals), they aspire to a situation in which no conflict would occur. Marxists aim for a conflict-free, classless society. Nationalists are confident that the people—or the nation, once allowed to rule itself—will be so unified that it will pursue its destiny without diverting from its chosen path. Anyone who might challenge this required unity is regarded, therefore, as disqualifying themselves as a member of the nation, or people, or classless, progressive society. The persistent blindness of Irish Nationalists to the existence of a significantly large population of Unionists in the north of Ireland, though a minority on the island, is evidence of this anti-political tendency in nationalism.

Republicans inspired by Rousseau wish to suppress the kind of politics based on competing sectional interests and party factions to ensure a harmonious pursuit of the common good as found in the general will. This was the shared view of the founder generation of the American republic. At the beginning, they declared themselves opposed to political parties, because parties replace the common good, the interest of the republic, with the good of the party—sectional interest. Thomas Jefferson is quoted as saying that if he could not go to Heaven but with a party, he would not go there at all.[14] However, Jefferson himself was instrumental in developing a party system, since it quickly became obvious that parties were very necessary in managing conflict: they enabled urgent issues of public relevance to be focused and clarified, unlike the situation with many individuals all pursuing the issues that they (or their constituents) considered important. A second advantage in a party system is the possibility of mobilizing support for policy and delivering the votes in Parliament or Congress. Practical considerations soon moved the idealists to a greater realism.

Knowledge

The poverty of the language available to our societies for managing conflict reflects general disregard for fundamental issues about the goods to be achieved in human society. These are the issues about what we want, how we want to live, what quality of relationships we desire to have with each other.[15] Our culture gives preeminence to the technical in many ways, but especially in our investment in knowledge. Pope Francis, in his letter *Laudato Si'*, makes this point convincingly in terms of the dominance of the technocratic paradigm.[16]

For the sake of what we might wish to do, to build and create, we invest a lot of effort in accumulating technical knowledge. This is primarily knowledge about materials, which enables us to exploit fossil fuels, wind and sun power, radioactive elements, microchip processors, and so on. The extent of our culture's investment in the accumulation of such knowledge is evident. There is no comparable investment by our culture in accumulating practical knowledge. To know what people want and what conflicted parties want would require a mastery of the languages in which people express their convictions and values. These include the languages of religious worldviews, in which people express their fundamental desires and their ultimate aspirations. A culture committed to managing conflict by political means would endeavor to be literate in what people want, what groups want, and their relevant histories. This requires complex hermeneutic skills, since we should expect it to be the case that people want many things, that their goals are diverse and often conflicted. Accordingly, it is not a matter of having an established, agreed principle or set of principles specifying a highest good or most fundamental set of needs from which guidance and directives might be drawn; that would be the model of technical knowledge.

Religious Worldviews and Religious Language

Good people wanting to do good things are in conflict with one another, because the goals they pursue are incompatible. This is the normal situation in government. For instance, cabinet ministers seeking more resources for their departments are in conflict. More money for education means less for security, or social welfare, or health. Conflict occurs because of the richness of the human good, the creativity of human agents, and the limitations of time, energy, and material resources for the agents to realize their plans and objectives. Of course, conflict also occurs because of greed, hatred, and the desire to dominate others. It is important that religious people, and Christians in particular, be free of the prejudice that conflict arises only from fault or sin on the part of some participant in the conflict. It is an important corrective for religious worldviews to accept that conflict can also arise from good people wanting to do good things.

Just as there have been philosophers (e.g., Plato, Rousseau, Marx) who have discounted conflict, so, too, there are theological accounts often drawing on eschatological visions of God's kingdom that regard conflict only in negative terms. Most religious visions, with their associated ideals, favor harmony, community, and peace—between the Creator and creatures, between all humankind, peoples, and states, and between humans and the rest of creation. Christian rhetoric often appeals to values, ideals, and visions of the good, immediately evoked by powerful symbols (swords into plowshares, the heavenly banquet, the healing of the blind and lame). But the relevant values and ideals cannot function as premises in arguments from which governments or other authorities can deduce suitable policy proposals. Christians must take care that their invoking of their ideals not distract from or frustrate the work of building viable proposals based on reliable practical knowledge of the issues.

The danger in this case is that religious language minimizes or even denies the reality of actual conflict, stressing instead the aspiration to harmony and community which it holds out as a promise. But the opposite danger is also linked to the use of religious language—namely, that it exacerbates conflict and polarizes the parties. Religiously inspired languages can be problematic in the face of conflict. Instead of recognizing what is common to the conflicted parties, the language of faith can stress instead the divisions, the differences between the insiders and the others. The familiar pairs of Jew and Gentile, believer and infidel, Christian and non-Christian, the *ummah* and the *kafir*, convey the separation. Common to these examples is the use of terminology that originates within one worldview, and which is used by sharers in that worldview to speak of those who are outside.

To be political in the proper sense, citizens require an appropriate language for conflict in which parties in conflict can speak *to* each other, and not simply speak *about* each other. The dangers with the latter are many. One is that the speaker can be misled into depicting the opponent in terms which that opponent does not recognize. These terms can be loaded with presuppositions from one side of the polarization. Another is that the opponent can be treated as an object, to be described, evaluated, analyzed, and discussed but not directly addressed. To speak *to*, and not simply *about*, each other in a conflict situation requires a degree of communality at least at the level of language. A shared language is required in which each in turn can have the status both of *speaker* and *spoken to*. It must be a language that is rooted in a common humanity.

Is there a common language in which we can speak across the divisions, and not only about those on the other side? Secularists have long advocated their stance as providing the needed neutral ground, but that neutrality is suspect. Alasdair MacIntyre, among others, has highlighted the illusion and the danger that people of faith may have sold the pass in conversations simply by accepting the ideology of a neutral language.[17] The politics of recognition and identity politics are built on the argument that the standard assumptions about the autonomous agent and the nature of practical rationality are not only not neutral, as they claim, but privilege one kind of identity and mode of experience, typically that of the masculine, Western individual.[18] However, the supposedly neutral language of the secularist is not the only stance. It is conceivable that the languages of faith themselves might still embrace a perspective that can recognize a common humanity beyond the divisions of faith allegiance. This more than anything else is the precondition for a political handling of fundamental conflict. Is it possible for people of religious conviction to transcend the divisiveness and polarization implicit and often explicit in their inherited languages without abandoning their religious worldview? Is there a possible perspective, rooted in a shared humanity, which acknowledges the religious dimension of human experience and so does not entail abandonment of deeply held convictions but enables a speaking *to* opponents and not merely *about* them? To ask these questions is not to fall into the trap of accepting that religious difference is the principal source of conflict. William Cavanaugh challenges the myth of religion as the source of conflict. We do not have to adopt the thesis that conflict emanates primarily from religious differences to accept the propensity of faith movements to be divisive, or to acknowledge the history of religious conflict, often violent in its expression.[19] Note, again, that my account of conflict points to incompatible goals and not to divergent comprehensive doctrines or worldviews.

The joint declaration by Pope Francis and the Grand Imam of Al-Azhar, Ahmed al-Tayyeb, in Abu Dhabi in February 2019, exemplifies the effort to seek common ground. Their joint statement, *A Document on Human Fraternity for World Peace and Living Together*, expresses a simple but sincere invitation to "all persons who have faith in God and faith in human fraternity to unite and work together so that it may serve as a guide for future generations to advance a culture of mutual respect in the awareness of the great divine grace that makes all human beings brothers and sisters."[20] A pity that their choice of title, as with Pope Francis's later *Fratelli tutti*, seems to discount women.

The Human Wisdom of the Decalogue

In the search for elements in religious worldviews that provide a foundation for dialogue across divisions, the Decalogue, the Ten Commandments, has been recognized as expressing the moral preconditions for human society. Reformed Christian theologian Paul L. Lehmann was concerned with the political implications of Christian faith. He had been a friend of Dietrich Bonhoeffer, and his own political involvement included resistance to the McCarthyism of 1950s America and engagement in the campaign for civil rights. Nancy J. Duff worked with Lehmann on his book *The Decalogue and a Human Future* and edited it for publication after his death.[21] She explains that the subtitle of the book carries a longstanding theme of Lehmann's writing and teaching: "Making and Keeping Human Life Human." Lehmann sees the commandments delivered by Moses as humanizing forces in the face of dehumanizing pressures on human life. Relationships of domination threaten to dehumanize both oppressors and victims. Duff explains that the commandments "have to do with how power is wielded among human beings—whether that means labourers who need time to rest, elderly parents who need to be honoured, or the poor who have been falsely accused and need to be defended in court."[22] With this emphasis on how power is exercised, the commandments' demands are addressed to the powerful. They protect the interests of the weak and vulnerable, but in such a way that the onus is on the powerful to secure their interests rather than on the weaker party to fight for their entitlements.

This twentieth-century approach to the Decalogue has its precedents in the medieval thesis that what Moses enjoined on the people as divine law was identical to what human reason might know as requirements of natural law. Thomas Aquinas was not alone among medieval authors in spelling out the relationship between what human reason knows by its own lights and what it is instructed to do by divine revelation or human law. From a very general precept that "no one should harm another," derived from the basic orientation of practical reason that "good is to be done and pursued and evil avoided," Aquinas recognized that the injunctions of the second tablet of the Decalogue made this more precise—not to kill, not to steal, not to falsely accuse, not to violate marital commitments.[23] Although presented in the biblical literature as part of God's covenant with his chosen people and so part of divinely revealed law, Aquinas considered that its general precepts were consistent with what humans were capable of knowing apart from special revelation, relying on the revelation of the good implicit in creation itself. In other words, violation of those norms prohibiting killing, theft, perjury, and adultery could be seen as a practical denial of a common humanity. Such a violation would be tantamount to the assertion that the other, the stranger or the enemy, was not entitled to the respect one would demand for oneself.

Alasdair MacIntyre has elaborated this thought in the context of contemporary disputes about what is owed to others. The context for his reflection is the failure to find agreement on the fundamental principles regulating social existence, also because the ethical theories espoused by different people are so incompatible. This experience provokes the question of whether there is in fact a natural law rooted in a common human nature. MacIntyre answers this challenge by reflecting on the preconditions for rational engagement between adherents of competing and opposed worldviews. Wanting to avoid a situation in which power determines outcomes, the only option for reasonable people is to enter into dialogue despite their differences, which are so fundamental as to make all dialogue problematic. Such discourse will not be possible unless participants are bound by rules. MacIntyre argues that "we will only be able to enquire together with such others in a way that accords with the canons of rationality, if both we and they treat as binding upon us a set of rules that turn out to be just those enjoined by the natural law."[24] The shared inquiry required for the reasonable resolution of intractable moral disagreements would have to recognize the good of truth as constitutive of the human good. The pursuit of truth, MacIntyre suggests, could not simply be instrumentalized to other goods and would have to be given a place in the overall plan of human life and activity, supported by appropriate virtues and rules.[25] Acknowledging that the pursuit of truth in the context of disagreement is precarious, the open and self-critical engagement with others must presuppose a trust that one will not be attacked, robbed, lied to, or otherwise taken advantage of. These expectations, when articulated as precepts, are identified as preconditions for rational inquiry, and so are not known as a result of inquiry. Here MacIntyre sees further the parallel to Aquinas's claims for the precepts of the natural law. His conditions for rational inquiry are like Aquinas's precepts, universal in scope, exceptionless, and the same for everyone. He concludes that theoretical argument cannot provide justification for these precepts but can attempt to show that they are presupposed by rational inquiry, and that any practical inquiry "which does not presuppose them fails in rationality."[26]

THE CATHOLIC CHURCH AND THE POLITICAL COMMON GOOD

If the common goods of a liberal democratic polity include a culture that accepts the prevalence of conflict and institutions for managing conflict, can these be accommodated within the Catholic church's overall vision? Is church teaching comfortable with conflict, its prevalence, and recognition of its inevitability? Considering the notion of common good as mentioned in *Gaudium et spes* (the set of conditions that enables each one and every community to achieve fulfillment),[27] we can ask whether the structures and procedures of liberal democratic regimes within pluralist societies belong among those conditions that comprise the common good. Are those structures and procedures to be valued and respected even when they lead to outcomes that the church authorities would judge are not for the common good? What is the relationship between the good pursued in the secular domain and the good pursued by the church?

Learning from Politics

Plato uses the metaphor of the ship to contrast democracy with good order, to the detriment of democracy. On the one hand, he describes the situation of the ship guided by a captain who knows his port of destination and has mastered the relevant navigation skills to reach it. On the other hand, he uses the image of a motley crew in which there is no single voice commanding obedience, but each one on board has his own view of where the ship should go and how it should be brought there.[28] In the face of this polemic it is difficult to make a case for a form of rule that is not based on an appeal to the ruler's unique knowledge, skill, or competence. But that is precisely what is required if we are to see the point of liberal democracy. There are plenty of persons or groups competing for power, claiming to have the relevant knowledge and competence. But there is no agreed criterion to decide which views are correct and who is entitled to rule. MacIntyre is correct in his analysis to this extent: the disintegration of a shared worldview and agreement regarding a hierarchy of goods makes it impossible for someone to be recognized as entitled to rule due to superior knowledge.

Contrary to the position taken by MacIntyre and other critics of liberal regimes, I argue that there is something truly valuable in the achievement of modern liberal politics. It represents the institutionalization of a distinctive way of managing social conflict. As argued earlier, the management of conflict is political when it renounces a primary reliance on coercion or domination and when it attempts to achieve conciliation through negotiation, argument, and persuasion. The political management of conflict will usually involve compromise. Only where there is a willingness on all sides to forego some of their objectives can political agreement be reached. This is not an argument in favor of liberal democracy based on any claim that democracy provides a way of reaching better, more rational, or more grounded decisions. Nor is it an argument in favor of democracy as such. It is simply a claim that the regimes with a commitment to handle conflict by talking mark a major step forward in human ordering of social life. These are *political* forms of rule, and the distinction allows us to remark that many nominally democratic regimes fail to be political insofar as they institutionalize the domination by the majority. "Winner takes all" attitudes operative in recent experiences illustrate this corruption of democracy.

Although conflict usually entails disagreement, not every disagreement leads to conflict. Disagreement occurs when parties in conversation are committed to incompatible propositions. There are different opinions and points of view. By contrast, conflict arises when people want things which, for one reason or another, they cannot all have. Circumstances of scarcity, incompatibility, or interdependence mean that some fail to get what they want if others succeed. *Gaudium et spes* has many references to disagreement: see §74, which locates the need for political authority in the coexistence of "widely differing points of view" (*in diversa consilia*) and the chaos to be avoided should everyone "follow their own opinion." Also, in §75, Christians are encouraged to "recognize the legitimacy of differing points of view" (*at inter se discrepantes, opiniones agnoscant*) and to respect those "who defend their opinions by legitimate means." Conflict as distinct from disagreement is also mentioned, but in such a way that the centrality of conflict to liberal democratic politics is overlooked. There are cases of conflict of interests, incompatible goals, when rulers place their own interests ahead of the common good (§73) and citizens pursue their own interests at the expense of the common good (§75). The problem with these cases is the implicit assumption that *there is an identifiable common good* being jeopardized by pursuit of special interests. Comparable texts in *Laudato Si'* concerning conflicts between sectional interests and the common good also seem to imply that the common good is a known quantity.[29] The normal case in liberal democratic politics is not considered—namely, where the challenge is to work out some way of managing the conflict between warranted interests and interest groups and there is no way of knowing in advance which interests are more justified than others. The cases of conflict in which good people pursuing worthwhile objectives prevent each other from succeeding exemplify this problem. As noted above, the administration of any well-functioning liberal democracy will face competing demands for resources—for health care, education, security, job creation, social welfare, defense, and pensions. Conflict is at the heart of democratic politics—that is, a conflict which is not simply due to moral fault or flaw, the inordinate pursuit of particular interests, and where the common good is not available as an already-known quantity to determine correct solutions.

Ignorance of the Common Good

Who knows what is for the common good? In chapter 4 we examined Aquinas's definition of law as "a certain ordinance of reason for the common good, made by him who has care of the community, and promulgated."[30] Recalling the analogical predication on which Aquinas relies, we can note how the divine lawgiver can know what is for the good of creation and the common good of humankind. However, for the instances of human lawmaking, the lawgiver is not blessed with complete knowledge of all aspects, nor with infallibility. The one who has care of the community has responsibility for the common good, and in Aquinas's world this was the prince or king, or in one case, the emperor. This phrase typically identifies the ruler in terms of their central responsibility—namely, to care for the common good of the community. Function, not structure or constitution, is the key to understanding political authority in this approach. Whatever form the constitution of the political community may take—principality, kingdom, empire, city-state, republic—those with authority in the community have responsibility to care for the common good. Inevitably, the predominance of monarchy or principality meant that the imagery for political authority was mostly of individuals exercising power.

Aquinas's influence on the development of Catholic thought resulted in an adoption of the same approach, even up to the social teaching of the church in the twentieth century. The state, governments, and political authorities are all reviewed in terms not of legitimacy, as conceived in the liberal tradition, or effectiveness or constitution, but relative to the common good. This is not to be seen as an essential definition, but it specifies a function, the obligation of which is not dependent on the moral goodness or legitimacy of the incumbent.

It is plausible to think that Plato's ideal of the philosopher king shaped Catholic notions of the responsibility of the prince in a culture in which the ruler was expected to know the good of the kingdom and pursue it. Augustine's framing of advice to Christian rulers on the model of the *pater familias*, the father of a family, incorporates a similar image. The prince, king, or emperor was assumed to know what was needed for the common good, and so could make and promulgate reasonable directives for the common good. In fact, the principle of *cuius regio eius religio*, adopted in the Peace of Augsburg in 1555, tacitly accepted that the good of the principality was what the prince thought was good for it.

The great advantage of this functional understanding of political authority was that it was applicable across a range of constitutions. As a result, revolutionary changes of regime did not require the church to rethink its teaching. A postrevolutionary regime was as obliged as the one it had replaced to serve the common good. It was thought that law should be reasonable and directed to the common good, whether made by a monarch, a triumvirate, or a parliament. The form of state or constitution was irrelevant; the function of political authority remained the same. But perhaps there was a hidden trap there? If something significantly different was emerging in the historical process with the creation of democratic institutions predicated on liberty, then reliance on the assumption of continuity of function could blind the church teachers to the nature of what they addressed.

Danger of Corruption

Limited knowledge is not the only or primary burden on democratic societies. They must also cope with conflict. Liberal democratic systems of government in pluralist societies are vulnerable to the kind of polemic evident in Plato, the disorganized mob attempting to sail a ship. There are individuals and groups mobilizing sources of power and influence, and politics is the struggle to find some conciliation between competing interests. That involves compromise, and compromise outcomes often fail to be rationally coherent. They seldom reflect an integrated set of goods sustained by a single vision of the good life. The muddling through of liberal democratic societies is also the achievement of a *modus vivendi*, a way of getting on together somehow. Seldom can it be said in such systems that conflicts have been resolved. Typically, the conflicts of interest persist, and the processes of negotiation and bargaining must be continued. Inverting von Clausewitz's famous remark, we can say that politics is war carried on by other means; parliamentary debate replaces the battles of a civil war. Just as Plato's polemic was telling against the ignorance of a democratic electorate, so, too, MacIntyre's polemic scores many hits against the conflict management of liberal democracies. He argues that there is no comprehensive vision of the good that embraces in a coherent unity all the particular goods pursued by groups within the society, and that in practice solutions are not generated by rational deliberation but by bargaining toward a compromise. The ever-present danger of corruption in such democratic systems is that the currency of problem-solving is not reason but power—the power of greater numbers or of greater wealth, or both.

If we accept that the whole citizen body has charge of the common good in a democratic polity, along with the representatives and officers elected or appointed for particular functions, we must acknowledge that the common good which they seek is not and cannot be a prescribed set of policies derived from a notion of the best or highest good. This is John Rawls's challenge in *Political Liberalism*: that we accept the fact of reasonable plurality as setting the context for politics. We must also accept that working out the actual set of projects that will constitute the society's common good will rarely, if ever, be conducted as a philosophy seminar, relying exclusively on reasoned argument in attempting to overcome disagreement, but will be the more or less satisfactory outcome of a contest of conflicting interests and a struggle for influence. While democratic politics, as Pope John Paul II insists, is not a way of determining what is true or right,[31] it is a means for parties in conflict to find some way of living together.

Admitting their ignorance of what policies in what areas of common life in what places and times would serve the common good, Christians and the church can nonetheless make a positive contribution to the process. Proposing the common good as a heuristic concept and articulating its criteria can help direct the process in a positive way.

Dynamic Sense of Common Good

The fourth chapter of *Gaudium et spes* deals with the political community and regularly cites the common good, but in one particular text there is a curious qualification. The term "common good" is to be "understood in the dynamic sense of the term."[32] Little is offered to explain this or to clarify what might be the other sense or senses used in other passages: Static rather than dynamic, or substantive as distinct from procedural? I suggest that this qualification is an admission of the vagueness or open-endedness in all the usages of the term in the context of the political community. It is an acknowledgment that the search for the common good is ongoing. In other words, it admits that the core idea of the common good is heuristic, naming that which is being sought but which is not yet known, although enough about it is known to be able to specify the program for its discovery. The specification of the common good as heuristic does not compromise the ontological commitments of the Catholic position, or, indeed, of Aristotle. Recall the discussion in chapter 2 considering Yack's separation of what citizens can negotiate as their common good from the philosophical knowledge of human goods in common.[33] Those who construct a theory of politics, and those who construct and implement institutions for achieving political goals, are engaged in creating something that might be labeled artificial. However, the fact of construction alone does not entail a denial of realism in a claim that what is artificial cannot be grounded in what is, whether human nature or nature in general. In understanding realism as commitment to the existence of a reality independent of human cognition, and to the view that this reality has its own order, it does not follow that invention or creation of theory or of institutions is without grounds in the nature of things. This is because the program of construction can at the same time be a process of discovery. The trial and error associated with the process of construction can provide the evidence for a conclusion that what works does so because it is grounded in what is appropriate for humans and their fulfillment. The dynamic sense of common good is related to such a project of discovery, and the concept of "common good" is itself heuristic in guiding the discovery. Enough is known about it to allow the application of criteria, exhibiting shortcomings in what is already achieved, or inadequacy in proposed candidates. The criteria proposed philosophically in chapter 1 also find expression in many of the church's advocacy stances—for instance, in making the option for the poor (first criterion) and in protecting the religious dimension in educational policies (second criterion).[34] Together they are succinctly expressed in the theme of *Populorum progressio* and *Caritas in veritate*, concern for the development of every person (first criterion) and of the whole person (second).[35]

Francis on Conflict

Pope Francis, in *Fratelli tutti*, acknowledges the reality of conflict. He appeals to his readers, especially Christians, not to run away from conflict but to engage in conflict in the hope of achieving a dialogue and a conciliation that avoids the destructiveness of violence. He has definitely moved the thinking of the church beyond the ambivalence we have seen in the confusion of disagreement and conflict in the Second Vatican Council's *Gaudium et spes*. At the same time, he invokes Benedict's placing of the dignity of the human person at the center of politics, along with commitment to the common good. The same difficulty persists, however, of mentioning the common good as if it were a quantity or content already substantially known. In facing the reality of conflict, Francis affirms his own approach encouraging engagement with opponents, citing previous authorities in support. In affirming the task of building social peace, he repeats the two central themes of the dignity of the human person and respect for the common good. But he also acknowledges the temptations when engaged in social action to seek "revenge and the satisfaction of short-term partisan interests."[36] This is a quotation from a speech he made in Bolivia in 2017, where the challenge of building social peace is very real. He quotes Pope John Paul II from *Centesimus annus* (1991, §14) to the effect that the church "does not intend to condemn every possible form of social conflict. The church is well aware that in the course of history conflicts of interest between different social groups inevitably arise, and that in the face of such conflicts Christians must often take a position, honestly and decisively."[37] Finally, he acknowledges that peace can be achieved in conflict: "Authentic reconciliation does not flee from conflict, but is achieved *in* conflict, resolving it through dialogue and open, honest and patient negotiation. Conflict between different groups 'if it abstains from enmities and mutual hatred, gradually changes into an honest discussion of differences founded on a desire for justice.'"[38] The cited passage is from Pius XI in *Quadragesimo anno*. Francis invokes his predecessors Pius XI and John Paul II to underline that acknowledgment of the reality of conflict as the context for the church's ministry is not new. In summary, we can see the position outlined in *Fratelli tutti* to include the following: (1) an acknowledgment of the reality of social conflict; (2) a challenge to engage in that conflict for the sake of human dignity and common goods; (3) recognition that such engagement will expose Christians to the temptations to resort to violence driven by hatred or desire for revenge; and (4) a commitment to renounce the use of force and engage in negotiation and dialogue.

CONCLUSION

This chapter began with a reformulation of Girard's question: How do we succeed (when on rare occasions we do succeed) in managing our conflicts such that they do not erupt in violence? How do we institutionalize the peaceful and peace-reinforcing management of conflict? My exploration of the nature of politics and its relation to conflict permits the suggested answer. We institutionalize the peaceful handling of conflict:

1. by valuing politics as activity based on the commitment to manage conflict by talking, and by acknowledging that such activity and its institutions are among our common goods—namely, the set of means and conditions for human flourishing
2. by valuing every human person as a transcendent value
3. by valuing the persons of character who are willing to put themselves forward as political actors, by valuing the skills and virtues they require, and including these among the aims of our educational systems
4. by valuing practical knowledge as much as we value technical knowledge and fostering the development of related human and social sciences

To the extent that we don't do these things, we leave ourselves vulnerable to those who can promise "to get things done," "whatever it may cost." And if we are not always at one another's throats, it is because there are persons in place, with character and virtue and appropriate skill and knowledge, supported by appropriate institutions, to facilitate the political handling of conflict. These common goods of persons, skills, knowledge, and institutions facilitate all our goods in common.

NOTES

1. René Girard, "Victims, Violence, and Christianity," *The Month* 259, no. 1564, 2nd n.s. 31, no. 4 (1998): 133.
2. Girard, 133.
3. Bernard Crick, *In Defence of Politics*, new ed. (London: Continuum, 2005).
4. James A. Schellenberg, *The Science of Conflict* (Oxford: Oxford University Press, 1982).
5. Recall the explanation of "state" presented in chapter 2 as a society articulated for action in the world.
6. Patrick Riordan, *Global Ethics and Global Common Goods* (London: Bloomsbury, 2015), 115–17.
7. Max Weber, "Politics as a Vocation," in *Max Weber*, trans. and ed. H. H. Gerth and C. Wright Mills (London: Routledge and Kegan Paul, 1948).
8. Zoli Filotas, *Aristotle and the Ethics of Difference, Friendship, and Equality: The Plurality of Rule* (London: Bloomsbury, 2021), 141.
9. Filotas, 8.
10. Filotas, chap. 1 and 140.
11. Filotas, 5.
12. Michael Sandel, *The Tyranny of Merit: What's Become of the Common Good?* (London: Allen Lane, 2020); Mark Carney, *Value(s): Building a Better World for All* (London: William Collins, 2021).

13. Crick, *In Defence of Politics*, chap. 5, "A Defence of Politics against Technology."
14. J. J. Ellis, *American Sphinx: The Character of Thomas Jefferson* (New York: Vintage Books, 1998), 144, 235–36.
15. The referents of "we" in this and similar sentences are the citizens of political systems.
16. Pope Francis, *Laudato Si'*, "On care for our common home," §§101–14, 2015, https://www.vatican.va/content/francesco/en/encyclicals/documents/papa-francesco_20150524_enciclica-laudato-si.html.
17. Alasdair MacIntyre, *Three Rival Versions of Moral Enquiry: Encyclopaedia, Genealogy, and Tradition* (London: Duckworth, 1990).
18. Charles Taylor, "The Politics of Recognition," in *Philosophical Arguments* (Cambridge, MA: Harvard University Press, 1995).
19. William T. Cavanaugh, *The Myth of Religious Violence* (Oxford: Oxford University Press, 2009).
20. Pope Francis, *Document on Human Fraternity for World Peace and Living Together*, Apostolic Journey of His Holiness Pope Francis to the United Arab Emirates, Abu Dhabi, February 3–5, 2019, https://www.vatican.va/content/francesco/en/travels/2019/outside/documents/papa-francesco_20190204_documento-fratellanza-umana.html.
21. Paul L. Lehmann, *The Decalogue and A Human Future: The Meaning of the Commandments for Making and Keeping Life Human* (Grand Rapids, MI: Eerdmans, 1995).
22. Nancy J. Duff, "The Commandments and the Common Life: Reflections on Paul Lehmann's *The Decalogue and a Human Future*," in *Explorations in Christian Theology and Ethics: Essays in Conversation with Paul L. Lehmann*, ed. Philip G. Ziegler and Michelle J. Bartel (Farnham, Surrey, UK: Ashgate, 2009), 41–42.
23. Jean Porter, "Does the Natural Law Provide a Universally Valid Morality?" in *Intractable Disputes about the Natural Law: Alasdair MacIntyre and Critics*, ed. Lawrence S. Cunningham (Notre Dame, IN: University of Notre Dame Press, 2009).
24. Alasdair MacIntyre, "Intractable Moral Disagreements," in *Intractable Disputes about the Natural Law: Alasdair MacIntyre and Critics*, ed. Lawrence S. Cunningham (Notre Dame, IN: University of Notre Dame Press, 2009), 3.
25. MacIntyre, "Intractable," 20–24.
26. MacIntyre, "Intractable," 24.
27. Second Vatican Council, *Gaudium et spes*, Pastoral Constitution on the Church Today, §26, 1965, https://www.vatican.va/archive/hist_councils/ii_vatican_council/documents/vat-ii_cons_19651207_gaudium-et-spes_en.html.
28. Plato, *The Republic*, trans. Benjamin Jowett (London: Sphere Books, 1970), bk. 6, 488a–489a.
29. Pope Francis, *Laudato Si'*, §54.
30. Thomas Aquinas, *Summa Theologiae*, vol. 28, trans. Thomas Gilby, OP (London: Blackfriars, in conjunction with Eyre and Spottiswoode, 1966), pt. 1–2, q. 90, a. 4.
31. Pope John Paul II, *Fides et ratio*, "On Faith and Reason," §89, 1998, https://www.vatican.va/content/john-paul-ii/en/encyclicals/documents/hf_jp-ii_enc_14091998_fides-et-ratio.html.
32. Second Vatican Council, *Gaudium et spes* §74: "commune bonum—et quidem dynamice conceptum."
33. Bernard Yack, *The Problems of a Political Animal: Community, Justice, and Conflict in Aristotelian Political Thought* (Berkeley: University of California Press, 1993), 170.

34. Patrick Riordan, "Europe's Common Good: The Contribution of the Catholic Church," in *Religion: Problem or Promise? The Role of Religion in the Integration of Europe*, ed. Šimon Marinčák, *Orientalia et Occidentalia* 4 (2009).
35. Pope Benedict XVI, *Caritas in veritate*, "Love in Truth," §8, 2009, http://w2.vatican.va/content/benedict-xvi/en/encyclicals/documents/hf_ben-xvi_enc_20090629_caritas-in-veritate.html, §58, emphasis in original.
36. Pope Francis, *Fratelli tutti*, "On Fraternity and Social Friendship," §232, 2020, https://www.vatican.va/content/francesco/en/encyclicals/documents/papa-francesco_20201003_enciclica-fratelli-tutti.html.
37. Pope Francis, *Fratelli tutti*, §240.
38. Pope Francis, *Fratelli tutti*, §244.

CHAPTER 7

UTOPIA AND APOCALYPSE

The theological clarification of the notion of the "secular" in chapter 3 on political Augustinianism suggests that states can be considered as placed along a spectrum where the poles are *closed to the transcendent* and *open to the transcendent*. As remarked in chapter 5, Pope Benedict has relied on secular language to encourage states to adopt the latter stance. Such a standpoint requires of states that they recognize the limits to their competence, notably regarding common goods. The common good corresponding to the civil authorities is that set of conditions for individual and communal flourishing, noted by the Second Vatican Council in *Gaudium et spes*, while the more extensive common good of ultimate fulfillment exceeds the competence of the state. However, history provides many examples of states that have claimed for themselves the right not only to define the ultimate end of humankind but to impose it coercively on their members. The themes of utopia and apocalypse addressed in this chapter allow for an examination of the distortion of the political common good and an illustration of the lack of openness to the transcendent that sometimes conditions how political leaders and institutions understand their power and status.

COMMON GOOD AS TOTALITARIAN

The standard objection to talk about the common good and common goods links this notion with authoritarian regimes. This was my experience over thirty years ago when I first wrote about this topic. Since the Fascists of Italy, the National Socialists of Germany, and the Communists of Soviet Russia had claimed to represent the common good of their respective peoples, it was thought impossible to use the term without evoking the aura of totalitarianism. In a way, this objection remained current in the form that espousal of common goods is conservative in upholding the status quo and so inevitably links to authoritarianism of some kind, even if the authority in question is the inertia that resists change. However, it was not just a case of risking being condemned by association, of appearing in a similar guise to those rejected forms of political culture; the critics suspected something fundamentally flawed in the language of the common good. Given the great upsurge of interest in human rights in the 1970s and 1980s, the suspected flaw in common good talk was both a neglect of human rights and a willingness to tolerate their violation in the name of public interests. Whoever spoke about political affairs in terms of common goods was tarred by association with the premise attributed to Jean-Jacques Rousseau, a significant proponent of a political common good, that people could be forced to be free. Whatever the adequacy of this interpretation of the political philosophical thought of the French republican, the standard interpretation in the English-speaking world attributed to him the view that it would be permissible to force people to accept the conditions of freedom. Isaiah Berlin was a significant contributor to the predominance of this view when he contrasted the notions of positive liberty and negative liberty.[1] The latter he saw as represented by the mainline tradition of English political thought, leading to those freedoms that are formulated in the human rights of freedom from all forms of discrimination. The rights to hold views and express and publish them, and to associate freely with others without interference from public authorities: these are the kernel of human rights asserted over against the state.

By contrast with negative liberty, which secures for individuals their scope for action free from interference by the state, positive liberty stresses the conditions for free action and points to forms of self-mastery, ensuring freedom not merely from external interference but from internal drives such as addiction or irrational enthusiasm. To be able to align one's actions with the demands of reason or with a vision of the self as one would wish to be is to be free in the positive sense, as Kant holds. The problem for Berlin arises when state authorities take exclusively to themselves the responsibility for interpreting what reason demands and the vision of self and society that is to be pursued. He does not deny that liberty must be curtailed to some extent in society, "since human purposes and activities do not automatically harmonize with one another," but there is a limit: "a certain minimum area of personal freedom which must on no account be violated." Those who followed Berlin in the emphasis on the question "How far does government interfere with me?" were inevitably concerned about any advocacy in favor of common goods as the purpose of public life and government itself, suspecting the threat of infringement on personal liberties.[2]

In social and cultural life, appeals to common goods were also being exposed as covertly oppressive. Feminists were reacting to the pressures on women to place themselves in service of the common good of their families, even if that meant sacrificing their own desires and ambitions. The objection was to the differential in the attitude toward women as distinct from men: mothers more than fathers were expected to sacrifice themselves for their children, wives more than husbands were expected to put in the work of fostering the relationship. The extreme form of oppression in the name of a common good was identified in the phenomenon of honor killing: women and girls killed to preserve the honor of a family, an honor they had supposedly violated. Examples of similar moral pressure could be found in other areas of social life, the workplace, industrial relations, and the church. The pressure to avoid conflict, to preserve an apparent harmony, required individuals to relinquish their own concerns or ambitions in the name of a common good they experienced as oppressive.

It is not surprising, then, that the language of common goods was suspect, and political philosophers in the liberal tradition avoided it completely. In fact, discussion of goods or values in general was avoided, since it was commonly believed that no agreement or consensus in society could be based on a shared view of the human good. Those occasions when political movements had succeeded in dominating all of society with an espoused vision of the good appeared as totalitarian, with the familiar consequences of destruction of human life and human goods. Any attempt to reintroduce a discourse about the human good and common goods would have to face this objection. It was of some benefit to the project to point out that the totalitarian regimes of Soviet Communism, German Nazism, and Italian Fascism were all totally secular based on a rejection of religion, whether Judaism or Christianity. But there are sufficient examples of religiously motivated oppression or forms of colonialist domination reliant on religious support to make it necessary to provide a defense of common good advocacy against the charge of totalitarianism.

Utopianism

A related charge to that of totalitarianism is utopianism. The visionary of the human good looks to the future when it is hoped that aspirations will be realized. Experience warns that the aspirations are illusory, and that the attempt to realize them in practice inevitably leads to disaster. This is an additional challenge. Is talk of the common good utopian? Does the common good perspective postulate an ideal end-state as a utopia, an ideally good place that does not exist and so traps its adherents to subscribe to an illusion? The ambiguity in the Greek root of the name conveys these two aspects: "eu," referring to the goodness of the place, and "u" referring to its nonexistence.

Discussion of utopian thought in the literature relies on several applications of the notion of utopia to the critique of modern political thought. For the most part, "utopian" is used as an evaluative term to dismiss political ideologies or the programs of some political parties. The point is to criticize the agendas pursued by relevant people or groups because, first, their projects can never be realized, at least in the sense in which they intend them, and second, their efforts will bring about consequences that are exceedingly worse than the situations they are attempting to remedy. In this context, the familiar saying "The best is the enemy of the good" is frequently quoted.

Religiously inspired visions of a good life are often said to be utopian, and so the evaluation of political ideas is frequently burdened with an assumed dismissal of religious thought. Christian thought, insofar as it relies on an eschatology often expressed in terms borrowed from apocalyptic literature, is most usually taken as the exemplar of religious thought with a political impact. *Eschaton* refers to the end, the end of time, and the end time; *apocalypse* refers to the style in which the events of the end are described, in terms of violence, destruction, upheaval, and terror. Metaphors and images borrowed from religious literature can be used to express political ideas.

In this situation, in which talk of common good is suspected of totalitarianism, utopianism, or denial of human rights, anyone seeking to mediate the view of the human good and of common goods as contained in the Catholic intellectual tradition is faced with a major challenge. How to speak of common goods in such a way that the noted excesses are avoided, as well as the unnecessary polarization of an individual's human rights and the common good of a society, or, indeed, of humankind? In line with the church's perspective, human rights of individuals belong among the constitutive elements of the common good. This is part of the challenge addressed in this book. In what follows, I review the dominant religious themes in Christian apocalyptic and eschatology before looking at the way they are transposed to political discourse. Are the common goods invoked in the Christian and specifically Catholic teaching about the end time (eschaton) directly relevant to political utopian visions? Are they abused or misused there? Hence it is necessary to separate arguments based on a critique of religious ideas and those directed to a critique of political ideas.

CHRISTIAN ESCHATOLOGY

A central doctrine of Christianity is the Resurrection—that Jesus rose from the dead, and that in his name the resurrection of all who die can be proclaimed to all humankind. This is more than the immortality of the spiritual or intellectual soul, a notion familiar from classical Greek thought. Eternal life promised by Jesus is life with God in the Resurrection. Various images in the Christian scriptures point to this. The judgment scene in the Gospel of Matthew chapter 25; talk of the home providing rest in Hebrews; the Johannine emphasis on eternal life, in the Gospel and his letters; Paul's announcement of the Resurrection as the core of his message: "If Christ has not been raised, then our preaching is in vain and your faith is in vain."[3] The problem arises because there is no clearly identifiable dividing line between the present condition in our continuing history and the condition that will obtain beyond history. Jesus himself proclaims both the coming of God's Kingdom—that is, the desirable end-state—and the fact that the Kingdom is already present. Hence Christian theologians write of the eschaton as "both-already-and-not-yet." Differences arise in reading the signs of the times, in the extent to which believers can recognize the presence or absence of God's Kingdom in current political arrangements. Differences also arise about the extent to which their Christian hope can ground confidence that their common efforts to promote the political (including technological and economic) well-being will have a good effect. To the complexity of these ideas we must add the doctrines on human sinfulness and the Fall. The human condition is not simply one of privation, of needing to learn, develop, and make progress in the direction of realization of potential and fulfillment of aspirations. There is also the perennial dynamism propelling in the opposite direction, bias and prejudice countering discovery and knowledge, selfishness undermining collaborative joint action, malice and ill will poisoning the care for others.[4] Even if Christians can proclaim God's forgiveness and the redemption of humankind from sin, they can still disagree about the role of sin in history, along a spectrum that ranges from a dualistic vision of a contest between good and evil pervading all human reality, with the emphasis on the battle to be fought, to a willingness to "find the good in everything," as the character of the Duke in Shakespeare's *As You Like It* puts it.[5] As well as those who see the pervasiveness of sin, there are those who concentrate on the ubiquity of grace. Accusations that some believers might throw at other Christians, that they want to create "Heaven on earth," are countered by charges that the other side can only see a "vale of tears." These charges and countercharges recur in political-philosophical debates about ideologies that for some critics are utopian and for their adherents are scientifically and rationally grounded.

The themes of resurrection, eternal life, and the fulfillment of divine rule in the realized Kingdom of God where peace and justice are complete, expressed in visions of a great banquet and an end to illness and death, belong among the key positive ideas of Christian eschatology. But the eschatological visions have a negative dimension also, in depicting the ongoing conflict between grace and sin, the rule of God and the rebellion against God, the life-sustaining forces of creation and the death-dealing forces unleashed by sin. This conflict will be resolved in God's favor, but the drama of that resolution is often depicted in the apocalyptic vision of a final destructive battle. This latter has been exaggerated in dualist or Manichean accounts of the battle of good and evil, and in some fundamentalist readings of the New Testament texts in the foretelling of a cataclysmic upheaval of created order. Of course, the Catholic tradition reads such texts differently—not literally but metaphorically. How are such ideas and images received in political ideology and discourse?

Political Reception of Apocalyptic

John Gray's book *Black Mass: Apocalyptic Religion and the Death of Utopia* offers an analysis of utopianism in politics. As the late Nicholas Rengger remarks in his mostly appreciative review, Gray is not the first to apply the categories of apocalyptic religion to modern politics.[6] Like many others before him, Gray notes how dominant political ideas in modernity, such as those of the party, the proletariat, the nation, or the state, play the role that God plays in religious thought. Eric Voegelin is one of those whose analysis precedes Gray's, and Rengger bemoans the neglect of Voegelin's contribution to such analysis, even though Gray does mention him. According to Rengger, "There seems in Gray's argument to be an elision of religion with *apocalyptic* religion that is merely stipulative."[7] Rengger contrasts Gray's approach with that of Voegelin, who also discovers the theme of apocalyptic in a good deal of modern politics, even where it is expressly nonreligious and non-Christian. But Voegelin attributes the influence not to religion as such, but only one version of it.[8]

Rengger's point is that while there is a validity in criticizing political ideologies as deformed religions, care must be taken that the criticism does not entail a sweeping dismissal of religion as such. He claims that Voegelin does not make the mistake of dismissing all religion as aberrant, and so might be a better guide to the critique of utopias rooted in apocalyptic religion than Gray. In a recent (posthumously published) article, Rengger argues more generally for the importance of recognizing the relevance of theological discussion for international relations. He focuses on Voegelin and an English theorist, Martin Wight, as exemplars from whom the discipline can learn.[9]

In his 1952 book *The New Science of Politics*, Voegelin identifies Gnosticism as the element in some forms of Christianity that has resulted in its deformation, but that has survived as secularized, immanentized visions of the eschaton.[10] Later presentations of his thought move away from this analysis in terms of Gnosticism, largely because scholarship in the historical phenomena of the movements known as Gnostic do not corroborate his original account. In a 1971 lecture (at Notre Dame University) to mark twenty years since publication of his book on the science of politics, Voegelin no longer designates Gnosticism as the exclusive source of the deformation of religion, specifically Christianity. He acknowledges other elements of modernity that are not traceable to Gnosticism. He sees the origins of modern epochal consciousness and its sacralization of the secular in the historical constructions of progress from darkness to light and from death to rebirth. *Aufklärung* ("enlightenment") and *renaissance*, in their different linguistic contexts, all contribute to the apocalyptic constructions of history.[11]

Other aspects of his analysis persist and seek attention. The process of dedivinization, which had its theological origins at least in Augustine's rejection of a purely theological interpretation of historical events such as the fall of Rome, provided a hermeneutic that could read political occurrences without attributing them to divine intervention. This process of dedivinization was carried over into the medieval period. But curiously, this dynamic of dedivinization was reversed in the modern period of the Renaissance, whose images of enlightenment, liberation from darkness and myth, and progress toward knowledge and mastery in freedom reintroduced the twin themes of an eschaton and an apocalyptic resolution. Originally religious ideas now had a new existence as designating an ultimate completion of history as brought about in a conflagration or violent revolution. The modern period in Voegelin's account saw the resacralization of the secular, reversing what had been achieved in the Augustinian and medieval dedivinization.

Voegelin analyzes the typical political movements of modernity as immanentizations in history of a transcendent eschaton.[12] Socialism, nationalism, and Fascism offer their adherents a vision of a glorious future in which whatever evil provoked their criticism of the present would be overcome. At the same time, the human as understood in the preferred description would be perfected, and human association would be complete. The leaders of the movements claimed some knowledge of these matters, and so functioned as the prophets communicating a revelation. The achievement of the glorious future required a changing of circumstances, or of the system, or of the situation within which politics was conducted, but such change of the environment would be sufficient to ensure any necessary change of the persons involved. The religious nature of the symbols of these political movements is recognizable once pointed out. There is a deliverance from evil, there is a community of the blessed (and possibly a mass of the damned), there is an achievement of completion which, in one way or another, assures happiness and the realization of human hope. There is the prophet who claims special knowledge, there is the requirement to struggle and even for the individual to sacrifice himself or be sacrificed for the sake of the common destiny, and there is the analysis of why some fail to share the faith.

These modern political movements, according to Voegelin, rely on a vision of an ultimate common good when they promise a flourishing of the whole nation, or of the proletariat in total, or, indeed, of all humanity. The problem is how such fulfillment could be imagined. To the extent that it happened within history, it would have to be confined to the well-being of those who were still alive to experience it. There would be a completion which would be enjoyed by some, but how might that be the fulfillment of those who did not live to see the success of their efforts? How might the achievement of communal flourishing at a certain point in time give meaning to the lives of those who had contributed to the success without benefiting from it? Voegelin identifies this as a fundamental question for every movement that claims to represent something universal, but always in a concrete place and time in history. The awareness of the universal is expressed in terms such as "humanity" or "the universal class." He writes, "It is a theoretical problem for every philosophy of history, since the universal order of [humankind] can become historically concrete only through the symbolic representation by a community of the spirit with ecumenic intentions."[13] This is as much a problem for religious as for political movements, to the extent that both claim to represent or encapsulate the universal.

Voegelin insists that the achievement of a consciousness of a unity of humankind was a historical event:

> There never was a [humankind] in evolution, its generations connected by cause and effect, accumulating a collective memory. Empirically, as far as we know, there were only concrete societies, geographically widely dispersed, with insufficient communications or none at all, their members blissfully ignorant of the supposed fact that they formed a unity of [humankind] accumulating a collective memory.[14]

The unity of humankind is real, but it is not to be represented as a linear story of progress, or enlightenment, or liberation. Any attempt to do so must face Voegelin's questions: "What profit is the perfect realm to those who do not live to see it? What happens to the generations of [humankind] who lived before the world became enlightened? Is it really the function of [humans] to 'contribute' to a Progress of which the profits will be reaped by future generations—to be a stepping stone for a rational world to come?"[15] He sees the problem particularly apparent in an extreme form of Islam, which reveals "the danger that beset all of the religions of the Ecumenic Age, the danger of impairing their universality by letting their ecumenic mission slide over into the acquisition of world-immanent, pragmatic power over a multitude ... which, however numerous, could never be mankind, past present and future."[16]

Despite the prevalence of symbols borrowed from the horizon of a transcendent eschaton, what these political forms reveal is the abandonment of a genuine relationship with the divine. In his discussion with Hannah Arendt about her book *The Origins of Totalitarianism*, Voegelin attempted to raise the question of whether liberalism was tainted with the same flaws as totalitarianism, despite all the differences between them.[17] To the extent that liberalism espouses an agnosticism about the divine ground of human existence, and excludes questions about it from the agenda of public discourse, it contains in Voegelin's view the same source of distortion that led to totalitarianism. Reason and revelation, philosophy and theology symbolize in various ways the same openness to the divine ground, the transcendent. Where this openness is lived and achieves articulation, it exhibits a tentativeness and uncertainty, a humility and honesty in stark contrast to the certainty claimed by the modern prophet. There is always a temptation for those who live by religious faith to seek and claim greater possession of the divine reality than is warranted. To live by faith is to live in hope of things not yet seen, and this is a source of discomfort and tension since it is not easy to sustain. The political movements of modernity have offered certainty to their adherents as well as the sense of communal bonding in the common project. But in doing so they make immanent to human history a reality that can only be located beyond history in the transcendent. This needs longer elaboration to be fair to Voegelin's views, and it requires some more analysis to avoid the exaggeration that would leave the eschaton only in the transcendent, and not at all in human history. But it is nonetheless useful as a critical tool to assess attempts to speak of the fulfillment through politics of human dreams.

Modern Political Movements

The political movements of modernity present themselves as movements of liberation, of deliverance, from ignorance and illusion, from poverty and deprivation, from oppression and exploitation. Nationalism, Socialism, and Fascism all exhibit in their distinctive ways the dynamic of liberation, with the promise of fulfillment. However, all have shown themselves to be illusory as political programs since there is no real basis for expecting that universal dehumanization or oppression will of itself transform into universal human fulfillment. That such a transformation is thinkable in the first place is only possible against the background of a religious worldview in which a divine drama provides the context for a human history. Hence the criticism of secular eschatologies that present their stories dressed up in what is essentially a religious format. They are disguised theologies without God.

Voegelin, in correspondence with Arendt, asks whether liberalism is also tainted with this illusory quality. Patrick Deneen's challenge to liberalism relies on a similar critique, to the extent that this political movement can be understood to have made promises of deliverance and liberation that have not been and perhaps never could be fulfilled.[18] Adrian Vermeule adds his voice to this line of criticism. In fact, Vermeule has made explicit how he sees the dominant liberalism as a religion with its liturgy. In a 2017 article in *First Things* titled "Liturgy of Liberalism," he reviews a book devoted to an analysis of this similarity between liberalism and totalitarianism, *The Demon in Democracy: Totalitarian Temptations in Free Societies* by Ryszard Legutko. His review praises the book's author for identifying this similarity between the experience of living under a Communist regime and living in a liberal regime embracing toleration to the point of enforcing conformity. In both, there is a destruction of tradition, dissolving traditional groups and institutions such as family and church, in the place of which people are offered identities as liberal citizens. Quoting Legutko, Vermeule writes, "Individuals forge this new identity by inventing and participating in ecstatic political rituals that aspire to combine perfect equality with perfect freedom. Especially prominent are politicized 'language rituals,' also a characteristic of life under communism; 'the more participants, the noisier the political rites, the more impressive seemed to be the performance of the entire political system.'"[19] A later article, from 2019, returns to this theme of the liturgical practices of liberalism and elaborates on the examples. In "All Human Conflict Is Ultimately Theological," Vermeule explains the distinctive nature of sacramental liberalism as essentially a religious movement that has its liturgy. This liturgy involves a public and conspicuous celebration of the defeat of the darkness, superstition, and authoritarianism of the past. This liturgy requires the repeated identification of a villain to be defeated ritually: "Sacramental liberalism *qua* religion requires not merely an overcoming of the darkness of pre-rational tradition, but an explicit, public, visible overcoming. The community of liberals must see that the forces of reaction have been vanquished, see that the vanquished see that, and so forth. The triumph of liberty and the defeat of liberty's foes must be common knowledge."[20]

Vermeule gives two examples of political behavior in the United States that illustrate this dramatized confrontation: "The first was the Obama administration's relentless attempt to force the Little Sisters of the Poor to either fund abortifacient contraceptives or, at least, to take action to pass the responsibility elsewhere."[21] This seemed to many at the time to be both unnecessary and counterproductive in antagonizing Christian voters who would give their allegiance to Donald Trump. The other was the intervention by the administration in the Supreme Court case *Obergefell v. Hodges*, which announced a constitutional right to same-sex marriage. In commenting on the chief justice's dissenting judgment, which objected to the gratuitous rejection of traditional views of marriage, Vermeule remarks that the judge did not know his role: "The Chief Justice betrayed a deep misunderstanding about what sort of activity he was participating in. He thought that he was participating in a legal decision. In fact, he was participating in a ritual drama—as the villain. The celebration of common-law liberal heroism, and its overcoming of the bigotry of the ages, requires the very aspersions that the Chief Justice thought gratuitous. They were an essential moment in the liturgy of liberalism."[22]

The behavior of liberals in constantly overturning received tradition is contrary to the political wisdom encapsulated in the expression *ragion di stato* ("reason of state"), as invoked by Vermeule. He identifies these reasons of political rule as the "principles and laws that no ruler can forever defy without undermining the very conditions of his rule."[23] Vermeule draws on the *ragion di stato* tradition as expressing a conception of the common good to be attained by a ruler, a tradition he notes arose from a Catholic response to Machiavelli, whose principal spokesperson was Giovanni Botero.[24] The ruler is advised in this tradition to secure "abundance, peace, and justice,"[25] and success in this ensures the stability and sustainability of their rule. As Vermeule represents the tradition, it advises caution in making changes to established mores and popular customs. This is also found in Aquinas's recommendation that the law should not be changed casually, since too-frequent change can undermine respect for the law and compliance with it. Prudence in making changes is important, and where changes are needed, the ruler should not draw attention to them with changes of names or titles. As Machiavelli himself counseled, the Prince must take care not to provoke needlessly the wrath of subjects by too-radical change or sudden disruption of their expectations.

Vermeule stresses these prudential factors because he wants to highlight the manner in which the American political establishment violates the elements of practical advice for maintaining rule guaranteeing peace and prosperity. He also wants to illustrate the problem that the mass of objectors to policy face if they try to oppose the imprudent rulers. Only if all together oppose the changes can they have a hope of success, but that is difficult to achieve in the absence of organization and coordination. This is the difficulty faced by citizens in the United States. They are faced with a liberal regime whose politics, according to Vermeule, "feature a continual dynamism, a putatively 'creative destruction' of tradition, that constantly undermines and disrupts pre-existing practices among the populace; under liberalism, dynamic change is itself the steady state."[26]

An understanding of the common good is proposed by Vermeule as a counter to a form of liberal regime that is constantly undermining received practices and traditions. That form of liberalism is accused of having the same flaw as totalitarian ideologies—namely, that they present themselves as forms of religion with a liturgy and a promise of fulfillment. The accusation faced in this chapter is that advocacy for the common good as a rhetoric of secular politics is also in danger of proffering a utopia, an illusory vision of a future in which all aspirations are realized. As such, an ideology claiming the label of the common good could also inspire a regime characterized by oppression and domination. This possibility underlines the need for greater precision in specifying what is meant by both "common goods" and "liberalism." The versions of liberalism and common goods that can warrant our endorsement have to be tightly circumscribed, especially when they are intended for use in a political context. In the secular political forum, we have seen the harms that follow from civil powers adopting the cloaks of religious authority and acting according to forms more appropriate to the sacred. One advantage of the *ragion di stato* approach recommended by Vermeule is the way it understands the limited role of civil authority. The object of action of civil authorities is identified as the forms of public order in which the goods at stake are clearly delimited, thereby confining the state's range of action within definite boundaries. Similarly, a regime that recognizes these limits on its scope of action could be termed liberal to the extent that it is respectful and protective of the freedoms of individuals, families, and communities to pursue their own vision of the good in their own established traditions, subject to respect for the good of public order.

IDENTIFYING AND REJECTING ILLIBERAL LIBERALISM

Voegelin's challenge to Arendt, asking whether the dominant orthodoxy of liberalism, no less than the various forms of totalitarianism, is a kind of religion offering an immanentized version of a transcendent eschaton, is answered by Vermeule. The form of sacramental liberalism that is committed to the creative destruction of traditions in such a way that the defeat of opponents must be demonstrated publicly reveals its essentially liturgical and therefore religious nature.

However, Voegelin himself did not provide a definitive answer but relied on a distinction between two forms of liberalism. A liberalism that accepted the dedivinization of political life as achieved in the Augustinian corpus, and also resisted the tendency to resacralize politics by imbuing it with immanentized versions of liberation and fulfillment, would not be guilty of the charge. To satisfy Voegelin's condition, a liberal regime espousing a liberal ideology would have to demonstrate an appropriate humility, a modesty only achievable with the realization of the limits to its own competence to address and answer questions about the transcendent. Trainor's account of the type of secular that is open to the divine source of being is appropriate here.[27]

On the other hand, a secular liberalism that is not only closed to the divine ground but offers its own immanentized version of a religious vision as a comprehensive doctrine would seem to be guilty as accused. As noted, to the extent that liberalism systematically excludes questions about the divine ground of human existence from the agenda of public discourse and not only from the day-to-day business of governing, it is an illiberal secularism, and contains on Voegelin's view the same source of distortion that led to totalitarianism.

Voegelin's answer predates a distinction later made by John Gray between the two faces of liberalism. Gray identifies two incompatible philosophies that claim the name of liberal. One is foundationalist, comprehensive, rooted in the belief that there can be a rational consensus on the ideal of the best life in which humans can flourish. The other is based on an acceptance of plurality of values and visions of human fulfillment and is oriented to finding means to peaceful coexistence. "In the first," Gray writes, "liberalism is a prescription for a universal regime. In the second, it is a project of coexistence that can be pursued in many regimes."[28] In elaborating this distinction, Gray notes how an espousal of pluralism is incompatible with a form of liberalism aimed at attaining rational consensus on the good life. He argues that if the thesis of value pluralism is true, then a liberalism that holds "that intractable disagreements about the human good can be resolved for the purposes of human law or public policy by a theory of rights or basic liberties" is indefensible.[29] His solution is to propose a view of liberalism as "the enterprise of pursuing terms of coexistence among different ways of life. Instead of thinking of liberal values as if they were universally authoritative, we can think of liberalism as the project of reconciling the claims of conflicting values. If we do this, liberal philosophy will look not to an illusion of universal consensus, but instead to the possibilities of a *modus vivendi*."[30]

John Rawls offers a similar distinction, although the differences are also marked. Rawls also juxtaposes a comprehensive liberalism with a more pragmatic version, in his case called political liberalism. Rawls concedes that his earlier work *A Theory of Justice* tends to offer a comprehensive account of liberalism, but that in acknowledging the legitimacy of a plurality of reasonable comprehensive doctrines in *Political Liberalism* he relegates his earlier account of justice to being just one candidate among several that could qualify as candidates for an accepted account of justice in the life of a pluralist society.[31] Where Gray advocates finding a *modus vivendi*, Rawls is not satisfied with finding some arrangement that works; he wants it to have in addition a rational elaboration that is moral, self-standing, and capable of being interpreted by citizens each from the perspective of their own comprehensive worldview. Philosophically speaking, these are different ambitions. But from my perspective they both exemplify the same originating concern with an acceptance of plurality and the search for some arrangement that allows for a peaceful coexistence and collaboration in support of a public order. In fact, with his further modification of his ideas on political liberalism as he faces the challenge of international relations, Rawls in *The Law of Peoples* accepts a *modus vivendi* as the basis for peaceful relations between peoples who do not and cannot espouse a version of liberalism.

Gray's accusation of apocalyptic utopianism is directed against recent political stances that could be seen as versions of the ideological rational consensus version of liberalism. Among his targets are the phenomena of neoconservatism and neoliberalism, insofar as these have been motivating ideologies for armed intervention in the world. He depicts the American interest in regime change in Afghanistan and Iraq, motivated by the desire to export the liberal values of self-determination and democracy, as "missionary liberalism" and "liberal imperialism." The idea of human rights provides the intellectual core of this form of imperialism and the rationale in justification, seeking support from contemporaries. Gray underlines this point: "Who dares deny that tyranny is bad, or question the ideal of a world based on human rights? After all, the claim that its values are valid for all of humanity is a cardinal principle of liberal philosophy."[32] This is the foundationalist version of comprehensive liberalism. Rights are emphasized in specifying the obligation of every state to protect the rights of its own people, and the government of a state that failed to deliver on its obligations of protection would forfeit its claim to legitimacy. The exigency of human rights overrides the claims of sovereignty, and the international community would be entitled to intervene militarily to secure the rights of those violated. This was the core of the doctrine of humanitarian intervention, a doctrine espoused by UK prime minister Tony Blair, who over six years took the UK into war five times.[33] Gray claims that Blair's motivation was ultimately religious, which provides evidence for Gray's thesis: "Blair believes in the power of force to ensure the triumph of the good. . . . In each case war was justified as a form of humanitarian intervention. . . . Blair justified these military involvements in terms of a 'doctrine of international community,' which he presented in a speech at the Economic Club in Chicago in 1999."[34]

Both neoliberalism and neoconservatism are utopian according to Gray. They both rely on the idea of human rights. But they differ on their understandings of the state's role. Neoliberals wish to minimize the size of the state, while neoconservatives assign additional significant roles to the state. On this latter view, shared by Blair, the state cannot be morally neutral. It must promote the good life, understood in moral terms, and acknowledge religion as a valuable collaborator, being a source of social cohesion on the neoconservative view.[35]

Gray discerns a change in the political culture of the United States. He interprets this change as the capture of government by a form of fundamentalism, leading to an illiberal democratic regime. The "power of faith" drives this fundamentalism, he claims, although the faith in question is not essentially a religious faith, a belief in God.[36] It functions similarly to religious faith but takes different forms for different groups. For liberal thinkers, it is a belief in human rights. For liberal thinkers of a legalist persuasion, it is a belief in the power of law, and the possibility of replacing the difficulties of political compromise with certainty of constitutional guarantees. For Trump and his followers, it is a belief in their victimhood and the rightness of their cause, and their entitlement to seek vindication. In each of these instances, there appears to be a form of utopianism as motivator, with a sense of certainty rooted in a confidence that the desired situation can and will be brought about. History is irrelevant; the complexity of facts on the ground is ignored. The assurance of faith overrides the skepticism and doubt that are associated with genuine political engagement with opponents, with those who think differently and desire different things.

Human Rights and Utopia

The concept of utopia is central to Samuel Moyn's thesis in his book *The Last Utopia: Human Rights in History*. Moyn maintains that the explosion of interest in human rights from the 1970s requires an explanation, since the standard account of the history of human rights is mistaken in relevant respects. He explains how the promotion and protection of human rights became the utopia of idealists who had experienced disappointment of their beliefs in other candidates, whether liberal progressivism, or Socialism, or Communism. The standard explanation of the origin of human rights, as encapsulated in the Universal Declaration of Human Rights (UDHR), promulgated in 1948, is that they arose from a desire to prevent the recurrence of the atrocities associated with the period of the Second World War, and so were associated with the reconstruction of national and international affairs following the devastations of the war. It is understandable that growing awareness of the horrors of the Holocaust, the extermination of the Jews and others, and the death camps, as well as of the violence conducted against civilian populations, would lead to an assumption that these were the motivating considerations behind the declaration.

Moyn's research into the history of the drafting of the UDHR reveals that the drafters did not explicitly mention the Holocaust as they corresponded with one another about their draft, nor was it a major point in the efforts to persuade states to adopt it. Glendon's study of Eleanor Roosevelt's role in the drafting of the declaration is consistent with this reading.[37] Another fact won from study of major newspapers in both the UK (the *Times*) and the United States (the *New York Times*) is that the term "human rights" seldom occurs in the newspapers' reports or in opinion pieces until 1977, when there is a great explosion in the number of occurrences in both sources. Why the sudden interest in a topic that had achieved relatively little attention in the thirty years of the existence of the UDHR? Moyn's study uncovers several aspects. First, the aspiration of many around the world as they looked to the formation of the United Nations and expressed their hopes for its focus on the dual ambition of ending colonialism and affirming the principle of self-determination. This hope was disappointed. The United Nations did not elaborate a policy of self-determination for peoples or an ending of colonialism. As Moyn puts it, "Human rights turned out to be a substitute for what many around the world wanted, a collective entitlement to self-determination."[38]

Second, Jimmy Carter's inaugural address as president of the United States in 1977 placed the promotion of human rights at the heart of his intended foreign policy. By this time, international lawyers had adopted the language of human rights to make sense of their discipline, driven not by the internal needs of their profession but adjusting to the pressures arising from social activists in Amnesty International. Moyn writes, "Indeed almost alone, Amnesty International invented grassroots human rights advocacy, and through it drove public awareness of human rights generally. Its contribution would reach its highest visibility when it received the Nobel Peace Prize in 1977, the breakthrough year for human rights as a whole, though it began its work years earlier."[39]

Moyn's publications on the origins and history of human rights talk have attracted considerable criticism, as noted by Nigel Biggar.[40] However, the relevance of his arguments to our project here is due to Moyn's use of the notion of "utopia" in explaining the great explosion of interest in human rights. In his view, the enthusiasm for individual human rights among the participants in an international movement was due to a reaction against a series of failures. The human rights project appeared attractive to idealists disappointed by the failure of their previously chosen goals, such as decolonization or Socialism. Human rights offered them "a pure alternative in an age of ideological betrayal and political collapse."[41]

Not only have those ideologies that attempted to appropriate the common good turned out to be illusory, but the reaction against them in terms of individual human rights is also now labeled an illusion, a utopia, by Moyn as an intellectual historian. In this chapter and in chapter 5, I have distinguished between two forms of liberalism as bodies of ideas, as well as between liberalism as a set of ideas and liberalism as a particular political regime. Insofar as a political and ideological regime is found to be disappointing, failing to deliver on its promises, shrewd critics attempting to develop an alternative in terms of the common good should be aware of the danger of generating yet another utopian vision.

CONCLUSION

This chapter begins with the question of whether talk of the common good or of common goods is utopian. Having explored what is meant by "utopian" and how the accusation of being utopian is made in recent literature, I return now to apply the question to the topic at hand. Utopian visions are attractive to their adherents because they point to an ideal state of affairs and raise the hope of achieving what is eminently desirable through a historical process of progress, or radical change, or revolution. The vision motivates involvement in political activity. The critique points to the illusory nature of such visions, since no historical process and certainly not political action on its own, can reach the end that is ambitioned. The critique goes further since the illusory nature of the visions is not the only ground on which they are condemned. The destruction caused by attempts to realize the unrealizable is horrendous, as is exemplified in the military interventions supported by the utopian dreams of neoconservatives. It is this aspect of the critique that links utopian thought to apocalyptic religion. As noted, however, critics of utopian movements differ in the extent of their ability to recognize the distortion or deformation of religion, especially Christianity, in the immanentized versions of a transcendent eschaton.

The criticisms of utopian thinking signal dangers for a form of religious and political thought that invokes a vision of an ultimate good. These dangers are present in those presentations of the common good that offer it as an alternative to failed utopias, such as (illiberal) liberalism. There can be no guarantee that a political movement that adopted the common good as its slogan and presented a corresponding vision of a just society would avoid the traps that have caught various political movements in history. This concern will be part of the reason for rejecting integralism as a political stance for Catholics.

The account of common goods offered here avoids the dangers for the following reasons. First, it offers a term of analysis and not a program of action. Attention to the good, to goods in common, is relied upon to understand and explain collaborative action. It is not directly prescriptive, specifying goods or a vision of goods that ought to be pursued. Second, while attending to goods, and to goods in common, it articulates criteria for clarifying when and why apparent goods are deceptive and are not truly good, and criteria for determining when and why what seem to be goods in common fail to be genuine common goods. Third, given that it is a futile question to ask why one should be reasonable in pursuit of goods, and in pursuit with others of goods in common, this account proceeds on the assumption that such a questioner, if genuinely raising the question, already accepts some standards of reasonableness since not any possible answer will satisfy, and so it goes directly to the exploration of the good. Fourth, it relies on the inherent attractiveness of the good and of goods in common, and so avoids, if possible, a positive injunction commanding pursuit of some good or other. It avoids, therefore, the mistake made by some critics in assuming that there is some attempt to derive an obligation from an assertion of good. The fact that tennis can truly be affirmed to be a good sport does not entail an obligation to play tennis.

NOTES

1. Isaiah Berlin, *Four Essays on Liberty* (Oxford: Oxford University Press, 1969).
2. Berlin, 124–26.

3. 1 Corinthians, 15:14, *The Holy Bible: Revised Standard Version Catholic Edition* (London: Catholic Truth Society, 1966).
4. See the section "Progress and Decline" in Bernard Lonergan, *Method in Theology*, 2nd ed. (London: Darton, Longman & Todd, 1973), 52–55.
5. William Shakespeare, *As You Like It*, in *Complete Works*, ed. W. J. Craig (London: Oxford University Press, 1969), act 2, sc.1.
6. Nicholas Rengger, "The Exorcist? John Gray, Apocalyptic Religion and the Return to Realism in World Politics," *International Affairs* 83, no. 5 (2007): 956.
7. Rengger, "Exorcist," 957, emphasis in original.
8. Rengger, "Exorcist," 956.
9. Nicholas Rengger, "Between Transcendence and Necessity: Eric Voegelin, Martin Wight and the Crisis of Modern International Relations," *Journal of International Relations and Development* 22 (2019).
10. Eric Voegelin, *The New Science of Politics: An Introduction* (Chicago: University of Chicago Press, 1952).
11. Stephen A. McKnight, "Gnosticism and Modernity: Voegelin's Reconsiderations Twenty Years After *The New Science of Politics*," *Political Science Reviewer* 34 (2005).
12. Voegelin, *New Science*.
13. Eric Voegelin, *Order and History*, vol. 4, *The Ecumenic Age* (Baton Rouge: Louisiana State University Press, 1987), 192. I note the historical context for Voegelin's use of exclusive terms.
14. Eric Voegelin, "World-Empire and the Unity of Mankind," *International Affairs* 38, no. 2 (1962): 181. The original formulation is adjusted to avoid gender bias.
15. Voegelin, "World-Empire," 185. The original formulation is adjusted to avoid gender bias.
16. Voegelin, *Order and History*, 198.
17. Eric Voegelin, *Religion and the Rise of Modernity*, ed. J. L. Wiser (Columbia: University of Missouri Press, 1998).
18. Patrick J. Deneen, *Why Liberalism Failed* (New Haven, CT: Yale University Press, 2018), 6.
19. Adrian Vermeule, "Liturgy of Liberalism," *First Things* (January 2017), https://www.firstthings.com/article/2017/01/liturgy-of-liberalism.
20. Adrian Vermeule, "All Human Conflict Is Ultimately Theological," *Church Life Journal* (July 26, 2019), https://churchlifejournal.nd.edu/articles/all-human-conflict-is-ultimately-theological/.
21. Vermeule.
22. Vermeule, "Liturgy of Liberalism."
23. Vermeule, "All Human Conflict."
24. Giovanni Botero, *The Reason of State*, ed. Robert Bireley, Cambridge Texts in the History of Political Thought (Cambridge: Cambridge University Press, 2017).
25. Vermeule, "All Human Conflict."
26. Vermeule.
27. Brian T. Trainor, "Augustine's 'Sacred Reign–Secular Rule' Conception of the State: A Bridge from the West's Foundational Roots to Its Post-Secular Destiny, and between 'the West' and 'the Rest,'" *Heythrop Journal* 56 (2015): 373–87.
28. John Gray, *Two Faces of Liberalism* (Cambridge: Polity, 2000), 2.
29. John Gray, "Where Pluralists and Liberals Part Company," in *Pluralism: The Philosophy and Politics of Diversity*, ed. Maria Baghramian and Attracta Ingram (London: Routledge, 2000), 95.

30. Gray, *Two Faces of Liberalism*, 33.
31. John Rawls, *A Theory of Justice*, rev. ed. (Cambridge, MA: Belknap Press, 1999); *Political Liberalism* (New York: Columbia University Press, 1996); *The Law of Peoples with "The Idea of Public Reason Revisited"* (Cambridge, MA: Harvard University Press, 1999).
32. John Gray, *Black Mass: Apocalyptic Religion and the Death of Utopia* (London: Allen Lane, 2007), 162.
33. Gray, 97.
34. Gray, 97.
35. Gray, 96.
36. Gray, 169.
37. Mary Ann Glendon, *A World Made New: Eleanor Roosevelt and the Universal Declaration of Human Rights* (New York: Random House, 2001).
38. Samuel Moyn, *The Last Utopia: Human Rights in History* (London: Belknap Press, 2010), 45.
39. Moyn, 129.
40. Nigel Biggar, *What's Wrong with Rights?* (Oxford: Oxford University Press, 2020), 76.
41. Moyn, *Last Utopia*, 8.

CHAPTER 8

IS TALK OF THE COMMON GOOD INEVITABLY PATERNALISTIC?

This question about paternalism is formulated generally, referring to any invocation of common goods. But since the Catholic church is one of the principal advocates for the perspective of common goods, the question initially can be more directly focused on the church: is the church paternalistic in specifying the common good as the purpose of the state? Following a clarification of what paternalism entails, and a discussion of solidarity, the question can be generalized to apply to any body that seeks the good of others, including the leaders of commercial businesses and politicians.

Chapter 7 notes the danger of a secular state being closed to the transcendent. This is not a danger for the Catholic church. Whatever challenges, risks, and temptations it faces—and they are many and various—the hope is that ecclesial language, liturgy, and symbolisms will continue to point to the divine. In the relationship between the sacred and the secular, explored in chapter 3, the church is differently placed than any state. The dangers of utopianism and apocalyptic, discussed in chapter 7, will not arise in the same way for the church as for the state. However, the context of relationships between sacred and secular, mapped out in chapter 3, suggests that there is a matrix of possible relationships between church and state, depending on where on the spectrum of the secular a particular state is positioned. Assuming the church does not find itself in the position of being persecuted and denied civil rights, its stance over against the state will not be simply prophetic and challenging. There will be potential for partnership and cooperation. In that cooperation there will be need for reciprocal respect and acknowledgment of diversity of interests and concerns. The danger for the church, drawing on its self-understanding as teacher, is taking on a paternalistic role, dictating to the state what its functions, obligations, and limitations should be. Perhaps there are other dangers also, but in this chapter I explore the question of whether the Catholic church, in teaching that the purpose of the state is to serve the common good, is acting paternalistically and inappropriately in the relationship with the secular state.

PATERNALISM

The topic of paternalism is often linked to that of patriarchy. If patriarchy refers to culturally embedded male domination, paternalism does not necessarily entail the gender link implied in the term but refers to the phenomenon of anyone *acting* on the assumption that they are entitled to determine what is the good for another. Of course, in a patriarchal culture, paternalism will most typically be exercised by dominant males. But there is no reason why the dominant characters determining the good for others could not be females. Usually, also, paternalism refers to *action* in the sense of interference in the affairs of another without their consent. This is evident, for instance, in the definition of the term advanced by Gerald Dworkin, who explains, "Paternalism is the interference of a state or an individual with another person, against their will, and defended or motivated by a claim that the person interfered with will be better off or protected from harm."[1] To ask about paternalism in the church's teaching stretches this meaning of the term, since the presentation of doctrine can hardly count as interference. At the same time, the various occasions on which the church or its ministers might be considered to act for the good of others without their consent are not the immediate focus of this reflection and will not be addressed (as, for instance, in the objections of some to the baptism of infants). The question posed focuses exclusively on the statements made in important documents of the Catholic church's ordinary teaching about the nature of politics and seeks to explore whether an unwarranted paternalism arises when the teaching authority of the church declares what is the good of political communities that are well able to determine their own good for themselves.

A prime example offered by the statement of the Second Vatican Council's *Gaudium et spes* §74 says that "the political community exists, consequently, for the sake of the common good, in which it finds its full justification and significance, and the source of its inherent legitimacy."[2] The church seems to be telling the state what its purpose and justification is. Does this not usurp the entitlement of a liberal democratic state to declare for itself how it understands its purpose and *raison d'etre*? Hence the question of this chapter: Is the church paternalistic in claiming to know what is the good of the political community?

Papal teaching on these matters is conscious of the danger of paternalism, as for instance in Pope Benedict's 2009 encyclical letter *Caritas in veritate*.

Pope Benedict expressly links the two terms "subsidiarity" and "solidarity" when writing of international development aid: "*The principle of subsidiarity must remain closely linked to the principle of solidarity and vice versa*, since the former without the latter gives way to social privatism, while the latter without the former gives way to paternalist social assistance that is demeaning to those in need."[3] Respect for the autonomy and responsibility of individuals and groups might result in their being left to fend for themselves unless that respect is balanced by a real concern for their welfare. On the other hand, Benedict warns that concern for the welfare of others can become a form of paternalism if it is not balanced by respect for their own responsibility to provide for themselves according to their own estimation of their needs. Hence the emphasis on pairing these two principles of solidarity and subsidiarity.

Pope John Paul II offers another pairing of key principles of Catholic social teaching (CST). In his encyclical *On Social Concern* (1987), he links solidarity with the common good. Solidarity, he writes, "is not a feeling of vague compassion or shallow distress at the misfortunes of so many people, both near and far. On the contrary, it is a firm and persevering determination to commit oneself to the common good; that is to say to the good of all and of each individual, because we are all really responsible for all."[4] We might immediately feel sorry for the victims of natural disasters such as earthquakes and tsunamis. However, such feelings alone would not be sufficient to qualify us as showing solidarity, on John Paul's view. Only if our response translated into providing both immediate assistance and ongoing support for reconstruction of their lives could we be said to show solidarity. This would be genuine solidarity, the ongoing commitment to working with victims for the sake of their well-being.

The danger of paternalism noted by Pope Benedict lurks in the uncritical attitude of solidarity, when helping agents and agencies determine what is good for others. Does the danger of paternalism also threaten when the teaching authority of the Church specifies the good of political communities? Hence the need to explore further the connection between solidarity and common goods. Is the idea of solidarity inevitably linked to the notions of need, suffering, or deprivation?[5] Both quotations from popes John Paul II and Benedict XVI above seem to presuppose such a link. John Paul II contrasts solidarity as a firm commitment to the common good with a simple emotional identification with suffering humanity. Solidarity would seem to be an attitude toward people in need. Pope Benedict makes the same connection when he argues that solidarity should be balanced by subsidiarity, so that the assistance given to those in need would not be demeaning or patronizing. Again, it has to do with an attitude to people in need. This element in CST is echoed in colloquial uses of "solidarity," as when people suffering from some debility or deprivation find common cause in their shared need and those who come to their support are also said to be in solidarity with them.

SOLIDARITY CLARIFIED

The relationship between solidarity and common goods requires further clarification. Concentrating on the fact that people choose for themselves the good they wish to pursue leads to a *practical* account of the good, that which is the object of choice and action. But people can be mistaken about what is for their good, and so the apparent good can be contrasted with what is truly good. A discussion of people's true good, an *ontological* account, might lead to the paternalistic danger identified by Pope Benedict—that some people think they know best what is for the good of others. After all, the principle of subsidiarity is formulated to protect the autonomy of individuals and their organizations against the (supposedly well-intentioned) paternalism of higher authority. This leads to the question of whether solidarity as a firm commitment to the common good rules out an ontological understanding of the good (*what is good for people, independent of their desires and choices*) and favors exclusively a practical account (*what people judge is good for them and accordingly choose*). I explore this question in detail in three steps. First, I use three distinctions to outline possible meanings of "solidarity." Second, I clarify the relationship between a metaphysical account of the good and a practical or ethical account. Third, I argue in favor of an understanding of the relationship between solidarity and common goods that allows room for a commitment to the goods of others of which they themselves may not be aware. The point is to secure philosophically the legitimacy of speaking of peoples' goods which those peoples may not (or not yet) have chosen for themselves. A further purpose is to secure the appropriateness of the Council Fathers pronouncing on the point of liberal democracy and Pope Francis pronouncing on care for the earth and care for the poor without falling into the error of paternalism.

Distinctions of Solidarity

Two popular misconceptions make it necessary to introduce several distinctions. One misconception is the spontaneous assumption that to tell people what is good for them is to *impose* on them a vision of their good against their will, which would be a grave violation of their autonomy or freedom. This is a concern held by many that makes them reluctant to speak of human nature as specifying the goods for people, and more critically, as grounding their human rights.⁶ The second misconception is the widespread assumption that a person cannot be in solidarity with other people without both knowing it and having chosen it as a commitment. These assumptions are both misleading and restrictive and should be abandoned. I introduce three distinctions to help with this. The first distinction is between the epistemic and the ontological; the second is between benefits enjoyed by all together and benefits to be enjoyed by individuals severally; and the third is related to the familiar distinction between the descriptive and the prescriptive, noting the difference between the evaluative and the prescriptive.

Epistemic and Ontological

The first distinction between the epistemic and the ontological enables us to recognize the difference between people united by shared awareness and feeling and people who have common interests, of which they may be unaware. With the term "epistemic," I refer to the shared consciousness of several people that they are united in having a common interest. When the term "solidarity" is used in this sense, the emphasis is on the shared consciousness, the awareness of members of the relevant group that they are linked with all others who share in the common interest. When the emphasis is on the knowledge and attitude of participants, the nature of the shared interest is secondary. The supporters of a football team cannot be unaware of their interest in their team winning a game or a competition. On the other hand, citizens may be unaware of the deliberations being conducted in a parliamentary or congressional committee—say, about a policing and crime bill—even though all would have interests at stake in the outcome of the deliberations. It can happen that very significant interests in the quality of social and political life may not be viewed with the same passion and personal engagement as other, more contingent interests. Accordingly, the intensity of the feeling among those in solidarity in some interest is not necessarily a good indicator of the importance of the interest in question.

"Solidarity" used in an ontological sense refers to the nature of the shared interests and their correlation with relevant populations, regardless of whether the people involved are aware of their interests and deliberately pursue them. For instance, if we consider the notion of the rule of law, it may be questioned whether in fact all the citizens and residents of a country are aware of what it means, and the degree of their interest in belonging to a regime conducted according to the rule of law. Let us assume that there will be some minimal awareness, at least to the extent that people in answer to a questionnaire would declare a preference for justice over injustice. The epistemic solidarity may not go much further than that. But the assertion of solidarity in an ontological sense explores the real interests of populations regardless of the relevant participants' awareness of those interests. The emphasis on interests tends to be overlooked given the way that the passion and feeling typical of the epistemic dimension more immediately demands our attention. However, it is worth noting how often campaigning groups who are seeking to mobilize support in some matter begin with the nature of the interest and then work to make the affected people aware of it. This process, associated with the work of Paulo Freire, has been given its own name: *conscientization*.[7] Becoming aware of the plight of women, or the poor, or the homeless, campaigners work at informing their relevant target group and increasing their knowledge of their situation, along with stimulating the realization that they have the power to do something about it. The hope is that recognition of the problem as a shared plight will lead the group to act together to change their situation. The ontological carries over to the epistemic. Only when recognized and espoused can the sharing of an interest become politically effective. A contemporary example is the fostering of awareness of environmental issues as being of interest to every person on the planet, since none can remain unaffected by contaminated air, earth, and water.[8] Pope Francis has contributed significantly to conscientization of the importance of caring for "our common home" in his encyclical letter *Laudato Si'*.

Agents and Beneficiaries

The second distinction of solidarity is drawn in terms of those whose interests are at stake and those who stand to benefit. On the one hand, there are cases in which the relevant interests are in fact the interests of each individual, the satisfaction of whom does not require the satisfaction of all other members of the group. For instance, all those who need kidney transplants share a plight and have common interests, such as that the method of allocating kidneys be transparent and fair. But when any individual patient successfully receives a transplanted kidney, the need is met, and the satisfaction of others' needs is not a precondition. Of course, one may continue to campaign in solidarity with fellow patients so that their needs might also be met. Contrasted with this, on the other hand, is the case of a labor movement agitating for more humane working conditions. The solidarity of trade unionists in the campaign is such that only an improvement of the conditions of all affected workers can satisfy the demands of any individual participant in the campaign. The satisfaction of the interests of all is a condition for the satisfaction of the interests of any one campaigner. The Black Lives Matter movement makes this point with its telling slogan: "No one is equal until all are equal!"

Sometimes the use of the term "solidarity" is confined to this latter case, in which the interest is shared and common in the sense that the individual's goal includes the achievement of the goals of others. It can of course be meaningful to address such cases, but it seems an unwarranted restriction of the term to demand that it be applied only to such cases and not others.

Descriptive, Evaluative, and Prescriptive Modes

The third distinction is a complex of three terms—the descriptive, the evaluative, and the prescriptive—and perhaps is best clarified with examples. In empirical descriptive mode, one might report as a fact that a government is comprised of a coalition of a smaller party and a larger party. In evaluative mode, one might say that it is good and praiseworthy (or bad and reprehensible) that the smaller party in question supports the government. In prescriptive mode, one might propose that other members of the parliament, whether independents or from marginal parties, should support the coalition government, or that the opposition should exploit policy differences and tensions between the government's coalition parties. The presuppositions of the last prescriptive mode include an evaluative judgment—for instance, that the actual coalition is a good arrangement. Another presupposition might be the empirical descriptive judgments that, in fact, not all agree on the value of the coalition, and that they are not all united in promoting the policies of the government. The evaluative says what is good (or bad); the prescriptive contains an imperative of what is (or is not) to be done. The evaluative and the prescriptive are often conflated, as if all normative speech were of the one kind, that the assertion of the goodness of some matter is equivalent to a command that the matter be pursued. It does not follow from my affirmation that marriage is a good that anybody ought to marry, or from my affirmation that Mary Jane would make a good wife that I should marry her.

When members of groups are conscientized to appreciate the reality of their situation, both factual and evaluative, they usually take steps to improve their circumstances. They address each other in prescriptive terms, speaking of what ought to be the case and what they see themselves as obliged to do. They also address relevant others, including authorities, in prescriptive terms, drawing out implications of what those others ought to do. However, at the heart of such prescriptive talk and fundamental to any assessment of its justification will be a set of evaluative judgments. Those judgments and the arguments based on them will have to invoke the real interests of both the speakers and the members of their audiences. The truth and adequacy of such judgments will depend on whether the invoked interests can be upheld as real, grounded in what is for the benefit of all affected.

Challenging Assumptions

With these three distinctions we can revisit the two assumptions mentioned earlier to clarify their distorting effect. The existence of an interest does not depend on whether, or how widely, it is recognized. However, for the political impact and effectiveness of existing interests, it is necessary that relevant groups become aware and choose to pursue them. In light of this, the assertion of the existence of an interest is evidently not an imposition of a view of a good on anyone, but it is an invitation to relevant people to recognize where their interests lie and to undertake relevant action. There can be a solidarity of shared interest between people otherwise strangers to each other which does not presuppose the conscious embrace of the particular interest by all concerned. But such interests, when affirmed, normally lead to an attempt to conscientize people so that their awareness of their bondedness with others is heightened and they pursue the realization of their real interests. This kind of solidarity does not entail any imposition of one view of their good on others but is consistent with allowing them free choice in response to what is discovered.

METAPHYSICS AND ETHICS

How might the real interests of people be known? It has become commonplace in liberal thought that there is no possible access to such knowledge. The reason for this is to be found in the heightened valuation of liberty or autonomy. The respect due to autonomy, reflected even in Pope Benedict's concern over avoiding paternalism in the assistance given to people in need, has become a dominant demand in liberal political thought. Ronald Dworkin, in his last great work, *Justice for Hedgehogs*, refers to the indignity of usurpation when someone decides for the good of another: "Authenticity is damaged when a person is made to accept someone else's judgment in place of his own about the values or goals his life should display."[9] Even the conception of the good as such, and not only specific goods, is considered a matter of choice for people. This point is disputed by critics like Michael Sandel, who question how it is possible rationally to choose one conception of the good in preference to another if the chooser is not already in possession of certain standards according to which one conception will appear superior to another.[10] This challenge doesn't seem to faze the liberal advocates who insist on the fundamental liberty to choose a conception of the good. Whatever might be the theoretical difficulties of such a position, it dominates in the actual jurisprudence of courts charged with deciding cases of religious liberty.[11] It is not surprising, then, if it dominates in the consciousness of typical students, who are extremely sensitive to the danger of imposing a conception of the good on anyone. These views, both popular and theoretical as well as legal, stress the practical understanding of the good, linking it with the object of choice. If, as in Aristotle's view, action is for the sake of some good, then this approach views action as rooted in an exercise of deliberate free choice for some object that appears attractive. The position is radical in seeing the possible object of choice as including the standards of goodness themselves. Obviously, this approach to the understanding of the good would be skeptical of an account of solidarity that stressed unacknowledged interests and would more likely give priority to the chosen and acknowledged self-identification with like-minded others. An epistemic rather than ontological notion of solidarity would suit them best.

There is an alternative account of the good that does not exclude the practical but also recognizes the metaphysical, by rooting human common goods in a view of human nature. Sophie Grace (formerly Timothy) Chappell summarizes the position in the context of a different debate: "Since we are all human, we all share the same nature. Since that nature is the same for all, the same things (the same goods) fulfill all of us. Our reasons and our motivations alike come from the goods: everything we have reason to do, we have reason to do because of its relation to the goods, and everything that we desire, we desire under the aspect of some good or goods."[12] Reference to human nature as a source of knowledge about what is good for humans typically provokes an antiessentialist reaction. In the context of debates about the United Nations' development work, Martha Nussbaum has challenged the simplistic assumptions of her colleagues in the rejection of any consideration of human nature. She acknowledges the anxieties that no one person's view of the good should be imposed on others, that no single culture should be allowed to dominate such that other cultures become marginalized in the specification of what is human, and that care should be taken so that the experiences of all should be considered. At the same time, she has argued very persuasively that the lack of an adequate account of the human would undermine two important attitudes that are the precondition for all development work: compassion and respect. Without a sense of the different other as nonetheless similar to oneself in fundamental respects, genuine compassion with the other as suffering or needy could not be maintained. Unlike pity, compassion requires a sense of equality so there can be solidarity with the situation of the other. The related attitude of respect similarly requires a recognition of those valued features of the other that can evoke the commitment to protect and foster, and not to harm.[13] She points to the fact that people, including the antiessentialists themselves, are able to recognize others as fellow humans even across historical and cultural boundaries. The reason is that it is possible to recognize certain common features that are thought to constitute a life as human, and she lists these as the capacities for human functioning.[14] Here and elsewhere, Nussbaum wishes to avoid being drawn into debates in metaphysics, but her version of Aristotle's account of human nature and social justice builds on elements that for Aristotle permits a metaphysical account of human nature as such.

Good Of, and Good For

Aristotle's view that all action is for the sake of some good is not to be read only in a practical sense but also in a metaphysical sense. The latter recognizes many instances of action in a material universe, not all of which presuppose the exercise of reason and of freedom. The growth of the bamboo, the flowering of the orchids, the leopard's pursuit of its prey are all instances of action in nature. Of these examples it can be said that each thing acts according to the kind of being that it is, whether it be in a process of feeding or growth or reproduction. The object of action in each case is specified by the kind of being in question, what we call its nature. The study of that nature allows us to discover the patterns of development and flourishing appropriate to the kind of thing being studied, and as adapted to its environment. And so we find out that meat is good for leopards, that sunlight is good for bamboo, and that the mimicry of bees is good for the pollination of orchids.

It is noticeable that "good for" is used in at least three different senses in this listing. First, there is the distinctive feature of the organism itself (Nussbaum's capacities), whereby it is fitted for good functioning in its environment—the speed of the leopard, the color and shape of the orchid's flower. Second, there is the object of the striving, be it the prey of the leopard or the sunlight for the bamboo, which will nourish it and allow it to thrive. And third, that thriving, that flourishing is in turn the good of the being in question. The leopard's speed is its good, the leopard's meal is also its good, and the leopard's well-being in having successfully exercised its propensity for the hunt is its good. These three features illustrating the idea that all action is for some good will be replicated in each kind of being, according to its nature and the kind of thing that it is. These examples from botany and zoology do not presuppose the exercise of freedom, but still allow for meaningful use of the generalized language of action and good. For humans, according to their nature, the kind of being they are, there are also attributes that qualify the human subject as capable of acting well, and those attributes include imagination, intelligence, virtues, and freedom. There are corresponding objects of action across the wide spectrum of possibilities open to humans. And in their succeeding in their projects they enjoy the goods of well-being, good functioning and flourishing. The botanist studying the orchid brings to the task the skills and competencies developed in training. The botanist has as a deliberate object the comprehension of the life cycle and reproduction of the plant. But in performing well, the scientist also perfects skills and achieves fulfillment, even if these are not part of the deliberately chosen focus. Nonetheless it remains true that the action is oriented to these goods, along with the intended good of the botanical investigation.

The important point of this elaboration is to recognize that the goods at stake in human action are not exhausted by the explicitly named objects of action, the goods that may be chosen. As well as the knowledge of the botany of orchids there is also the flourishing of the botanist. As well as the athlete's trophy there is also the well-being of the athlete. In these examples, the specific object of action is matched with an achieved well-being that will not have been the object of action in the same sense. But also, in each of these examples, while the contrast is drawn in terms of the interests of specific individual agents, reflection shows that there are communities of people in institutions providing social context and support for the individuals' activities and successes. An individual's success and flourishing might also be a high point for the relevant community or institution. The science of botany and the scientific community of botanists are enriched by the discoveries of individual researchers. There can be a communal flourishing in the achievements of individuals.

Levels of the Good

The same three distinct levels of the good for individuals outlined here, summarized as capacity, performance, and flourishing, can also be found in the communities of persons who cooperate, either spontaneously or within institutions or organizations. Shared or common capacities, collaborative performance, and successful completion and enjoyment are constitutive parts of the goods in common in cooperation.

This brief discussion reveals the complexity of good invoked in the traditional attention to common goods. The goods in question are not simply the acknowledged and deliberately envisaged objects of pursuit in the practical sense of goods, although these are definitely included. When the common good is labeled on the one hand as the integral development of every person and of the whole person, and on the other hand as the set of conditions that enable individuals and groups to achieve their proper fulfillment, much more is invoked than what people can identify as their own chosen goals. Many elements and dimensions normally taken for granted are included in speaking both of integral fulfillment and of the conditions for flourishing. However, these aspects are not specified in detail, because the claim that there is an appropriate fulfillment for humans and for their communities does not entail that the relevant fulfillment has already been achieved, or that its constituent elements are already exhaustively known. "Exhaustively" is added here in this formulation, because of course there is sufficient human experience available to enable us to identify in broad outline what will constitute human flourishing and what its conditions are. Whether we follow Martha Nussbaum in listing the capabilities for good human functioning or the various theorists, such as David Oderberg, who list the forms of human good, we can say in general terms what can make for a good human life.[15] This is not to claim that every individual must exercise all the listed capacities or realize instances of all the basic goods. To say that there are distinctively human ways of being fulfilled and that those ways have their conditions is not to claim to know how any individual will realize their potential.

This approach to the good acknowledges that there are limits rooted in human nature and in the nature of our environment to what can be said to be good for humans. Accordingly, the freedom to choose one's conception of the good cannot mean an individual is free to ignore those limits set by nature, wherever they might be discovered to lie. This latter qualification is important, as many heated debates today are conducted around the question of the limits set by nature—for instance, regarding sex and gender. To refer to such limits is not to claim that we already know what they are, nor to foreclose the project of investigation and discovery.

WORKING FOR THE GOOD OF OTHERS AND PATERNALISM

If the argument above is correct, then it can be an act of solidarity to work for those goods of others of which they themselves might not be aware. To do so is not necessarily to impose a conception of their good on people, but instead to empower them to the point at which they can accept their responsibility to decide for themselves how they are to live. Taking that decision may also at times involve adopting a more nuanced conception of the human good, as a previously accepted conception, formed in childhood or in an ideologically shaped education, may be discovered to be limited or distorted and insufficient to guide adult responsibilities. This kind of event could make sense of the expression of "choosing one's conception of the good."

Medicine

Many professionals find themselves in the position of working for the good of others where those others are not in a position to evaluate what is proposed to be done on their behalf. Professional ethics in medicine requires that physicians and surgeons, where possible, obtain the consent of their patients for the treatment proposed. For that consent to be meaningful, patients must be informed of the nature and duration of the proposed therapy, and its likely risks and possible side effects. Medical personnel should make themselves available to answer any questions and, if necessary, facilitate obtaining a second opinion. However, despite the availability of online diagnostic aids, patients rarely, if ever, attain the levels of knowledge, competence, and experience of the professionals, and so the consent given is based on trust. The trust offered is not blind, since the patient can rely on the professional accreditation of the medical staff, their public reputation and prior record, and the existence and operation of standards of accountability and professionalism in the various fields of medicine. Accordingly, the oncology patient submits to the regime of radiation and chemotherapy, placing great trust in the professionals.[16] It is not only the trust of their patients that provides the physicians, surgeons, and other medical staff with the assurance that the treatment they offer is genuinely for the good of the patients. They also rely on the institutional assurances that their knowledge and training are well-grounded and periodically updated and their therapies are supported by research. Also, regimes of quality assurance and accountability confirm them in the confidence that their work for the good of others is commendable. Trust is a good in common in that patient-doctor relationship. The shared standards and institutions that support the trust between doctor and patient are also valuable goods in common that must be sustained.

Business Entrepreneurs

The professionals in health care provide us with a model of what it means to work for the good of others, where those others cannot and do not specify their own good in concrete detail. What model would apply to leaders in business or in politics? Business leaders in market economies have traditionally relied on consumer choice to validate their investment decisions. If the consumers don't want the product, they won't buy it, so the business will fail. Business is successful when it manages to meet a consumer demand; hence, market feedback is taken as providing business leaders with the assurance that their action is for the good of others. The entrepreneur doesn't have to decide on behalf of others what is for their good; consumers express their own decisions as to their good by exercising choice in the marketplace. "Commercially tested betterment" is the label given by Deirdre McCloskey to the resulting social development when innovation is tested in markets and acceptance confirms its beneficial nature.[17]

There is no need here to review the debates around these claims. Suffice it to mention that no society will accept the instrument of the market as the sole, the ultimate, or (even) the appropriate instrument for determining social good. There are, for instance, blocked exchanges, certain goods we will not allow to be bought or sold, such as human beings, human organs, national secrets, justice, or the loyalty of politicians or soldiers.[18] Then there is the concern about the acknowledged capacity of business to generate false needs with the result that resources that might be better used in meeting genuine needs are diverted to satisfy artificially generated demands.[19] The reality of market failure—that is, the inability of the market mechanism to provide public goods—is another reason why societies will not rely on markets alone for determining their good.[20] And finally, the externalities of market exchanges, especially the negative impact on third parties and other goods such as the environment, make it necessary to restrict the functioning of markets. But these standard qualifications are largely accepted in practice. Businesspeople know that their freedom to pursue their own good by serving the goods of others must be done within politically set parameters. The political question must address the appropriate parameters for ensuring that the market serves the common good, and we will return to this question in chapter 9.

Politicians

Political leaders in democratic systems rely on a ploy similar to that of business leaders in claiming warrant for their decisions for the good of others. Just as consumer feedback in the market is taken to reassure business leaders that their products cater to the good of their customers, so, also, does the ballot box offer politicians some assurance that their decisions indeed cater to the voters' good. This argument is supposed to be decisive, but for similar reasons to those summarized earlier concerning reliance on the market, reliance on voters' choice is not a guarantee that the leadership shown is for the common good. For one thing, a democratically elected politician holds a post because they are elected to it by a majority. In other words, the candidate has persuaded many constituents, for one reason or another, to give their vote. Assuming (and it is a big assumption) that the majority have given their vote for the same reason, and assuming further (another big assumption) that their reason is tied to the furtherance of their sectional interest, the elected politician is given no assurance that their policy is for the good of all. The qualifications in this sentence echo the realization that mixed-motivation voting confuses the intelligibility of outcomes of polls: it is not unambiguous how a particular outcome is to be interpreted.[21] It may be for the benefit only of the majority, whose good in some cases may well be detrimental to the good of all. Given the tendency in many democratic systems, partly driven by the dynamics of television campaigning, to concentrate attention on the personality of the politician and not on policies, success in elections cannot be claimed as confirming support for those policies. The vote may have been cast in many cases because one candidate was preferred to another, without consideration of policy. When it is noted further that the composition of the electorate may be manipulated—by gerrymandering, by blocking the registration of some voters, or by enabling the registration of many new voters—then it is even less plausible that the success at the ballot box represents confirmation that the politician's policies are for the good of all. Returning to the simplest case, that the majority have in fact voted to support a single policy, thinking that this policy is in their best interests, it remains possible that they are in fact mistaken—or misled—in the identification of those interests.

Granted these features of democratic elections, electoral success alone is not a reliable indicator to the political leaders that their decisions are for the good of all. For that, cogent arguments in public debates about the particular and sectional goods, as well as common goods, at stake on certain issues, is the only pathway to such assurance. Deliberative democracy is elaborated as a corrective to the limitations of relying solely on procedures, and as a pathway to realizing the values of social justice and common good as formulated in many state constitutions. Advocates for deliberative democracy make the case that reasoned argument among voters, sustained throughout the electorate, is the only assurance available that democratic processes are providing direction for the good of all. They argue that it is important for real democracy that outcomes are just, but that following proper electoral procedures alone does not guarantee just outcomes.[22]

On this pathway, proposals would have to be argued for in terms of their contributions to the good of all, and not only the good of some sector. Counterarguments would have to be considered and answers to possible objections explored. For instance, it would not be sufficient to assert that the development of a mining industry in a region will lead to overall economic progress. What forms that contribution to progress would take should be elaborated in some detail. Will the excavated ore be processed in the region, or exported? What share of the revenues will accrue to the local region, the national government, and the private corporations? Will the revenues be only in the form of charges and taxes, or will there be structures of co-ownership? Will those structures allow for a veto by the local community to protect its interests? What assurances can be given in relation to the impact on the natural environment, including ground and surface water, runoff, disposal of waste or slag, and the atmosphere? The quality of discussion and debate required to ensure an honest and genuine deliberation shows that the legitimacy of ultimate decisions as democratic and for the good of all cannot be assured by victory in an election or a plebiscite.

Even with these provisos about the requirements of democratic legitimacy, many critics of deliberative democracy claim that it is excessively modeled on the conduct of an academic seminar, and that the cognitive dimension is given too much importance.[23] In the conduct of actual politics, real interests confront each other with a power imbalance. Critics claim that the reliance on deliberative democratic strategies in the hope of an open and fair discussion of the issues would be naive in the face of such a power imbalance. More agonistic theorists of democracy advocate developing strategies with a view to redressing the imbalance of power. While this is perfectly correct, it brings its own dangers. Gabardi comments that such advocates tend to overlook "the dangers of tribalization and violence generated in the wake of a more agonistic politics."[24] To the extent that it concedes to the economic and political opponents that the nature of the contest is one of power against countervailing power, it risks forfeiting the appeal to core democratic values concerned with the political handling of conflict.

Proponents of an agonistic view of politics must be careful in practice not to so exaggerate their point that they provide the opponent with the excuse to be even more violent. The examples of the Civil Rights Movement led by Rev. Martin Luther King Jr. in the United States and Mahatma Gandhi in India, among others, underline the importance of retaining the "moral high ground." In a conflict in which force is met by force, the stronger force will usually triumph. In a conflict in which force is met by reasonable argument and nonviolent resistance, force may win, but it will not have legitimacy, and may lose out in the long run. In a conflict in which reasonable argument is met by argument, there is a possibility, but not a guarantee, that the better argument and the more reasonable case will prevail.

How might a case be made against powerful interests whose proposals to develop mining put at risk the ancestral domains of indigenous peoples and the environmental resources of a forested landscape and clean water? Invoking the common good in making such a case means appealing to the criteria that are at the heart of common good analysis. It relies on showing first that proposals are objectionable when they fail to consider the warranted concerns of affected people and groups. When those people are not admitted into the deliberations about matters that concern their livelihood and survival, or when their participation is tolerated only as cosmetic gesture, then the decisions arrived at cannot enjoy the stamp of legitimacy. These are the concerns of *solidarity*. Common good arguments rely secondly on spelling out the dimensions of human good that are jeopardized by a narrow-minded or one-sided emphasis on economic values. When the values of traditional culture are relegated to the sidelines as of no significance in comparison with the prospect of greater prosperity (but for whom?), or when the long-term benefits of a healthy environment, including the maintenance of forests and securing clean water, are discounted in balance sheets focused on short-term returns, then the second criterion of common good analysis is invoked. These are the concerns of *subsidiarity*. In support of the people and their communities who are unjustly treated in such decision-making, and in support of the human goods that are violated or jeopardized, critics of objectionable policies need to be imaginative and flexible in bringing their case to the attention of national and international publics. At the same time, while not abandoning their grounds in the application of the common good criteria, they may have to be prepared to resort to nonviolent forms of protest, including civil disobedience.

Could advocacy for the common good fall into the trap of paternalism, and is there a danger that supporters of the common good might impose their view of the good on others? In this final section I have been considering how different professionals who in their various ways are concerned with the goods and well-being of other people might answer the charge of paternalism. Politicians might be inclined to rely on electoral success as the source of their assurance that they respond to the good of their constituents with the agreement of those constituents, but the survey of criticisms directed against this view of democracy shows the limitations of such a defense. Ultimately, only good reasons can provide the grounding of legitimacy on which democratic politicians might rely. The same holds true for advocates of the common good who find themselves opposing the policies proposed by business and political leaders. The accusation of paternalism directed against those advocates must be baseless if their arguments are grounded on the two criteria of the common good. Are there such people or groups, as mentioned in application of the first criterion, who have been excluded? Are there people whose warranted concerns have not been adequately represented or answered in the deliberations? Are there such dimensions of human goods, as mentioned in application of the second criterion, that are disparaged or insufficiently protected, or otherwise discounted in comparison with more prominent concerns? In either case, an accusation of paternalism is misplaced, since the whole point of the advocacy is to ensure that no one and no group is excluded and that they can have all their concerns adequately considered. It cannot be a usurpation of the responsibility of people for their own good to act to ensure that those people are included in deliberations and that their concerns are given adequate hearing. It cannot be a usurpation of the care that others should have for their own good to spell out the neglected dimensions of that good so that those others may be faced with real choices.

CONCLUSION

I have explored the question of whether the church's view of politics might be in danger of paternalism—the church knowing best what is for the good of the political community, which it might not have chosen for itself. This led me to the question of whether solidarity as a firm commitment to the common good rules out an ontological understanding of the good and favors exclusively a practical account. A first section reviewed relevant distinctions of solidarity. The validity of assertions of interests-based solidarity was affirmed. The second section considered debates about knowledge of the good and whether an ontological account rooted in a view of human nature is compatible with human autonomy. This developed the argument in support of the legitimacy of assertions of solidarity in the name of common goods that may not yet be acknowledged by the people concerned. In the third section, a survey of forms of professional responsibility for the good of others enabled a clarification of the role of political leaders. Reliance on procedural correctness alone is not sufficient to ensure the legitimacy of policies. Even with the cogent criticisms of an excessively cognitivist approach to deliberative democracy, there is no way around the task of engaging in the evaluation of proposals and policies in terms of the common good. That evaluation relies on the two criteria of the common good, whether all affected persons and their concerns have been included and adequately addressed, and whether all relevant dimensions of the human good have been respected in the deliberation and the conclusions. Since these criteria are oriented to the inclusion of all affected persons and the inclusion of the full range of their legitimate concerns, any accusation of paternalism must lack foundation, given that the goal is the empowerment of those people and groups to secure their own interests. Any political community which attempts to exclude itself from the specification of its purpose in terms of the common good will expose itself to critical review: Which aspects of human goods will it denigrate or deny space to, and which persons or groups will it exclude from a share in the benefits of cooperation?

NOTES

1. Gerald Dworkin, "Paternalism," *The Stanford Encyclopedia of Philosophy*, Fall 2020 ed., ed. Edward N. Zalta, https://plato.stanford.edu/archives/fall2020/entries/paternalism/.
2. Second Vatican Council, *Gaudium et spes*, Pastoral Constitution on the Church Today, §74, 1965, https://www.vatican.va/archive/hist_councils/ii_vatican_council/documents/vat-ii_cons_19651207_gaudium-et-spes_en.html.
3. Pope Benedict, *Caritas in veritate*, "Love in Truth," §58, 2009, http://w2.vatican.va/content/benedict-xvi/en/encyclicals/documents/hf_ben-xvi_enc_20090629_caritas-in-veritate.html, emphasis in original.
4. Pope John Paul II, *Sollicitudo rei socialis*, "On Social Concern," §38, 1987, https://www.vatican.va/content/john-paul-ii/en/encyclicals/documents/hf_jp-ii_enc_30121987_sollicitudo-rei-socialis.html.
5. Patrick Riordan, "Human Solidarity in Need and Fulfilment: A Vision of Political Friendship," in *Solidarity Beyond Borders: Ethics in a Globalising World*, ed. Janusz Salamon (London: Bloomsbury, 2015).
6. Chris Brown, "Human Rights and Human Nature," in *Human Rights: The Hard Questions*, ed. C. Holder and D. Reidy (Cambridge: Cambridge University Press, 2013), 24.
7. J. L. Elias, *Conscientization and Deschooling: Freire's and Illich's Proposals for Reshaping Society* (Philadelphia: Westminster Press, 1976); Paolo Freire, *Pedagogy of the Oppressed* (London: Penguin, 1985).
8. Willis Jenkins, *The Future of Ethics: Sustainability, Social Justice, and Religious Creativity* (Washington, DC: Georgetown University Press, 2013).
9. Ronald Dworkin, *Justice for Hedgehogs* (Cambridge, MA: Harvard University Press, 2011), 212.
10. Michael Sandel, *Liberalism and the Limits of Justice* (Cambridge: Cambridge University Press, 1982), 60–64.
11. Roger Trigg, *Equality, Freedom, and Religion* (Oxford: Oxford University Press, 2012), 104–5.
12. Timothy Chappell, *Knowing What to Do: Imagination, Virtue, and Platonism in Ethics*. (Oxford: Oxford University Press, 2014), 125.
13. Martha Nussbaum, "Human Functioning and Social Justice: In Defense of Aristotelian Essentialism," *Political Theory* 20, no. 2 (1992): 208–9.
14. Martha Nussbaum, *Women and Human Development: The Capabilities Approach* (Cambridge: Cambridge University Press, 2000).
15. David S. Oderberg, "The Structure and Content of the Good," in *Human Values: New Essays on Ethics and Natural Law*, ed. D. S. Oderberg and T. Chappell (Basingstoke, UK: Palgrave Macmillan, 2007), 129.
16. Marek Kohn, *Trust: Self-Interest and the Common Good* (Oxford: Oxford University Press, 2008), 72–74.
17. Deirdre Nansen McCloskey, *Bettering Humanomics: A New, and Old, Approach to Economic Science* (Chicago: University of Chicago Press, 2021), 58.

18. Debra Satz, *Why Some Things Should Not Be for Sale: The Moral Limits of Markets* (Oxford: Oxford University Press, 2010).
19. Emile Perreau-Saussine, "What Remains of Socialism?" in *Values in Public Life: Aspects of Common Goods*, ed. Patrick Riordan (Berlin: LIT Verlag, 2007).
20. Richard A. Epstein, *Principles for a Free Society: Reconciling Individual Liberty with the Common Good* (Reading, MA: Perseus, 1998).
21. Jonathan Wolff, "Democratic Voting and the Mixed-Motivation Problem," *Analysis* 54, no. 4 (1994): 193–96.
22. Amy Gutmann and Dennis Thompson, *Democracy and Disagreement: Why Moral Conflict Cannot Be Avoided in Politics, and What Should Be Done about It* (Cambridge, MA: Harvard University Press, 1996), 27.
23. Wayne Gabardi, "Contemporary Models of Democracy," *Polity* 33, no. 4 (2001).
24. Gabardi, 557.

CHAPTER 9

FRAUGHT COMMON GOODS

INTEGRAL ECOLOGY, HUMANE ECONOMY

My project in this book is to show that a liberal political stance is compatible with adherence to the Catholic faith and the church's social teaching. I take issue, therefore, with authors who present the common good as a sectarian concept in a polarized debate in which liberalism is seen as the enemy. I take issue also with liberal theorists who reject the theoretical value of any concept of the common good as relevant for understanding social and political reality. In opposition to movements such as integralism or political Augustinianism, I defend a Catholic understanding of common goods that is comprehensive enough to embrace a variety of political stances, including a liberal one—in the classical and contemporary European sense, not the American sense of the term. Central to my approach is a positive evaluation of liberalism, understood as a tradition of thought about how societies should be governed that is predicated on the centrality of human freedom. Human freedom is a fundamental good, and any form of government that respects, promotes, and facilitates human freedom is capable of being a common good. From the Catholic tradition I focus on *Gaudium et spes* on the common good, Pope Benedict on the dignity of the human person and associated fundamental freedoms, and Pope Francis's encyclicals on the existential challenge of sustainability in the face of climate change.

My fundamental premises are as follows: From Aquinas's analogical use of the notion of common good, as explored in chapter 4, we see that the common good of a liberal state would be a limited though genuine good in common. The law of a liberal political community would not attempt to make people good in an unrestricted moral sense but would have a more limited agenda of securing the society's survival and preventing harm to its members. In this, the similarities with the thought of the liberal John Stuart Mill are noted. Considering Pope Benedict's emphasis on the dignity of the human person as being of transcendent value and warranting the rights acknowledged by the UDHR,

I raised the question in chapter 5 about the most appropriate political system to achieve his vision. A liberal regime espousing the values of the person would have to be a candidate. The discussion of political Augustinianism in chapter 3 shows that Augustine's theology can be read such that the secular is not necessarily opposed to the sacred. A spectrum of possibilities can allow for cases where the secular is open to the sacred, and not only the opposite pole where secular means rejection of religion. Illiberal secularism is not the only form of either liberalism or secularity and is objectionable on standard liberal political grounds of unreasonableness.

REHABILITATING MILL

In this chapter I return to the rejection of liberalism, and to the criticism of J. S. Mill to situate the discussion of fraught common goods of integral ecology and humane economy. Patrick Deneen blames Mill for many of the problems he identifies. He claims that the world we live in today is the world Mill proposed. He supports this claim by pillorying Mill's opposition to "custom," his advocacy of "experiments in living," and his elitism. Adrian Vermeule underlines the accusation that liberal regimes disparage tradition and custom.[1]

In my view, tradition or custom is objectionable if it is relied upon as answer to a challenging question—say, "Why do we treat women this way?" or "Why are black people treated this way?" Mill is right to point out that appeal to custom is an insufficient answer in such cases. As for experimentation, it was not a recommendation to experiment with drugs, or with casual sex, or with financial speculation. Given the many innovations, technological and political, that were causing upheaval in nineteenth century British society, destroying customary ways of life, it was necessary to find ways to adapt. Not all attempts at accommodation would be successful, and it would be important to test what worked and what did not, according to Mill. His model for experimentation is the scientific one, expecting a strict recording of performances and outcomes. His elitism seems misguided to us in the twenty-first century, but against the background of his experience of working for the East India Company, we may understand his concerns. After all, people still distinguish between developed, developing, and less-developed nations, and Rawls in his *Law of Peoples* also distinguishes between decent, impoverished, and rogue peoples. There is much to object to in Mill's writings, but I believe that Deneen's treatment of him is unfair.

Take, for instance, the following passages from Mill's "Considerations on Representative Government" (1861). Mill is contrasting the citizen of

Athens and the modern citizen regarding their democratic credentials. The sentiments expressed here are worthy of Deneen himself in bemoaning the deficiencies of our modern experience. According to Mill, the ancient Greek citizen was called upon "to weigh interests not his own; to be guided, in case of conflicting claims, by another rule than his private partialities; to apply, at every turn, principles and maxims which have for their reason of existence the common good.... He is made to feel himself one of the public, and whatever is for their benefit to be for his benefit."[2] By contrast, the modern individual, according to Mill, "never thinks of any collective interest, of any objects to be pursued jointly with others, but only in competition with them, and in some measure at their expense. A neighbour, not being an ally or an associate, since he is never engaged in any common undertaking for joint benefit, is therefore only a rival."[3] The contrast is offered in the context of Mill's argument for representative government, since the ideal of direct participation by all could only be realized in a very limited degree.

Can we not see Mill as a possible ally in upholding the importance of common goods and of public interest, and in resisting the atomization of social order to the private interests of individuals? This is how I regard him, and I also read his proposals on experiments in living differently than Deneen. I follow Elizabeth Anderson and Robert Kane, two philosophers whose reading of Mill on this topic presents a very different picture. Robert Kane, renowned for his work on free will, has made experiments in living a key feature of his moral philosophy, renaming them as value experiments.[4] Insofar as the good life can be said to be the objective of decisions and plans of life, it cannot be known fully in advance but must be discovered empirically, he argues. Through their experience, people come to determine where their good lies, and they correct and develop their conception of that good as they try out various possibilities. Kane appeals to Mill for his account of value experiments as essential to the moral life, lived as a quest for fulfillment. Values are discovered, known, and reflected on, and not simply chosen. This emphasis on the discovery of what works for us, as individuals and as groups, is significantly different from the currently predominant stress on autonomy in moral theory as well as in popular opinion. Liberty, the freedom to choose one's own way of life for oneself, and—more fundamentally in the views of some—the freedom to choose one's conception of the good are the pressure points in public debate as well as in the interpretation of the law. Kane, following Mill, shifts this emphasis away from the exercise of choice to the progress in discovery of what is good. He sees it as more a matter of knowing than of deciding. Knowing the good, the discovery of what contributes to our well-being and good functioning is his focus. This resonates with Aristotle's focus on agreement on the good. Liberty is a condition for the pursuit of the good; it is not itself the point of it all.

John Stuart Mill is most widely known for his advocacy on behalf of liberty. It is commonly forgotten, however, that for Mill liberty was not an end in itself but a necessary condition for the discovery of forms of life that were conducive to human well-being. Pace Deneen, it was not simply that Mill wanted people to be free from custom, the social pressure of disapproval, or the constraints of legal regulation so that they could do their own thing. He wanted them to be free to pursue their vision of the good, so that their experience of trying something out would lead to discoveries, of benefit not only for themselves, but for society. The precondition for society learning from the experience of its members was open public discussion and reflection on what had happened, and how others might learn from the attempts of some to discover better ways of living. Many who invoke Mill's patronage for their advocacy of freedom conveniently forget his expectation that their experiment not be a purely private matter but an opportunity for humankind to learn about how to live more decently and more fully. Again, the context of upheaval in traditional English society should not be forgotten. The popular reception of his essay *On Liberty* (originally 1859) ignored the call for analysis and reflection and adopted merely the insistence that the freedom necessary for experimentation was not to be curtailed except to prevent harm to others or to society. Were we to apply Mill's original proposal in full, it would require elaborate detailing of what was attempted and how it did or did not succeed, and whether the venture contributed to human progress. What is entailed in this last aspect would need to be made explicit, and this in turn would require public debate that could not be silenced merely by invoking liberty, or expense, or some form of cost-benefit analysis.

Liberal thinkers who consider only questions of right to be public matters and consign all questions of the good to the private domain are not consistent with Mill. Fair interpretation of his writing does not support such a public-private separation. He expected people to learn from each other's experiences about the human good in a very public process. That public process required freedom of speech and open debate to test the validity of claims made.

In his advocacy for liberty, Mill explicitly rejects any appeal to a natural right to liberty—what he calls an abstract right: "It is proper to state that I forego any advantage which could be derived to my argument from the idea of abstract right, as a thing independent of utility. I regard utility as the ultimate appeal on all ethical questions; but it must be utility in the largest sense, grounded on the permanent interests of man as a progressive being."[5] To understand this notion of "utility in the largest sense," it is helpful to reflect on how Mill, after experiencing a profound depression, came to distance himself from the narrow sense of utility as he had been raised to pursue it by his father, James Mill, who was guided by the philosopher Jeremy Bentham.

Elizabeth Anderson has suggested that we should consider Mill's reflections on this matter as an example of the kind of reflection on experiments in living that he advocated.[6] In other words, he himself had been an experiment. He had been educated and raised according to Bentham's utilitarianism. Bentham postulated that pleasure and pain were the two great motivators of human action, so that a hedonic calculus could enable individuals and society to work out the best paths of action, leading to the greatest happiness of the greatest number. Raised in this philosophy, he had the opportunity to experience how unsatisfactory this doctrine and plan of life were in practice. Anderson argues that Mill's reflection on his own experience provides a model for how, in general, experiments in living might be reflected upon and analyzed. Mill's attempt to live according to Bentham's philosophy led to a crisis which drove him to reshape his lifestyle and revise his understanding of the good. As Anderson remarks, it was both a crisis of life, since the pursued good of happiness was not achieved, and a theoretical crisis, since the espoused theory could not explain the suffering encountered.

The discovery of Wordsworth's poetry and the affective support of Mrs. Harriet Taylor, whom Mill was later to marry, made him realize that his life's goals were not adequately characterized as the optimized pursuit of pleasure and avoidance of pain. He needed a different account of the human good to help him make sense of his experience. What is significant here is not so much his revision of utilitarianism as his discovery of the learning process. Mill extrapolated from his own personal experience to identify the importance for people of following a similar trajectory of discovery of the limitations both of their conception of the good and of their experience. Experiments in living, Mill believed, should be facilitated so that people could discover superior conceptions of the good.

The point here is not to claim that Mill has succeeded in formulating a comprehensive account of the good. The point instead is to acknowledge his achievement in recognizing the process of discovery and developing a social philosophy open in principle to the discovery of ever more satisfactory accounts of the human good. Generalizing from this dynamic enabled him to reconsider the kind of being the human is. Mill shifts from the simplistic description of the human agent as a seeker after pleasure or satisfaction and an avoider of pain to a more complex model that recognizes behind the motions of pursuit and avoidance an underlying dynamic of development. Mill redefines utility in the largest sense as "grounded on the permanent interests of man as a progressive being." "In proportion to the development of his individuality," he writes, "each person becomes more valuable to himself, and is therefore capable of being more valuable to others."[7] In this notion of development we see reflected Mill's own experience of change in himself, his own growth in awareness encompassing new dimensions of experience, and his growth in understanding as he modified his theory of utility.

Mill is by no means beyond criticism for his arrogance vis-à-vis what he considered to be barbarian and undeveloped peoples, as well as for his elitism in dismissing the collective mediocrity of the masses. But his basic insight continues to warrant attention—that people are always capable of becoming more, and liberty must be assured them so they will not be blocked in their development. The exaggerated individualism of his view of development also deserves critical comment, but this weakness does not undermine the main point here, which is to highlight the discovery of a dynamic of growth and make it the focus of individual and social learning.

Is it plausible to suggest that a whole society might engage in the kind of experiential learning that Mill envisaged? Can a society learn from its own history, viewing it as a series of experiments in living? Is this not what is essentially going on in the literature in which authors appeal to their readers to attend to common goods and the well-being of all, including the good functioning of the political and legal systems, instead of private and sectional interest? Certainly we can detect in Deneen's book a call to review the experience of living under a specific liberal regime and its failure to deliver on the promises it seems to hold out. Is this not what is essentially Deneen's concern, that we would review the experience of liberalism and its failure to deliver on its promises? Far from Deneen's interpretation of Mill, that "everywhere, at every moment, we are to engage in experiments in living," it is much more a recommendation to review our history as if it were an experiment, to evaluate our performance and experience and learn from it. Deneen evaluates the experience of living under liberal regimes negatively, and proposes pathways to alternative lifestyles such as the Benedict Option. Adrian Vermeule relies on a similar analysis but suggests a different pathway.

POPE FRANCIS AND LAUDATO SI' *ON INTEGRAL ECOLOGY*

I suggest we can read Pope Francis's encyclical letters also as calls to reflect on our experience, identify where we have gone wrong, and seek alternative pathways that might help us correct our mistakes. I am not claiming that Pope

Francis was influenced by Mill, but I hope to show the similarities between what Francis does and what the liberal author proposes. Francis points to the need to reflect on how we treat our common home, on the mindsets that guide our politics and communal behavior, and on how we run our economies as we use the resources made available to us to provide for what is needed for a decent life. As is widely acknowledged, Francis uses the See-Judge-Act model for the reflection on our experiments in living. Introduced originally by a Belgian cardinal for use by the Young Christian Workers, it was adopted in liberation theology and various pastoral contexts.[8] The three steps include attending to elements of our experience, analysis in terms of causes, and prescriptions for action.

Pope Francis's application is to the environmental crisis of climate change. There is no need to review the survey of environmental devastation and the impoverishment of many of the world's marginalized societies. This has become even more part of our consciousness following the Synod on the Pan-Amazon Region. I move straightaway to the "Judge" phase, where the critique is offered. A focus of Francis's critique in *Laudato Si'* (2015) is the "technocratic paradigm" as a mindset that sustains the exploitative behaviors of humankind in relation to its planetary home.[9] This is a mindset, a spiritual reality, as the shared meanings and values of communities and cultures, and the solution requires a complete overhaul of cultural and technological norms and institutions. This mindset pervades the dominant orthodoxies in social sciences, including politics and economics. At the heart of these mindsets is a distinctive position on the human good, especially on the impossibility of any conception of the good life informing decision-making in the economy and in political life. Pope Francis points to the need for a review of common assumptions about the good and calls for a critique of operative conceptions of the good in economics and politics and their related scientific disciplines. The need for critique is evident from the dynamics of resistance and rejection with which philosophical challenges are rendered politically powerless. Francis is aware of these difficulties as signaled in the encyclical where he comments on the blocks to dialogue and insight, usually leveraged by vested interests.[10]

Linked to the critique of the technocratic paradigm is the demand to review the relationship between economics and politics. The attempt to rely solely on the market for solutions with such instruments as a market for carbon or institutions of cap and trade illustrates the tendency to prioritize economics over politics. Critical thinkers agree with Francis in advocating political rather than primarily economic measures. Institutions of deliberative democracy for social choice are needed.[11] Pope Francis writes in *Laudato Si'*, "Politics must not be subject to the economy, nor should the economy be subject to the dictates of an efficiency-driven paradigm of technocracy. Today, in view of the common good, there is urgent need for politics and economics to enter into a frank dialogue in the service of life, especially human life."[12] This emphasis on a deliberative society pursuing the meaning of the good life for which the economy is merely instrumental reaffirms central concerns of Catholic social teaching (CST). For instance, Pope John Paul II, in his letter *Centesimus annus* marking the centenary of *Rerum novarum* in 1991 insists:

> The economy in fact is only one aspect and one dimension of the whole of human activity. If economic life is absolutized, if the production and consumption of goods become the center of social life and society's only value, not subject to any other value, the reason is to be found not so much in the economic system itself as in the fact that the entire sociocultural system, by ignoring the ethical and religious dimension, has been weakened, and ends by limiting itself to the production of goods and services alone.[13]

This pithy statement locates the economic within a larger sociocultural system and expects that the values of the market will be subject to other values. Similarly, in reflecting on the end of the Soviet Union, like liberalism itself, another big experiment in human living, Pope John Paul II, in *Centesimus annus*, does not celebrate the victory of capitalism but notes how it can only be supported if embedded in a strong juridical framework. Asked whether capitalism could be endorsed as a model for development, he offers a qualified, positive answer. The qualification is that the "freedom in the economic sector" must be "circumscribed within a strong juridical framework which places it at the service of human freedom in its totality, and which sees it as a particular aspect of that freedom, the core of which is ethical and religious."[14] It is not only that economic freedoms require a strong legal framework, such as the securing of private property rights and the enforceability of contracts, in order to function well. Those framing legal structures should function to ensure that the exercise of economic freedoms serve a moral purpose, such as the flourishing of human communities. As discussed later in this chapter, the dynamics of deregulation have contributed to the weakening of the inherited legal constraints on market activity, and the facilitation of sectional interests in appropriating the benefits of economic activity.

The adequacy of inherited and currently functioning legal frameworks is now queried by Pope Francis in the context of the global environmental crisis. What can be the appropriate "strong juridical framework" to ensure that the care for our common home is not undermined by our economic activity?

How to formulate the values or higher purposes, relative to which that activity of wealth production and distribution can be evaluated?

Combining these two perspectives—Mill's liberal philosophical analysis of the requirement to learn from our experience and our experiments in living, and Pope John Paul's demand that our economic activity be constrained within a strong juridical structure—we can sharpen the question in terms of common goods: What can we learn from our experience of how economic activity delivers or fails to deliver common goods for our societies?

Is Neoliberalism the Same as Economic Liberalism?

Pope Francis identifies neoliberalism ("individualism, consumerism, globalized technocracy")[15] as a mindset that needs correction. While there are many like Pope Francis who use the term in a pejorative sense, it is difficult to find authors who explicitly defend the stance of neoliberalism as a political philosophy with implications for the structuring of the economy and society. David Harvey, a Marxist critic, offers the following helpful account: "Neoliberalism is in the first instance a theory of political economic practices that proposes that human well-being can best be advanced by liberating individual entrepreneurial freedoms and skills within an institutional framework characterized by strong private property rights, free markets, and free trade. The role of the state is to create and preserve an institutional framework appropriate to such practices."[16] How is this account of "neoliberalism" distinguishable from classical "liberalism," understood as a combined economic and political system? Deirdre Nansen McCloskey, whose book title *Why Liberalism Works* indicates her stance, declares her satisfaction with Harvey's definition: "I entirely agree with his definition of (neo)liberalism. So understood, it's the same as the old, classical liberalism of Adam Smith and J. S. Mill."[17] In her view, it is consistent with Adam Smith's 1776 proposal that everyone be allowed to pursue their own interest in their own way as the best means of assuring equality, liberty, and justice.

The newness signaled by the "neo" may be the associated policy recommendation to deregulate. As Harvey's definition notes, the state has a positive role in providing an institutional framework to support economic activity. Beyond the supportive role, liberals expect state interventions in markets to be kept to a minimum for two reasons: because the "state cannot possibly possess enough information to second-guess market signals (prices) and because powerful interest groups will inevitably distort and bias state interventions (particularly in democracies) for their own benefit."[18] Supported by this ideology, many economies have undergone the changes of "deregulation, privatization, and withdrawal of the state from many areas of social provision."[19] The term "creative destruction" was coined by Joseph Schumpeter to describe the impact of competition within markets whereby inefficient and uneconomical producers will be put out of business. Harvey uses the term to describe the broader impact of neoliberalism. Prior institutional frameworks, divisions of labor, social relations, welfare provisions, and ways of life and thought have been destroyed by neoliberalism. At the heart of this destructive force is the substitution of the contractual relations of the marketplace for all previously held ethical beliefs.[20] These criticisms are echoed by many authors from a Catholic standpoint, such as Patrick Deneen,[21] Adrian Vermeule,[22] and Matthew T. Eggemeier and Peter Joseph Fritz.[23] However, "creative destruction" is not without its supporters. A French publication translated into English continues the defense of Schumpeter's account: *The Power of Creative Destruction: Economic Upheaval and the Wealth of Nations*.[24]

Kevin Vallier's essay "Neoliberalism" in the *Stanford Encyclopedia of Philosophy* denies some of the charges made against it.[25] Vallier identifies the principal authors who have contributed to the distinctive political philosophy at the heart of neoliberalism and provides a positive overview of the position as a coherent political doctrine. The authors are "F. A. Hayek, Milton Friedman, and James Buchanan, all of whom play leading roles in the new historical research on neoliberalism, and all of whom wrote in political philosophy as well as political economy."[26] Vallier provides three criteria for the construction of his account: "First, the term 'neoliberalism' should be used to denote a fairly coherent set of positions. Second, it should be used to capture the views of those figures most often associated with the position. Finally, we should focus on capturing the most serious and even-handed uses of the term, such as by academic historians, rather than more popular and pejorative uses of 'neoliberalism.'"[27]

Vallier first dismisses four elements associated with the position by its critics. He denies, first, that neoliberalism is an ethos, writing that it is "a view about the design of social institutions, and not a particular ethos of social life."[28] The authors cited say little about how to live well. Their main emphasis is on the freedom to pursue what one values, including the view that free societies need people prepared to act on fundamentally *religious* impulses. Second, Vallier denies that neoliberalism is a school of thought within utilitarianism. All three of the authors reject that association. Third, the authors also deny the identification of their position with libertarianism, as exemplified by Robert Nozick's positing of natural rights as fundamental to determining the nature and limitations of the state. According to Vallier, "Neoliberals instead focus on the consequence-based arguments for liberalism without adopting consequentialism. They simply rationalize liberalism in part based on the claim that liberalism has good consequences."[29] He notes the historical origins of neoliberalism after the Second World War in reaction to communism, fascism, and social democracy: "Neoliberals sought to confine state power to a range of functions much more limited than that undertaken by extensive states of these three varieties. Hayek's work on informational systems was a response to communist central planning. Friedman's monetarism was a response to Keynesian macroeconomic policy. And Buchanan's public-choice research program was a response to the economics of general equilibrium and market failure economics."[30] The fourth misapprehension is to label neoliberalism as a form of ideal theory. The authors' reasons are grounded in a skepticism about human capacities to know the ideal and a realism about human noncompliance with ideal standards.

In their self-description they see themselves as defenders of human freedom and the freedom of small groups such as the family over against the state. They position themselves in the tradition of liberalism, but for their contemporary critics they appear as a distortion of that classical tradition, not for what they write but for the policies adopted in their name. Putting it differently, while Vallier draws on the founding authors to present a relatively stable political philosophy, their critics attack a dynamic and variable political ideology associated with the policies of certain politicians, political parties, and governmental regimes.

To the extent that the political philosophy of neoliberalism as outlined by Vallier is an adaptation of a liberal political philosophy in modern circumstances, I can endorse its fundamental commitments, which I see as harmonious with the Catholic church's emphasis on subsidiarity. Edward Hadas points out that the dynamics of statism, whether on the right or the left, drive toward an ever-greater role for the state that squeezes the institutions of civil society such as the church and the family; these dynamics therefore inevitably threaten to violate the principle of subsidiarity.[31] Given the economic power of corporations and the dominance of market forces, states are relatively powerless in modern circumstances unless they have the advantage of scale, such as the United States or the European Union. In fact, part of what must be learned by reflecting on recent experience is the extent to which the state and its lawmaking powers have been captured by vested interests, either to remove regulation originally intended to serve the common good or impose new regulations facilitating selective interests. This, indeed, is the danger the liberal thinkers warned against.

THE NEED FOR REGULATION ACCEPTED

There is no reason why liberalism cannot accept the need for regulation, and many forms of liberalism do. The enforcement of competition is one major reason why regulation of markets is warranted. Far from Adam Smith being a defender of unregulated markets, as is often asserted, he believed that regulation was essential to protect the populace and oblige merchants to compete.[32] Appropriate regulation preventing cartels and ensuring competition is needed. Other reasons can be found for regulation of various forms, as in the standardization of weights and measures, and prohibition of harmful products. As Jonathan Wolff records, "It took the Adulteration of Food and Drink Act of 1860 to stop publicans putting salt in beer and bakers chalk dust in bread in the UK. Competition between brewers, or between bakers, seeking their own self-interest, did not do the trick."[33] Consumers could not identify the flaw in the product.

Take the example of Samuel Plimsoll (1824–98), an English politician and social reformer. To him we owe the Plimsoll line, a line painted on the hulls of ships to mark the limit of safe loading. His efforts were directed especially against what were known as "coffin ships": unseaworthy and overloaded vessels, often heavily insured, in which unscrupulous owners risked the lives of their crews. How to ensure that only seaworthy and properly loaded ships would take to the sea? The Plimsoll line was the solution. It was visible, and overloading was recognizable before ever a ship left port. That is a regulation regarding safety and conditions of trade that we would not want to see removed. Tragically, it took a long time to have it adopted, since British shipowners well-represented in Parliament were content to recoup the insurance and were not at a financial loss when ships foundered with loss of cargo and crew.[34]

Regulations of various kinds are part of doing business. Neoliberalism's interest in pushing back the boundaries of the state and removing such regulations as hindered freedoms without compensating benefits have appeared in the guise of deregulation as a fundamental rejection of all regulatory constraint. Where liberals of different hues have been able to accept necessary regulation, campaigning neoliberals seem opposed to constraints in principle. This is a simplification and exaggeration, but the experience of recent decades bears out its core of truth. Deregulation is the catchword of the program of reform initiated in the era of Thatcher and Reagan that has carried through into the twenty-first century. Regulations of every kind are targeted and removed. And so we can ask, in the terms of Pope John Paul's recommendation: How has the restructuring of the juridical framework by the policies of deregulation advanced or jeopardized the common good? In the following sections I review several cases.

Regulation of Banking

William Kingston records how limited liability was first introduced in an Irish law in 1782. Its purpose was to facilitate investment in innovative technologies with a view to producing useful goods and services.[35] That "Anonymous Investors" Act ensured that, in the case of failure, the liabilities incurred by businesses in creating and marketing their product would be limited to the extent of their initial investment. Prior to this, personal responsibility for debt was the norm. In cooperative ventures, considered as partnerships, each partner was jointly and severally liable for any debts that might be incurred by their business. Because this system of unlimited personal responsibility by each of the partners was a major deterrent to investment in innovation and industry, it was changed. However, the 1782 act explicitly denied limited liability to bankers and others dealing in money, and this denial was copied in the 1855 British law creating limited liability. (The Irish and British parliaments had been combined in 1801.) French, Spanish, German, and Belgian legislation adopted it later in the century. New York had adopted it in 1811. However, lobbying by financial interests in the UK achieved a reversal of the exclusion of banking in 1879. The good reasons for the exclusion had not lost their plausibility.

What was the reason for the exclusion of banking? It was recognized that dealing in money was significantly different from dealing in goods. For example, in the latter case, holding stock would be a cost, while in the former, holding money would not be a cost. This constraint on banking activity ensured that bankers were assiduous in determining loans. They would take care to whom and on what conditions they lent money, since they and their bank were at risk of losing in the event of bad debts.[36]

The success of financial interests in achieving a change in the law reflects a dynamic that would function throughout the subsequent century. Juridical constraints in place to ensure that the market functioned to serve the common good, including the good of investors, were weakened or dissolved in favor of the interests of financiers. The original purpose of limited liability was to facilitate technological innovation and the development of industry, including the building of the railways, and the assumption behind this was that the satisfaction of human need was for the common good. However, the change in law favored the interests of financiers rather than those of industry and the common good. Instead of financing technical innovation, owners of capital could choose to speculate in financial products. In effect, the poachers had succeeded in getting control of the law the gamekeepers relied upon to protect the public good.

The same dynamic is evident in the later change in the laws regulating the responsibilities of auditors. A fascinating example is how accountants made rules to suit themselves. Kingston narrates how the auditing (accountancy) profession succeeded in getting the publicly established standards of best practice changed to standardized box-ticking procedures. This replaced the requirement that professionals exercise personal judgment. As a result, practitioners were freed from personal liability for mistaken judgment. Now all they needed do to protect themselves was demonstrate that required procedures had been followed. Another change in standards that had very negative consequences for the public good was the restriction that auditors only had to report actual losses incurred by a bank or business, and not any expected losses. As a result, auditors were signing off on the accounts of banks that were due to make serious losses and, in some cases, to fail. But the auditors had nothing to answer, they claimed, since they had complied with requirements, a defense which the House of Lords inquiry into the 2009 banking crisis in the UK did not accept but could do little about. Kingston reports on the self-interested parties succeeding in capturing the lawmaking processes and shaping the focus of concern.[37]

American Deregulation of Banking

Reflection on recent experience suggests that our societies are very poor at learning from experience. The failure of the financial sector and governmental regulators to learn from the Enron crisis of 2000 is staggering, given that the problems at the heart of the 2008 subprime mortgage credit crisis were very similar to those encountered in the earlier Enron debacle. In both cases, the treatment of debt as an asset was central.

The instruments developed for packaging and marketing mortgage debt are reminiscent of the Special Purpose Entities (SPEs) developed by the Enron executives, which enabled them to present debits as assets. Enron had been innovative in developing financial instruments such as derivatives and SPEs. SPEs "are financing vehicles that permit companies, like Enron, to, among other things, access capital or to increase leverage without adding debt to their balance sheet."[38] But these were the specific instruments that enabled Enron and its auditors Arthur Andersen to defraud the stakeholders. The crisis showed up the failure of the regulatory regime of internal and external auditing, and of the combination of market assessors and business journalism.

Instead of revealing the deception, the assessors and journalists turned out to be complicit in conveying the impression that Enron was solid. Similarly, in the summer and autumn of 2007, the new techniques of "securitization" (whereby lenders packaged their mortgages and other loans into marketable securities), although they had been very popular with investors in the early years of the decade, suddenly became widely suspect because the real risks involved were concealed by the instruments. The debates arising in these contexts provoke the question of the common good.

In favor of deregulation is the fact that some regulations introduced to protect consumers or encourage competition have had unintended negative consequences. Some systems of licensing and patenting have created monopolies and prevented competition. But other regulations, initially introduced to prevent catastrophes such as bank failure or a repetition of the great crash of 1929 and the subsequent depression of the 1930s, were removed without consideration of the consequences.

One of the lessons learned in the United States after the 1929 crash was the wisdom of separating commercial and investment banking. The US banking acts of 1933 and 1935 required banks to opt for one designation or the other, and those registered with the Federal Reserve as commercial banks, offering loans to customers and taking deposits, were prevented from engaging in trading in stocks. They were prevented from dealing in companies' stocks either on behalf of customers or for themselves; they were also prohibited from underwriting or distributing such company shares, or affiliating (or sharing employees) with companies involved in such activities. On the other hand, these regulations prevented securities firms and investment banks from taking deposits. Banks of all kinds put pressure on legislators to remove these limitations, and eventually, with the adoption of deregulation policies, they were freed from those constraints in their pursuit of profit. The collapse of the banking sector in the 2007–8 catastrophe was the direct result of the deregulation.

George Soros uses strong language in speaking about those who were responsible for the crisis, referring to "unscrupulous lenders" and "predatory practices."[39] But "the regulatory authorities lost the ability to calculate the risks involved."[40] The same inability to really understand what was happening led the rating agencies to take the same easy way out as the regulatory authorities: they simply believed and repeated the self-assessment of the issuing banks. Soros's main target is the market fundamentalism that favored deregulation and confidently assumed that the markets, left to themselves, would bring about a satisfactory situation for all. The general weakening in the regulatory regime coincided with the development of new instruments for packaging and marketing debt. These were made possible because of the new technologies in computing and mathematical modeling. Just at a time when complexity and speed required new forms of regulation, the regulatory authorities were being dismantled as a matter of policy. The impact of the crisis was undeniable.

In facing the crisis, governments on both sides of the Atlantic refused to allow the free market to work to its natural conclusion. Morris documents the inconsistency in the stance taken by the greatest advocates of market freedom. Before the crisis, Alan Greenspan had argued for the ability of markets to police themselves and dismissed the anxieties of those who "raise[d] the specter of . . . a chain of defaults."[41] Later, Greenspan argued before Congress that the ordinary processes of the market could not be allowed to follow their course when it threatened the survival of certain strategically placed firms who should be rescued by state intervention.[42] The inability of banks to meet obligations and the failure of the market to provide resources to meet demand should lead, in the normal course of events, to default and bankruptcy. But on the judgment of the political authorities, some institutions have been "too big to fail," and so the federal authorities in the United States, and the Bank of England and the Treasury in the UK, intervened to save the banks in crisis.

Commentators warn of "moral hazard," the counterproductive effect of giving the impression that risky deals will never have to face the consequences of failure, thereby encouraging more reckless trading. As a result of this security, granted by the fact that some losses will be socialized—that is, borne by the taxpayer and society in general—operators in the financial markets have been able to take greater risks, earning themselves larger fees and bigger profits. This means that financial services have not really been operating in a truly free market, but in one underwritten by the assurance of ultimate rescue.[43] Here lies the dishonesty of some free market advocates: the refusal to admit the reliance on social support and ultimate state-assured security while maintaining that the benefits are solely due to the operations of the market.

Morris examines the case of an American bank, Countrywide Financial, rescued by a state agency, the Atlanta Federal Home Loan Bank, in 2007. It highlights the issue of whether such banks are risk-taking enterprises or public utilities. If treated as public utilities underwritten by government, there would have to be tighter control of bank risk-taking.[44] Deregulation made the crisis possible because of the removal of constraints for ideological reasons. The crisis illustrates the need for regaining regulatory control of these markets for debt. The framing question has to be how such markets benefit the greater good. The same question has been posed from experience of the operation of financial markets.

Value-Taking by the Financial Sector

Mariana Mazzucato, professor of Innovation at University College London, challenges the standard justification for the takings of the finance sector, which is that it contributes to the efficient allocation of capital to productive investment opportunities. Her book *The Value of Everything: Making and Taking in the Global Economy* builds on earlier publications in which she challenges the assumption that the private sector alone is responsible for the creation of wealth. She documents the contribution of public institutions to major innovations.[45] According to Mazzucato, most established firms finance their research and development from internal resources such as retained profits, and do not depend on financial markets.[46] Furthermore, initial financing for start-ups is rarely provided from the finance markets, as investors are only willing to become involved once chances of success have been established by initial performance. The enormous expansion of the finance sector, if it were contributing to the efficiency of investment in productive activity, might be expected to have resulted in a corresponding growth in returns on productive investment. In fact, Mazzucato records that only 15 percent of the funds generated in financial markets go to businesses in nonfinancial industries.[47] It appears that the enormous earnings in the finance sector are largely due to the churning of stocks by fund managers who benefit by charges on purchases and sales regardless of whether these have any impact on productive activity. Mazzucato's study also shows how this development in finance has infected the industrial sector, since any proposals to invest in new production will be compared with rates of return on the financial markets, and so resources are diverted in some cases.[48] This observation resonates with Kingston's argument about the self-destruction of capitalism, summarized in the subtitle of his book: *Technology Displaced by Financial Innovation*. The seduction of large earnings in the financial markets draws capital away from investment in technological innovation.[49]

The World Bank and Deregulation

The ideology of deregulation was adopted by the World Bank in the 1980s and imposed on developing countries as a condition for receiving development support from the World Bank and the International Monetary Fund. As a former chief economist at the World Bank, Joseph Stiglitz confronts the uncomfortable reality that the bank's policies in insisting on privatization, deregulation, and the removal of protective measures had catastrophic impacts on the economies of many developing countries, and instead of resolving crises in many cases made them worse.⁵⁰ As the title of his book suggests, the dynamics of globalization appear as destructive rather than productive because of the features associated with neoliberalism. These are the ideology of deregulation, the systematic removal of constraints on the free operation of market forces—that is, the liberalization of trade and financial markets—and the demand that state intervention be minimized. The Vatican's 2018 statement of considerations on the economic-financial system echoes the same concern: "Where massive deregulation is practiced, the evident result is a regulatory and institutional vacuum that creates space not only for moral risk and embezzlement, but also for the rise of the irrational exuberance of the markets, followed first by speculative bubbles, and then by sudden, destructive collapse, and systemic crises."⁵¹ It was too easily forgotten that much of the regulation in place had been put there to prevent bubbles and their consequences.

If we take Mill's suggestion or Pope Francis's See-Judge-Act model seriously, we have to review this and similar histories to establish what happened; evaluate it in terms of who benefited and who was excluded, and what the impact was on human goods and social life; and then determine what is to be done. In doing this, our political deliberations will not be able to avoid conflict. The initial conflict is to be expected in the attempt to rescue politics, understood as the management of conflict by talking, from being colonized by the bounded and limited rationality of economics.

Signs of Change?

Pope John Paul II wrote that market freedoms should be constrained in a juridical structure to ensure they serve a higher purpose. This seems to be echoed in a book about values published by the former governor of the Bank of England, Mark Carney.⁵² He argues that we cannot cope with crises such as those of credit, COVID, and climate unless we uphold and foster values. Economy and politics must be surrounded by a strong moral framework. Carney's book resonates with that of another eminent public figure, Jean Tirole, the 2014 French Nobel Prize winner for economics, who in 2017 published *Economics for the Common Good*.⁵³ In both cases, respected figures familiar with the worlds of business, finance, and government regulation argue for the need to balance markets with morals. They have slightly different terms, with Tirole advocating the common good as the horizon providing markets with their purpose and Carney arguing for values as delineating the comprehensive context in which the distinctive economic values should be situated. Both arguments are welcome as reinforcing the Aristotelian and Catholic appeal to ends and purposes to enable us to transcend the bounded rationality of economics. However, in both cases the argument is weakened by a poor mastery of ethics, and the cases they make require an account of human goods and values, and of common goods, that neither delivers. Both authors agree that a simplistic utilitarianism is unsatisfactory, but that is not enough to provide the needed account of human goods, values, and ethical principles.

On issue after issue—climate change, labor market regulation, survival of the Euro and the European Union, digitization, regulation of intellectual property, and innovation—Tirole demonstrates that the issues addressed in the economic debates are not matters of concern to economists alone. The handling of these issues directly affects the quality of human social and political life impacting everyone. Policy decisions cannot be driven by economic considerations alone but depend on the political vision of the kind and quality of life a society desires for itself. In effect, then, the book is a challenge to those political cultures that in recent decades have delegated to market forces the decisions about what is to be fostered in cultural and political life. The marketization of education is an example that will be addressed in chapter 10. While Tirole does not doubt the usefulness of markets in serving social purposes, he highlights the need for discussion about what those purposes are and what we would want them to be. The common goods are not simply given, and the failure to make them explicit and widely endorsed across society results in a hijack by sectional interests, ensuring that the interests of some are secured at the expense of others.

Mark Carney is too nice in what he has to say about how markets can contribute to solutions, and his remarks about how financial markets have caused the problems are too general in tone. He describes how "markets can go wrong" and how "following the global financial crisis, many supposedly rugged markets were revealed to have been either cosseted or corrupt."[54] But this does not deliver the kind of analysis that would help identify the source of the problems. He does not engage in the review of these experiments in living that Mill demanded. With reference to the purpose of financial markets, Carney writes, "Financial capitalism is not an end in itself but a means to promote investment, innovation, growth and prosperity. Banking is fundamentally about intermediation—connecting borrowers and savers in the real economy."[55] Although he mentions Mazzucato's book, he ignores her arguments that financial markets facilitate "taking" and not the creation of innovation and prosperity. As noted earlier, she documents how small a proportion of finance as mediated by the markets is directed toward facilitating innovation; investors only direct their wealth to new enterprises once they have proven their success. Carney's book is that of an establishment figure who wishes to continue to be acceptable to that establishment, and so is careful not to be seriously critical. There are helpful suggestions about regulation. But there is no analysis of how the deregulation policies of recent decades have removed constraints that had the purpose of securing values against economic dominance. "Regulation" is in the index, but not "deregulation."

Deirdre McCloskey's Defense of Liberalism

Deirdre Nansen McCloskey is an outspoken defender of liberalism as a culture sustaining the economy. What she wishes to defend is liberalism as facilitating "commercially tested betterment."[56] She takes every possible opportunity to remind readers of the achievements of what Marx called the bourgeois mode of production in lifting an increasing proportion of a growing world population out of poverty. The quality and quantity of foods, materials, and resources available to people living in poverty in the twenty-first century is a multiple factor greater than that available to the poor of the eighteenth century. This enormous change, "the Great Enrichment," has been largely due to the influence of a set of ideas that shaped human society and social collaboration. Those ideas form what McCloskey calls the "bourgeois virtues": a suspicion of social hierarchy, an affirmation of equality of persons, and a demand for liberty, for the freedom to "have a go" and attempt to realize some idea for the improvement of tools and equipment and how things are done.[57] Not all such ideas prove successful, and it is the testing of their products in the marketplace that confirms their usefulness. Commercially tested betterment is made possible by a culture that allows individuals and groups the freedom to take a risk and try something out. Schumpeter's creative destruction is accepted as a corollary of such enterprising economy; for example, the development of the automobile eventually put a lot of people out of work: some breeders of horses, makers of carts and carriages, and the leatherworkers engaged in producing harnesses, saddles, and whips. Other paid jobs were made possible, but there is no denying the destruction and disruption.

McCloskey is not the only defender of economic liberalism who celebrates its achievements in reducing poverty.[58] She stands out from the others in espousing a Christian stance and showing how her commitment to liberalism is compatible with her faith and with a loving concern for those who are disadvantaged or experiencing poverty. She also engages robustly with critics who rely on a theological critique to reject liberalism. She reviewed Patrick Deneen's *Why Liberalism Failed*, and her own book, published the following year, might be taken as a rejoinder: *Why Liberalism Works: How True Liberal Values Produce a Freer, More Equal, Prosperous World for All*.[59]

She is very confident that allowing people the freedom to act in pursuit of their own interests will contribute to the dynamic of "betterment," improving the quality of life available to people. That some regulation of markets is necessary she would not deny, but while she warns against the dangers of too much regulation, she does not address the risk associated with too little regulation, nor with the harmful consequences of overzealous deregulation.

CONCLUSION

Given the demonstrated propensity of big corporations and economic interests to capture regulative authorities and influence state policy, political culture requires deliberation about the values and desired quality of public life the market economy should serve. That deliberation presupposes a literacy in the good and the goods of common life, so that where and when deliberation is possible citizens are well-resourced to express their vision and aspiration. For this purpose, and to meet the task set by Pope Francis in *Laudato Si'*, we need a fuller account of goods appropriate for articulating our vision and values.

The reforms Francis calls for require not simply a relativization of the technocratic paradigm but a revision of the understandings of the human good that pervade all our human sciences and our economic and political practices. In terms of the myriad goods in common, there is no shortcut in the form of a convenient rule of thumb or litmus test to determine the justifiability of actions or programs. In concrete cases, participants must be able to enter into a detailed examination of what is proposed and what might be the expected consequences, both intended and unintended, and so provide an evaluation of the action or program. Robust public discourse is required, not the technological application of some preformed instrument of decision-making.

It should be evident from my argument so far that I am not upholding a conception of common goods as a solution or panacea. It does not provide us with a content from which we can deduce or otherwise derive solutions to our pressing problems. It is much more useful as a tool of analysis, and its role is programmatic. "The common good" in its most generalized sense I introduced as heuristic in chapter 1, naming something we are in the process of pursuing and discovering on the way. But the fact that it is still only vaguely known, essentially unknown, does not entail that we have nothing to go on. We have two criteria that can help us identify failings and limitations in our efforts to achieve common goods. These two criteria have philosophical formulations: no persons or groups excluded systematically from a share in the goods we pursue together, and no genuine dimension of human good excluded systematically from the range of goods we pursue together. In the parlance of CST, these criteria also appear as the values of solidarity and subsidiarity.

My argument through these chapters is largely provoked by an upsurge of interest in the common good in a wide literature in several disciplines and areas of concern, including the criticism of neoliberalism. I share many of the concerns that have motivated the literature. As evidenced in the list of examples to which I apply Mill's notion of experiments in living with his recommendation that we learn from experience, I draw attention to the harms caused by deregulation policies. But I do not share the blanket condemnation of liberal economic policy. In fact, as understood along the lines of Vallier's qualifications, noted earlier, neoliberal economics can be consistent with the Catholic principles of solidarity and subsidiarity. The achievement of market economies in delivering millions of people from poverty is not to be denied, and this capacity for betterment must be welcomed and facilitated. Solidarity with those now excluded requires this. Encouragement of free market activity is not to be read as giving license to multinational corporations or big tech, but, consistent with the principle of subsidiarity, it enables people to exercise their initiative and take their opportunities to generate wealth.

What emerges from the discussion of recent economic experiments in living is that the political horizon sustaining regulatory frameworks has been too weak to counter the lobbying activity of vested interests. Democratic structures of lawmaking have been hijacked to facilitate risk-taking underwritten by public money, and value-taking instead of fostering innovation. This has conferred a tone of legality—tragically, in the case of the World Bank—on policies that have worsened rather than improved the situation of poor countries. One evident lesson for Christians who are critical of the detrimental impact of what they label as neoliberal policy is that they need to engage in political education and consciousness-raising campaigns to ensure that there is a significant countervailing power of numbers. The breakdown of strong juridical frameworks in the cause of deregulation has been achieved by democratic means, conforming to procedures. Apart from procedural correctness there is also deliberation, the examination of reasons for and against proposals. Relying on procedure has not protected our societies from the destructive impact of deregulation. This suggests the need for what deliberative democracy advocates: widely dispersed opportunities for discussion of issues. For that, a constituency is required that possesses the literacy and facility to consider proposals in terms of goods and values. To ensure the protection of a strong juridical framework for our economic freedoms, as John Paul II demanded, our societies need to implement

Mill's proposal of reflection on experience and that any conclusions be submitted to open debate. In fact, we can rely on Mill's writings to demand of liberals that they be more faithful to liberal principles.

NOTES

1. Patrick J. Deneen, *Why Liberalism Failed* (New Haven, CT: Yale University Press, 2018), 146; Adrian Vermeule, "All Human Conflict Is Ultimately Theological," *Church Life Journal* (July 2019), https://churchlifejournal.nd.edu/articles/all-human-conflict-is-ultimately-theological/.
2. John Stuart Mill, *Utilitarianism, On Liberty and Considerations on Representative Government*, ed. H. B. Acton (London: Dent, 1972), 233.
3. Mill, 234. Mill's assumption that the Athenian citizen and the Victorian neighbor were male is explained by the historical context.
4. Robert Kane, *Ethics and the Quest for Wisdom* (Cambridge: Cambridge University Press, 2010).
5. Mill, *Utilitarianism, On Liberty*, 79.
6. Elizabeth Anderson, "John Stuart Mill and Experiments in Living," *Ethics* 102 (1991).
7. Mill, *Utilitarianism, On Liberty*, 131.
8. Justin Sands, "Introducing Cardinal Cardijn's See-Judge-Act as an Interdisciplinary Method to Move Theory into Practice," *Religions* 9 (2018): 129.
9. Pope Francis, *Laudato Si'*, "On Care for Our Common Home," §101, 2015, https://www.vatican.va/content/francesco/en/encyclicals/documents/papa-francesco_20150524_enciclica-laudato-si.html.
10. Pope Francis, §54.
11. John O'Neill, *Markets, Deliberation and Environment* (Abingdon, UK: Routledge, 2007), 185.
12. Pope Francis, *Laudato Si'*, §189.
13. Pope John Paul II, *Centesimus annus*, "On the Hundredth Anniversary of Rerum novarum," §39, 1991, https://www.vatican.va/content/john-paul-ii/en/encyclicals/documents/hf_jp-ii_enc_01051991_centesimus-annus.html.
14. Pope John Paul II, §42.
15. Austen Ivereigh, *Wounded Shepherd: Pope Francis and His Struggle to Convert the Catholic Church* (New York: Henry Holt, 2019), 237.
16. David Harvey, *A Brief History of Neoliberalism* (Oxford: Oxford University Press, 2005), 2.
17. Deirdre Nansen McCloskey, *Why Liberalism Works: How True Liberal Values Produce a Freer, More Equal, Prosperous World for All* (New Haven, CT: Yale University Press, 2019), 245.
18. Harvey, *A Brief History of Neoliberalism*, 2.
19. Harvey, 3.
20. Harvey, 2.
21. Deneen, *Why Liberalism Failed*.
22. Adrian Vermeule, "Integration from Within," review of *Why Liberalism Failed*, by Patrick J. Deneen, *American Affairs* 2, no. 1 (Spring 2018), https://americanaffairsjournal.org/2018/02/integration-from-within/.

23. Matthew T. Eggemeier and Peter Joseph Fritz, *Send Lazarus: Catholicism and the Crises of Neoliberalism* (New York: Fordham University Press, 2020).
24. Philippe Aghion, Céline Antonin, and Simon Bunel, *The Power of Creative Destruction: Economic Upheaval and the Wealth of Nations*, trans. Jodie Cohen-Tanugi (Cambridge, MA: Belknap Press, 2021), 81.
25. Kevin Vallier, "Neoliberalism," *The Stanford Encyclopedia of Philosophy*, Summer 2021 ed., ed. Edward N. Zalta, https://plato.stanford.edu/archives/sum2021/entries/neoliberalism/.
26. Vallier.
27. Vallier.
28. Vallier.
29. Vallier.
30. Vallier.
31. Edward Hadas, *Counsels of Imperfection: Thinking through Catholic Social Teaching* (Washington, DC: Catholic University of America Press, 2021), 85–88.
32. Adam Smith, *An Inquiry into the Nature and Causes of the Wealth of Nations*, ed. R. H. Campbell and A. S. Skinner, 2 vols. (Indianapolis: Liberty Fund, 1981), 145, 267.
33. Jonathan Wolff, *Ethics and Public Policy: A Philosophical Inquiry* (London: Routledge, 2011), 174.
34. Nicolette Jones, *The Plimsoll Sensation* (London: Little, Brown, 2006).
35. William Kingston, *How Capitalism Destroyed Itself: Technology Displaced by Financial Innovation* (Cheltenham, UK: Edward Elgar, 2017).
36. Kingston, 103.
37. Kingston, 111–14.
38. R. J. Craig and J. H. Amernic, "Enron Discourse: The Rhetoric of a Resilient Capitalism," *Critical Perspectives on Accounting* 15 (2004): 842.
39. George Soros, *The New Paradigm for Financial Markets: The Credit Crisis of 2008 and What It Means* (New York: Public Affairs, 2008), 120, 147.
40. Soros, 117.
41. Cited in Charles R. Morris, *The Two Trillion Dollar Meltdown: Easy Money, High Rollers, and the Great Credit Crash* (New York: Public Affairs, 2008), 54.
42. Morris, 55.
43. Morris, 153.
44. Morris, 154.
45. Mariana Mazzucato, *The Value of Everything: Making and Taking in the Global Economy* (London: Allen Lane, 2018). Her earlier book was *The Entrepreneurial State: Debunking Public vs. Private Sector Myths* (London: Anthem Press, 2013).
46. Mazzucato, 104.
47. Mazzucato, 109, 136.
48. Mazzucato, 160.
49. Kingston, *How Capitalism Destroyed Itself*, 99.
50. Joseph Stiglitz, *Globalization and its Discontents* (London: Penguin, 2002), 13–18.
51. Congregation for the Doctrine of the Faith and Dicastery for Promoting Integral Human Development, *Considerations for an Ethical Discernment regarding Some Aspects of the Present Economic-Financial System*, §21, (2018), https://www.vatican.va/roman_curia/congregations/cfaith/documents/rc_con_cfaith_doc_20180106_oeconomicae-et-pecuniariae_en.html.

52. Mark Carney, *Value(s): Building a Better World for All* (London: William Collins, 2021).
53. Jean Tirole, *Economics for the Common Good*, trans. Stephen Rendall (Princeton, NJ: Princeton University Press, 2017).
54. Carney, 478–79.
55. Carney, 481.
56. Deirdre Nansen McCloskey, *Bettering Humanomics: A New, and Old, Approach to Economic Science* (Chicago: University of Chicago Press, 2021), 58.
57. Deirdre Nansen McCloskey, *The Bourgeois Virtues: Ethics for an Age of Commerce* (Chicago: University of Chicago Press, 2006).
58. Martin Wolf, *Why Globalization Works* (New Haven, CT: Yale University Press, 2005).
59. Deirdre Nansen McCloskey, "Why Liberalism's Critics Fail," review of *Why Liberalism Failed* by Patrick Deneen, *Modern Age* 60, no. 3 (Summer 2018).

CHAPTER 10

CULTURE AS COMMON GOOD

Jean-Jacques Rousseau once startled his enlightened contemporaries by suggesting that science and education did not lead to the development of society but to the corruption of humanity. Opposing the progressive views of the Encyclopedists, who were confident that the amassing and publication of knowledge could only lead to the betterment of society by suppressing ignorance and prejudice, Rousseau argued that the opposite was the case. The world of the intelligentsia was shocked, but it rewarded him with a prize for his essay. Rousseau drew on the same themes in later writings, affirming the goodness of humankind and the distorting and corrupting influence of society.[1] A similar shock was experienced by the intellectual establishments of the UK and the United States following the outcomes in 2016 of the Brexit referendum in the UK and the election of Donald Trump as president in the United States. These outcomes seemed to reflect fundamental divisions in their respective countries, and many commentators, including Michael Sandel, remarked on the correlation of the divisions with educational attainment.[2] But this correlation was interpreted in two different and opposed ways.

One interpretation suggested that the more educated voters had the intellectual resources to identify and dismiss hype and bluster, and to assess policy and character instead. The implication of this account is the regrettable one that in both elections, ignorance, prejudice, and fear won the day. The alternative reading discounted this version as the self-validation of the educated and saw their qualifications as giving access to an elite group in society that had long been able to manipulate the levers of influence to gain advantage for themselves. The conclusion from this interpretation was that the excluded, ignored, and discounted classes of blue collar and service workers, as well as the unemployed, had finally had enough; they had rebelled against the self-serving elite of society and demanded that their concerns be taken seriously by the establishment and government "for a change." This latter interpretation has prevailed over the intervening years.

Just as Rousseau's essay shocked his enlightened contemporaries, so, too, this realization of the divisive impact of the educational system has shocked our societies. Whichever of the two interpretations one wishes to accept, there remains a serious question to be addressed about the role played by our educational systems in the construction of the political culture. Academics engaged in education must wonder if their institutions and efforts are contributing to a division in society or helping to foster unity. Does education contribute to our common good? Does educational attainment lead to a privileged elite and so divide the successful from the unsuccessful? In the presence of so many centrifugal forces pulling society apart, should not education be a counterinfluence and not another source of division?

SANDEL ON MERITOCRACY

Michael Sandel's *Tyranny of Merit* raises the same question. I have remarked on the thinness of his conception of common goods, but the analysis of the problem generated by the adoption of meritocracy at the heart of educational and professional systems is profound. On close reading it appears that neither merit nor desert are the tyrant, but the elaboration of the notion into the social ideology that would have society and the economy structured as a meritocracy. It is meritocracy that has become toxic and tyrannical. The toxicity arises from the widespread assumption fostered by a meritocracy that those who succeed have deserved their success, and those who have not succeeded equally deserve their fate. This assumption results in a sense of entitlement and pride among the successful, and humiliation and loss of self-esteem among those who have "failed."[3] The public display of success and failure results in a loss of solidarity and any sense of interdependence within society. Sandel cites British sociologist Michael Young's book *The Rise of the Meritocracy* (1958), acknowledging that Young foresaw the consequences of implementing a policy of equality of opportunity in generating "hubris in the winners and humiliation among the losers."[4] Far from supporting such a policy, Young points to its dangers as a source of social division. The gap between rich and poor, he suggests, would be deepened because the wealthy would be convinced of their entitlement to their wealth while the poor could have no consolation in the thought that they had lacked opportunity. Instead, they would be confronted with the realization that they were inferior and hence had failed. Young, Sandel records, forecast a political backlash, predicting that "the less-educated classes would rise up in a populist revolt against the meritocratic elites." Sandel comments further: "In 2016, as Britain voted for Brexit and America for Trump, that revolt arrived."[5] Michael Young in his eighties took to print again in 2001 to bemoan the British Labour Party's espousal of meritocracy under Tony Blair, who promised "to create real upward mobility, a society... open and genuinely based on merit and the equal worth of all." Young's rejoinder in the *Guardian* newspaper pointed to the consequence that a society based on merit would expose many to the judgment that they had no merit, and that they deserved what they got—that is, failure.[6]

Such references in Sandel's book point to the relevance of its thesis to British society and politics, but the main thrust of the argument is directed against the meritocratic culture in the United States, where going to college plays such a major role in determining earnings and social standing. The hope that education would facilitate social mobility and lead to greater equality by ensuring that workers could compete and succeed in a global economy has been frustrated. Those who have been well-resourced have been well-placed to benefit from greater opportunity, but that has not resulted in greater equality. Sandel's chapter "Success Ethics" documents how the language of "rising" as exemplified in social mobility has dominated in the rhetoric of progressive parties, reinforcing the logic of the marketplace that rewards winners and punishes losers.

Scholastic Aptitude Tests (SATs) were introduced to ensure equality of opportunity and replace the arbitrary influence of extraneous factors in the allocation of university places. The idea was that parents' class position, wealth, or connections should not privilege their children's chances of accessing education. Only the candidates' demonstrated ability should count in the distribution. However, as Sandel argues, drawing on many studies, those families with wealth and other advantages can ensure that their children are well-resourced to take the test, so that the fairness of the selection process is compromised. "SAT scores track wealth," he argues.[7] Reform of the testing system is not the issue, but the destructive impact of a meritocratic culture. Inequality is further entrenched, with the added prejudice that the successful claim their success due to their own efforts and talents while the unsuccessful are left to face the reality of their failure without any consolation that they are not personally to blame.[8]

Because educational achievement and credentials are so determinative of earning capacity, the measures of success and failure are not simply the certificates attained but the income and wealth associated with success in a competitive market economy. The hubris and sense of entitlement that the culture of meritocracy lends to wealth exacerbate the growing inequality in our societies. As Sandel remarks, "The more we think of ourselves as self-made and self-sufficient, the harder it is to learn gratitude and humility. And without these sentiments, it is hard to care for the common good."[9] Solidarity and the bonds of community are also dissolved by such attitudes, so the possibility of shared responsibility for the quality of social life and the deliberation about communal purposes is diminished—hence Sandel's appeal that we face the failures of meritocracy and technocracy and strive to reimagine a politics of the common good.[10]

That the allocation of jobs and university places should be based on merit, that equality of opportunity should prevail across society, that access to education is crucial for fostering equality, that educational qualifications are the capital of the poor and their key to advancement—these are convictions shared by many socially concerned citizens who put themselves at the service of others. Sandel's book challenges them to reflect on some of the unintended consequences of this social philosophy. Surprisingly, a concentration on fostering social mobility via education coupled with a commitment to meritocracy can have the consequence of worsening the situation of those worst-off in society, who are made to feel they are to blame for their lack of success and deprivation of all the social and economic rewards of success. And those who should be motivated to help are inoculated against their responsibilities to share their good fortune by the self-satisfied conviction that they are entitled to their advantages as justly earned.

EDUCATION AS A GOOD: PRIVATE, PUBLIC, CLUB

To consider these questions, it is helpful to distinguish the ways in which education can be a private good, a public good, a club good, and a common good. These terms were introduced in chapter 4, but here they are applied to the reflection on education. The key policy innovation in third-level education in the UK in the twenty-first century is the marketization of education. Other inherited communal assets are also being marketized: what formerly were deemed public goods in the UK are now being treated as private goods in the cases of public transport, water supply, and, to some extent, medical care, social welfare, and even the prison service.[11] Just as the UK government has privatized these, so it is attempting to privatize third-level education. The key question, then, is whether it is better for the common good that education be regarded primarily as a private good or primarily as a public good.

"Public good" is a technical term in economics and is not identical with common good. Market failure is the usual context for the introduction of the notion of public goods. Market failure refers to those goods or services that cannot be supplied via the market because no entrepreneur can undertake the cost of supplying the good when there is no assurance that beneficiaries will pay. Who will provide street lighting by way of the market when citizens can enjoy the benefit of the lighting once it is in place without having to pay? The market will not deliver this good, so we rely on public authority to provide it. It recovers payment for this and other services (defense, justice, etc.) via taxation, and not by means of quid pro quo payments in exchange for each usage. Public goods are nonexcludable (once they are in place it is not possible to exclude some categories of people—everybody sees the traffic lights, even those driving untaxed cars) and nonrivalrous (adding more people to the enjoyment does not diminish the benefits of those already included). By contrast, private goods are both excludable and rivalrous. In between there is a spectrum including the categories of commons and club goods.

In several ways, of course, education is a private good. The certificate obtained at the end of the course is definitely private, with the graduate's name printed on it; the school or college place is private, especially where there is scarcity or quotas. These are excludable and rivalrous goods. This is the aspect which attracts the attention of state administrators: they believe that efficiency can be achieved by encouraging the market in the goods—namely, places on courses and qualifications at the end. And a market requires competition, so the state has encouraged private enterprises to enter the market in the expectation that the newcomers, by offering students attractive alternatives, will oblige the existing universities to compete on quality and price.[12]

As well as being a private good, in other respects education is also a club good: the English expression of the "old school tie" acknowledges this. Once graduated from a school, one can rely on the support and patronage of fellow alumni. A club good is excludable but nonrivalrous: others not from the same school can be excluded from the preferential treatment, but the inclusion of others from the same school is nonrivalrous and hence tolerable, since no individual is disadvantaged. The question for educators raised earlier, from the recent experience of voting patterns, is the extent to which we are creating club goods. Are we forming and reinforcing the elite as a distinctive section of society?

Is education a public good? When levels of literacy, numeracy, and oracy (the ability to express oneself eloquently in speech) in a society are high, when the electorate in a democracy is capable of discerning issues of policy and exercising critical judgment about candidates and their programs, when print and broadcast media carry a quality of debate about relevant issues that goes beyond sloganeering and name-calling, then we see the benefit of education as a public good. Once it is in place, all people benefit, and no one is disadvantaged by the addition of further participants to the enjoyment of this quality of public life, although its long-term survival depends on the new additions bringing a comparable capacity and willingness to engage in public life on the terms on which they are admitted.

Another way in which education can and ought to be a public good is related to the achievements of the rule of law. The rule of law itself is also a public good in being nonexcludable and nonrivalrous: once in place, it is there for everyone, and no one can be disadvantaged just because others are treated according to the law. A relatively high level of education in a populace is a fundamental precondition for the rule of law. Public officials in their various roles and capacities will not do justice unless they are sufficiently skilled and competent, and sensitive to the obligations arising from the human rights of the people with whom they must deal. Without the capacity to imagine themselves in the position of the other, to think their way into the mindset of peoples from other cultures and traditions, citizens in our world will be unable to deal with the challenges posed by the presence of a great variety of cultures and religions. In this sense education is a public good.[13]

Can this dimension of education be achieved by privatized educational systems? Our societies are being subjected to a vast social experiment, "an experiment in living" in Mill's sense, in which students, and indeed our universities, are being conditioned into the attitudes of the marketplace. It is not the skills of citizenship, of neighborliness, of dialogue partners that are valued above all by students and their parents and patrons, but the marketable, transferable skills that make one a valued commodity in the labor market. The values of service, the sense of obligation to benefit those less well off, the duty to put one's privileged assets to use for the good of others are undermined by the officially reinforced attitude that the education has been paid for. It is property, a possession to be used or exercised at the whim of the owner. Students will exaggeratedly claim to have earned their degree through their own hard work, not attending to the many social contributions to their advancement for which no payment has been made. Here, too, an economic term can highlight the dimensions that are not taken into account. In the maintenance of any education system there are "externalities," costs borne by some of the stakeholders that are not compensated in the market. It is irrelevant to the economic consideration that those costs are willingly borne by educators, including many who are religiously motivated. The point is that the concentration on the marketing of education as a private good prioritizes and reinforces the economic attitude to understanding education, and in that mindset certain elements such as externalities do not appear and hence are likely to be overlooked and forgotten. A culture of education provision is being fostered that will be unable to sustain our inherited educational institutions that have relied on very different values.

EDUCATION AS COMMON GOOD

Having reviewed the ways in which education can be a private, club, and public good, we must inquire in what ways it can be a common good. Applying a distinction introduced in chapter 8 and invoked in earlier chapters, we can consider two cases: practical and ontological. The *practical* sense is that wherever people cooperate for some good, they have a good in common, a common good. That good in common might be a private good (college places for our children), a club good (networks for alumni), a collective good (any school's ambition for its students), or a public good (high levels of educational attainment conditioning political discourse and widespread respect for the rule of law). Perhaps the less obvious but more important way in which education is a common good is the *ontological* sense of good. Education as a perfection or fulfillment of individuals and communities enables persons to *be* more and to realize to a greater extent their human potential. What fulfills people is for their good, enabling them to flourish. Education is not narrowly limited to academic achievement, of course; it also includes personal formation and empowerment for relationship of all kinds, including the political friendship of citizenship. Accordingly, since education enriches human flourishing in the fullest sense, it deserves to be part of the *practical* common good, that which we deliberately name as the point of our cooperation. Aristotle would agree with this because of his acknowledgment of political friendship as the bonding relationship between citizens, which should, in turn, be the practical concern of legislators concerned about the characters and qualities of citizens.[14]

If people are to be capable of acting as responsible citizens in a very complex world, they must learn to live alongside differences of many kinds. They must learn to understand themselves and their traditions as situated in a plural and interdependent world. This means they must be capable of operating at two levels: they must be comfortable in their own tradition and be at home with their distinctive identity; on the other hand, they must be capable of meeting others from differing backgrounds in the public forum on a basis of understanding, respect, and tolerance. There is a tendency to regard the public forum only as a marketplace or bargaining table where different interest groups meet to compete for power. Of course, the competitive nature of interest-group politics cannot be denied and must be allowed its place. But this form of politics alone will not serve the common good. For a different style of politics, another form of encounter must be possible in which, despite their differences, people can engage with one another as fellow citizens, or simply as fellow humans. Debate and dialogue are contrasted with bargaining and deal-making. Dialogue and debate presuppose a commitment to fostering an alternative space for political engagement to the competition for power in which the stronger is sure to win. The stronger can be the more passionate; more numerous; more manipulative; more resourced, financially and otherwise; and better organized and mobilized.

Education is a public good when relatively high levels of literacy and numeracy and competence for engagement in political discourse are widespread in society, supporting the vibrant public debate of deliberative democracy while sustaining tolerance and respect.[15] However, increasing divisiveness in the political cultures of the UK and the United States suggests that education may be functioning not as a public good and therefore a real asset to common life, but as a club good, hardening division and reinforcing the advantages of the elite. Accordingly, the question about the potential divisiveness of educational attainment in our political communities is provoked. Divisiveness within the educational institutions themselves, with the phenomena of no-platforming and the attempted silencing of some opinions, underlines the urgency of the question. That our education systems may be failing to secure public spaces for genuine political debate, and also failing to inculcate the rhetorical skills and practices of reasoned discourse, suggests the need to make the public good of education the common good of our collaborative efforts. Without the public goods of some shared meaning and shared values, our political culture will not be able to sustain trust, liberty, and the benefits they make possible.

REINFORCING THE GOOD OR CONTROLLING THE BAD?

As noted in chapter 6, conflict is endemic and inevitable, and will always provide the context for a political response. In that discussion, the focus was on the fact that good people wishing to achieve good things will sometimes be in conflict with one another because their goals are incompatible. But perhaps this conflict is more radical than I have allowed.

Broadcast and print media daily bring us stories of domination, exploitation, and abuse. At the same time, we find stories of exceptional heroism, dedication, and commitment to the well-being of others. One set of stories depresses us and leads to a sense of despair; the other set encourages and inspires us and leads to a sense of hope for humanity. Generous commitment to the good of others is found alongside the willingness to deceive and take advantage of the gullible and the vulnerable. Goodness and badness, virtue and malice, cooperation and exploitation all coexist in our societies and have done so throughout history. Rutger Bregman, in *Humankind: A Hopeful History*, strives to highlight the goodness of humanity, countering literature that emphasizes the opposite—the undeniable inhumanity expressed in the history of vice, violence, war, domination, and exploitation.[16] He makes the case that humans, for the most part, are decent; supposed evidence to the contrary is challenged in detail. He notes the polarization in the philosophical literature—for instance, between Thomas Hobbes and Jean-Jacques Rousseau: Hobbes sees political order and the civilization it engenders saving humans from a life in the state of nature that is "solitary, poor, nasty, brutish and short," and Rousseau, by contrast, sees society as the source of corruption of the naturally good human. The debates continue, taking various forms in different contexts, as in the debates of nature versus nurture in psychology or education. Bregman will not be the last to reactivate the question of human goodness, innate or acquired. With our theological resources of doctrines of sin and grace, we may be tempted to translate these debates into theological disputes and mirror the polarization into extremes: human nature wounded by original sin versus human nature completely corrupted by sin; justification that elevates the human versus justification as juridical imputation that leaves human nature in its depravity.[17]

It is also helpful to consider the problems we humans create for ourselves by being good, and by being good at what we do. For instance, in the context of Pope Francis's *Laudato Si'*, on care for the planet as our common home, much use is made of what is called the tragedy of the commons, as discussed in chapter 4.[18] A commons shared by many (grazing land, water supply, the seas and their stocks of fish) is destroyed because each commoner acting independently calculates rationally how best to use the commons for their own advantage. Even in the context of a regulation to conserve the commons, each one reasons, "If I cut back my use and nobody else does, then there is no point in my doing so; I would suffer a loss that benefits no one. But if everybody else cuts back on their use, then my overgrazing or overfishing will cause only marginal harm and no one participant will suffer a loss." From the perspective of individual rationality, it makes no sense to accept constraints: whatever the others do, the individual does best by defecting.

Hence the use of "tragedy" in the dramatic sense: there is a flaw in heroes that leads to their self-destruction. In the tragedy of the commons, the flaw is in the very precious human strength of rationality understood in terms of achieving benefits to the actor. It is not the only inherent flaw in our constitution: Shakespeare's *The Merchant of Venice* reminds us that the hunger for justice can be destructive unless modified by mercy; his other Venetian play, *Othello*, exhibits the dangers of too much love if not tempered by wisdom. Such dramas help us identify the risks posed by our strengths, our virtues, and learn to minimize them.

Elinor Ostrom and other authors have shown how the care of the commons can be managed in small-scale, traditional societies so that the threat of tragedy, at least from the source of excessive individual rationality, cannot arise.[19] All commentators acknowledge that distinctive issues arise as the human population increases, and different societies must live as neighbors in an ever more crowded space. Where the other appears as a stranger, or as a member of a different tribe or linguistic group, one can no longer rely on the shared norms of the home group or the standard sanctions of shaming to ground one's attitude of trust. The question, then, becomes how trust can be fostered and sustained in large-scale groups. There are great advantages to be had from large-scale group cooperation, as the affluence of our developed societies demonstrates. Even in the face of major threats such as the COVID-19 pandemic that exposed the vulnerability of our complexity, we must rely on large-scale cooperation in treating victims, managing the spread of the disease, and seeking remedies in vaccines or treatments. The risk of free riding increases with the growth of complexity: the temptation to enjoy the benefits of cooperation without sharing the costs through taxation increases. Hobbes's proposed solution of the sovereign who enforces the rules is our societies' typical resort, but with the evident result that it does not work. Compliance with the law and avoidance of prosecution were not enough to prevent the 2007 credit crisis in our complex financial system that had disastrous consequences for the real economy. Compliance with the law is not sufficient to ensure that corporations who make their profits in the national economy contribute their fair share via taxation to the costs of maintaining social order. External policing is not a reliable means of guaranteeing the levels of trust required in large-scale cooperation, as found in our developed Western societies.

Rose on the Importance of Culture

David C. Rose locates the solution to the dilemma in what he calls culture.[20] By "culture" he means the set of tastes and beliefs that are formed in a generation of a society's children before they have developed the rational capacities of discrimination and choice to determine for themselves what they want. Rose places a lot of weight on the training that young children receive from their parents, a training that inculcates tastes and forms the habits of willing and thinking such that character is shaped. Young people who are cultured in this sense are guided by a sense of duty that morally constrains even what they might consider as options for action. Free riding on the cooperation of others can be minimized if people hold the view that it is wrong opportunistically to take advantage of others' goodwill at the expense of the common good. "What's in it for me?" or "What do I stand to lose?" are not, then, the spontaneous reactions of those invited to make an effort in a common project. A prerational formation of trust enables widespread forms of cooperation and reduces transaction costs. Such trust can counter the dynamics of individual rationality that point agents to their golden opportunities, occasions when they can exploit the benefits of cooperation without getting caught and paying a penalty. In large-scale societies there is not the spontaneous, sympathetic identification with the other, who might be a victim of harm, since the anonymous mass that bears the costs of free riding is not any nameable person.

Almost as if he were responding to Bregman's optimistic account in *Humankind*, Rose insists that it is not a matter of "either-or," that humans have both good and bad impulses. Forming a civilized society is not about making people willing to act on their good impulses, he writes. "Civilization, instead, depends on making people unwilling to act on their bad impulses. The closer a society can get to having people not act on bad impulses—that is, to having a very strong ethic of duty-based moral restraint—the more civilized the society will be, the higher will be its level of social trust, and the more it will support mass flourishing."[21] Rose has little confidence in the power of moral advocacy (preaching at people and trying to persuade them to be good), and argues instead for the cultural transmission of values and duty in early childhood. This stance echoes what Aristotle has to say in his ethics when he remarks that anyone desiring to make progress in the study of ethics must be well-trained in their habits. Such a person will be able to grasp first principles, recognizing them as resonating with what is already absorbed as taste.[22] Rose reflects further on the relationship between generations whereby one generation is in a position "to determine the prevailing moral beliefs" of the subsequent generation.[23] It follows that the large-scale cooperation and its benefits in any society at a particular time are reaping the fruits of investment made by earlier generations in child-rearing and the transmission of culture. This is often taken for granted and in danger of neglect, not least because the costs of investment in the next generation borne by parents are not going to deliver benefits directly to their own children as adults. Society at large will be the beneficiary.

Society in this respect is a commons. In the case of this commons, the risk of tragedy is very real. The failure of parents to make the investment in the inculcation of moral restraints in their children results in a deterioration and disintegration of the institutions of a high-trust society—but only in the course of time, once the generation of children who have not acquired the duty-based moral constraint are themselves adults. In the intervening years, enough of the formed culture from earlier generations will survive to carry the institutions. Repairing the damage arising from a loss of culture will not be done quickly: it, too, will be a matter of generations, but where will the motivation for the relevant investment be found when the characters who can recognize the scale of the damage lack the cultural resources to act?

These reflections give plausibility to the Benedict Option as a movement motivated to support parents who face the challenge of raising children with characters formed with duty-based moral constraint. Given the countercultural nature of this challenge, the supportive point of the movement is evident. Rose has a different focus, considering the society-wide and civilization-wide need. He emphasizes the fundamental role of culture for the maintenance of a high-trust society, which in turn is fundamental to well-functioning political and economic systems. High levels of trust can emerge naturally in small-scale communities in which people know each other and anyone's reputation for trustworthiness conditions whatever form of cooperation they can engage in. But this level of trust is not achievable in large-scale societies in which people are strangers to one another. A prerational formation of trust enables widespread forms of cooperation and reduces transaction costs. Such trust can counter the dynamics of individual rationality that point agents to their golden opportunities, occasions when they can exploit the benefits of cooperation without getting caught and having to pay a penalty.

In large-scale societies there is not the spontaneous sympathetic identification with the other, who might be a victim of harm, since the anonymous mass that bears the costs of free riding is not any nameable person. Rose argues for free market democracies as producing mass flourishing, including the benefits of a liberal democratic order and the prosperity that arises from the production and wide distribution of goods and services. "Many of the institutions required for a free-market democracy," he writes, "require a high-trust society."[24] Rose underlines his case by quoting Jon Elster on the importance of institutions for sustaining society: "Institutions keep society from falling apart, provided there is something to keep institutions from falling apart."[25] For Rose that "something" is culture, "a sufficiently strong and widespread ethic of duty-based moral restraint."²⁶ The absence of such an ethic and its replacement by a culturally institutionalized consequentialism centered on individual market rationality, and by a culturally institutionalized emphasis on the individual's rights and freedoms, undermines the common good. The common good is at stake when agents are inclined to do what they know to be wrong but justify their choice because it promises to deliver the best outcome. People convincing themselves that "being moral requires behaving in untrustworthy ways as a means to the end of undertaking laudable actions" erodes willingness to trust each other and undermines the common good.²⁷ It cannot be emphasized strongly enough: in this instance the common good *is* the shared trust sustaining social institutions and the flourishing they make possible. But it also is used to refer to "mass flourishing," a term borrowed from the Nobel Prize–winning economist Edmund Phelps, which in the forms of general prosperity and freedom supports the "good life."²⁸ Rose does not consider this meaning of common good explicitly, though his oblique reference to Aristotle's notion of the good life as the point of politics supports this reading. Nevertheless, Rose's focus is on the common good of culture as the means to, and condition for, a high-trust society, and so instrumental for the purpose of mass flourishing.

Rose's target is a mindset that Elizabeth Anscombe labels "consequentialism"—namely, the willingness to do what is wrong and known to be wrong by claiming it to be the correct moral option in the circumstances.²⁹ This term has undergone a change in meaning: for John Finnis it is the most general category of ethical positions that determine the goodness of actions in terms of consequences only to the exclusion of all other factors, whereby utilitarianism is one example of a consequentialist approach in relying on the notion of utility to measure those consequences.³⁰ In Anscombe's usage, the term applies to the acceptance of abhorrent or evil means such as murder because of beneficial consequences anticipated or achieved. Rose's argument links the conditions for the flourishing of a modern society to the inculcation of attitudes in children that make them resistant to the tempting idea that it is all right to do wrong if one thinks that there will be big beneficial consequences if one does so. The tempting idea to be resisted is that the ends justify *any* means. On such an ethic (if it can be called that), nobody could ever be trusted to keep their promises, if they might gain from breaking them.

Formation of Citizens

Luke Bretherton, in a study of the regeneration of democracy, considers the character of citizens. Going beyond the contributions of parents and family,

Bretherton identifies faith communities as among the vibrant sources of virtue as required by democratic politics. As he puts it, "Good politics needs good people, and the formation of good people needs a good politics."[31] He relies on the language of virtue to characterize goodness and points to the formation of good character through participation in the practices of institutions and organizations. Drawing on his study of broad-based community organizing with the organization London Citizens, he can point to the faith-based communities that are its members. Consistent with Saul Alinsky's practice in Chicago, the congregations of churches, synagogues, and mosques, among others, have proved to be the most accessible and readily mobilized groups for community organizing. "Community" in this case denotes the "coming together by mutual agreement of distinct institutions for a common purpose without loss of each of their specific identities or beliefs and practices."[32]

Does that "common purpose" refer to a common good? Bretherton explains in a footnote that he prefers to use the term "common life" rather than common good. He writes, "Although some notion of a 'common good' may still operate as a regulative ideal, an all-encompassing 'common good' can only ever be a deferred horizon of possibility rather than a plausible political reality under conditions of a fallen and finite political life."[33] He is willing to speak of common goods, or goods in common, in the plural, and one example of such is the commitment to democratic politics as a shared good.[34] "Deferred horizon of possibility" is an interesting way of formulating the idea of heuristic. "Deferred" points to what is in the future but out of reach; "horizon" suggests its comprehensive nature, including all relevant elements that can come within the range of human attention; and "possibility" underlines that we are dealing here with something that can be realized, not a utopian chimera. He echoes the distinction made throughout this book drawing on Aristotle's remark that there are as many goods in common as there are forms and instances of cooperation. The unique, singular, common good is elusive, all the more so as modern political forms of state have replaced the Greek city-state, and the modern forms can no longer ambition the high moral purpose of achieving the good life simply through the moral formation of its citizens. However, as Bretherton's discussion underlines, even modern political forms are dependent on the quality of character of their citizens, but it is not the business of the modern liberal state to undertake such formation directly. Were it to do so, it would compromise its commitment to liberty, its foundational value. Civil society and its constituent institutions, such as families, churches, charitable organizations, sporting and cultural clubs and societies, and schools and universities, are the formative and nurturing context for the character building of good persons. As an agency with an indispensable role in promoting the common good, the state should facilitate the conditions in which civil society's institutions can function as described, and above all refrain from obstructing them in their doing so. Here is an important reason why Catholics can and should support a liberal state that functions to support civil society's institutions.

As Bretherton's title indicates, democratic politics is not simply a good to be valued but a vulnerable asset to be protected and secured. The multiple threats to democratic politics are evident, with the increasing influence of technocrats and professional communicators and administrators depriving citizens of direct access to public deliberation. Powerful interests such as those of business and the financial markets set the agenda for politics, while complex issues in health care, social welfare, education, and culture leave the nonprofessional at a loss as to the best way to proceed. Immigration, international relations, and defense policy all pose major issues for contemporary politics in such a way that the individual voter can feel daunted and incompetent to form a judgment. Resurrecting democracy attempts a revival of politics by recovering the experience of direct action, participation in campaigns for worthwhile and achievable goals, that will enable citizens and their organizations to realize the extent of their power and competence. This is an adaptation of MacIntyre's proposal to build community, but in this case to engage in politics instead of opting out—the Pope Benedict Option rather than Dreher's Benedict Option.

Reflecting on his experience of involvement as an organizer with London Citizens in East London, Bretherton stresses the priority of a practical over a theoretical approach to the possibility of democratic politics. He is not formulating a theory or ideology that might compete with other ideologies for the power and opportunity to implement their vision. Instead, he points to the experience that shows that people of different religious faiths or political worldviews can be partners in campaigns to achieve concrete objectives that all value. The response to the financial crisis in 2008 provides a good example. London Citizens was a group of more than 150 institutions representing approximately fifty thousand people in London. Bretherton notes, "The institutions were made up of schools, synagogues, churches, mosques, trade unions, university departments, and other civil society institutions spread throughout London."[35] Considering the hardship experienced by many as they faced high interest rates on credit card debt, rising rents, and stagnant wages, London Citizens committed itself to concrete proposals, the principal one of which was the living wage. Coming from their different institutions, all were able to endorse the idea that a living wage was the best means of ensuring that the working poor would not be forced into debt to make ends meet. The campaign for the living wage (as distinct from a legislated minimum wage) continues.

One of the most valuable contributions of Bretherton's book, all the more important because it draws on the experience of organizing, is to challenge polarizations of the secular and the religious in models of democracy that exclude religion from public life. Bretherton argues for a revised meaning of "secular," according to which religious groups have an essential place in politics: "One of the aims of this book is to provoke greater critical reflection on the question of what kinds of secularity are amenable and conducive to democratic politics."[36] Experiences of organizing show that a wide range of models of secular settlement is possible. For instance, over 60 percent of the member institutions of London Citizens in 2008–12 were Christian, and over half of those were Catholic. Over half the constituent institutions in this civil society organization were congregations of faith communities. This reality on the ground shows that religion, far from being a private affair, is present in the public space, and it helps to constitute that space by the form of its presence. Difference and diversity remain, but conversation on issues of common concern build relationships of solidarity. The construction of the shared public space as a secular space is as much a product of faith convictions and religious practices as it is of the inherited anticlerical or atheist assumptions of postenlightenment modernity.[37] This vision resonates with the elaboration of the secular attempted in chapter 3 in considering political Augustinianism. What Bretherton describes is a concrete realization of the vision of *Gaudium et spes*, where people with different visions of human fulfillment can nevertheless cooperate to secure the means and conditions that will facilitate individuals and groups in pursuing a flourishing life. He maintains that "the politics of a common life occurs when no single tradition of belief and practice sets the terms and conditions of such shared speech and action, and the generation of a faithful and pluralistic pattern of secularity is a negotiated, multilateral endeavor."[38] His experience and reflections provide examples of a secular space that in Trainor's terms is open, facing toward and not denying the transcendent, but also not claiming its authority.

Bretherton observes that democratic politics requires moral convictions, and that such convictions require moral traditions with practices sustaining visions of common life based on respect for the dignity of the other. But convictions are not in the gift of democratic politics, they are presupposed by it. Echoing Rose on culture, Bretherton reminds readers how politics depends on the work of moral formation done by parents, establishing tastes and convictions in children. Democratic politics is not the forum for child-rearing, so it "must find ways of creating space for the kinds of moral formation that are a condition of its own possibility."³⁹ Rose's discussion views culture as a necessary means for the sustaining of institutions in a well-functioning society. The end is the flourishing of that society, its prosperity, the good life. However, as noted in chapters 3 and 4, from a theological perspective, the good functioning of human societies is not the ultimate good, but is subsidiary to the transcendent interests of human beings. At the same time, culture may also be viewed as an end, and so a common good of action, when we recognize the validity of Rose's argument and take steps to reinforce the dynamisms that generate and sustain culture. For instance, support for parents, including a heightening of awareness of their importance for society, might be among the means adopted for the promotion of the goal of reinforcement of the duty-based ethic of restraint.

Böckenförde Challenges Liberalism

Rose's concern for culture is anticipated in a different realm of discourse by Ernst-Wolfgang Böckenförde, a former judge of Germany's Constitutional Court. He formulates a paradox that subsequently bears his name: "The liberal secular state lives on premises that it cannot itself guarantee. On the one hand, it can subsist only if the freedom it consents to its citizens is regulated from within, inside the moral substance of individuals and of a homogeneous society. On the other hand, it is not able to guarantee these forces of inner regulation by itself without renouncing its liberalism."⁴⁰ In other words, a liberal state cannot survive unless it is sustained by a political culture in which some elements are constantly at work, strengthening and renewing the civic virtues of citizens and fostering their shared meanings and values. How citizens shape their common life constructs a social capital of shared understandings and expectations, as well as the virtuous habits of citizens. These provide the life breath of a liberal democratic system. If the democratic state attempted to impose convictions or enforce virtues, it would contradict its own core values. The political community might continue to enjoy the cultural capital inherited from the past without being aware that it was being exhausted, consumed without being renewed. Böckenförde warns that this poses a particular dilemma for a liberal state, because it simply assumes the reasonableness and autonomy of its citizens without addressing questions of character formation, fearing accusations of perfectionism or paternalism.

The political common good is worked out by citizens as they shape their common life. In a sense, it is constructed through the process of deliberation. Some aspects of what is constructed, such as the social capital of shared understandings and expectations, as well as the virtuous habits of citizens, are built by the activity and the process without necessarily being the deliberately pursued goals of the process. They occur as by-products. Where the goals pursued are common goods in a practical sense, the characters and virtues of citizens are common goods in an ontological sense.

Many responded to Böckenförde's arguments by pointing to the partnership between the churches and the states of Germany, insisting on the major contribution made by faith communities to sustaining the democratic culture. However, while Böckenförde, himself a Catholic, always admitted his own faith commitment, he did not present his analysis as a defense of religious values or practices. Instead, his point was that the resources that sustain democratic politics and a liberal legal and political order are generated in fora that are outside the control of the state. The organizations of civil society take many forms, from families to sports clubs to schools as well as religious bodies. This point has been clarified in subsequent literature.[41]

CONCLUSION

Our exploration of common goods has led us to a discussion of education. This is provoked by the questions of whether our educational systems have contributed to the divisions in society and whether they have reinforced the polarization that so many authors writing about common goods identify with regret. Sandel has focused the question on meritocracy as a strategy for social mobility and fostering equality, but suggests that it is counterproductive, undermining social cohesion and exacerbating inequality. The discussion has proceeded by recalling distinctions, introduced earlier, between the Aristotelian practical philosophical account of goods and standard economic categories of types of goods. We distinguish further between two Aristotelian accounts: a practical account seeing an intended object as the end of action and an ontological account identifying the fulfillment of the agent as ancillary end, though often not deliberately ambitioned. Among the economic categories are private, public, and club goods. Using the Aristotelian practical notion of the goods of cooperation being goods in common, all of the economic categories could, on occasion, be goods in common for collaborators. Hence it is possible to see how education can be at the same time a private, public, or club good in economic terms, and a common good for relevant collaborators. The qualification of possibility is important, however, since it is conceivable that these also fail to be common goods. If it is the case that education as a private and club good is part of a dynamism that undermines social cohesion, that functions to exclude, and not simply exclude but to damage further those excluded, as Young and Sandel suggest, then the first criterion can be invoked to demonstrate that the goods in question are not common goods. Furthermore, when the pursuit of private and club goods, even as objects of cooperation, undermines public goods of culture, including the presuppositions of social life and cooperation, then they cannot simply be validated as common goods.

Common to the three authors surveyed is a recognizably Aristotelian theme, although Aristotle is not explicitly cited as an authority by any of them. Rose, Bretherton, and Böckenförde, in their respective contexts, acknowledge the importance of character formation as a precondition for an adequate politics. Rose sees the first steps in child-rearing as critical, as children are helped to acquire the skills of self-restraint. This is the essential condition for culture, without which large-scale trust in society and the consequent good functioning of institutions would be impossible. Where Rose concentrates on the role to be played by parents, Bretherton acknowledges the contribution of civil society organizations, including churches and voluntary organizations, in forming the characters of citizens. These, in turn, are essential for a well-functioning democracy. Böckenförde makes a similar point, but specifically with the perspective of a liberal democracy in mind. Combining all three, we can generalize that civilization and generalized trust, participation in democracy, and the enjoyment of the benefits secured by a liberal legal and political regime are all conditional on dynamics that the liberal democratic state receives from elsewhere, and that it cannot provide for itself without compromising its values. None of the three proposes that the state or civil authorities should take it upon themselves to provide the necessary moral formation. On the contrary, both Böckenförde and Bretherton are explicit in affirming that the liberal state could not attempt to do so without violating its own principles. But all argue for the need, also on the part of the state, to respect those agents in civil society—parents, families, church communities, and other organizations—that can and do provide for the formation of citizens.

Sandel's criticism of meritocracy as encouraging attitudes that undermine solidarity for the common good is consistent with this attention to the preconditions for satisfactory social and political existence. When people are encouraged by their upbringing to consider themselves as self-made and self-sufficient, they are unable to acknowledge the extent to which they have been the beneficiaries of the efforts of others and of their society, to which they owe gratitude. Sandel makes the point that gratitude and the associated humility in recognizing one's dependency are essential sentiments for caring for common goods.[42] The possibility of shared responsibility for the quality of social life and the deliberation about communal purposes is diminished. Sandel's appeal that we face the failures of meritocracy and strive to reimagine a politics of the common good is a challenge to reconsider educational policies in terms of their fostering or frustrating solidarity, bonds of community, and our common goods.[43]

The goods in common for which we in our political communities cooperate can be characterized as both practical and ontological. Under the latter heading are those instances of individual and communal flourishing that may not actually have been the chosen objective of action. The botanical team's research project into orchids may have achieved its goal, resulting in papers and monographs published. The flourishing of the team members and their supportive institutions is also a good achieved, although perhaps not adverted to. Noting this complexity, we as citizens and members of organizations as well as churches can see the value in articulating the goods of flourishing so they can be incorporated into the range of practical objectives that are our social and political common goods. Among the common goods of our cooperating, we can draw attention to the following, which are in danger of being taken for granted:

- the childcare and character formation provided by parents and guardians
- the formation for citizenship provided by families and churches, and religious, sporting, and other organizations
- the educational provisions that ensure the basic skills of literacy, oracy, and numeracy to all children
- teachers at all levels and their qualities of dedication and expertise, ensuring the excellence of pupils' and students' experience
- the institutions in which reflection on and debate about the curricula and the methods and purposes of education are conducted

The list could become more detailed and be extended to cover many other areas of cooperation. But this short list illustrates the point of *Gaudium et spes* in addressing the set of conditions that enable individuals and communities to flourish. The list also highlights the extent to which the principal agents of collaboration for these goods in common are parents and citizens and ordinary people in their social lives, and not primarily the state or its officers acting in an official capacity. How the state facilitates these goods in common will depend on circumstances, but in general its role should be subsidiary, assisting and supporting the agents in civil society.

NOTES

1. Jean-Jacques Rousseau, "A Discourse on the Arts and Sciences," in *The Social Contract and Discourses*, trans. G. D. H. Cole (London: Dent, 1973).
2. Michael Sandel, *The Tyranny of Merit: What's Become of the Common Good?* (London: Allen Lane, 2020), 116–19.
3. Sandel, 183.
4. Sandel, 30.
5. Sandel, 119.
6. Sandel, 152.
7. Sandel, 164.
8. Sandel, 174.
9. Sandel, 14.
10. Sandel, 112.
11. Guy Standing, *Plunder of the Commons: A Manifesto for Sharing Public Wealth* (London: Pelican Books, 2019), 27.
12. Roger Brown and Helen Carasso, *Everything for Sale? The Marketisation of UK Higher Education* (London: Routledge, 2013); Andrew McGettigan, *The Great University Gamble: Money, Markets and the Future of Higher Education* (London: Pluto, 2013).
13. Martha Nussbaum, *Cultivating Humanity: A Classical Defense of Reform in Liberal Education* (Cambridge, MA: Harvard University Press, 1997); Martha Nussbaum, *Not for Profit: Why Democracy Needs the Humanities* (Princeton, NJ: Princeton University Press, 2010). See also Elizabeth Anderson, "Fair Opportunity in Education: A Democratic Equality Perspective," *Ethics* 117 (2007).
14. Aristotle, *Politics*, trans T. A. Sinclair (Harmondsworth, UK: Penguin, 1962), bk. 7, c. 7; see Sibyl A. Schwarzenbach, "On Civic Friendship," *Ethics* 107, no. 1 (1996); John Cooper, "Political Animals and Civic Friendship," in *Aristotle's Politics: Critical Essays*, ed. R. Kraut and S. Skultety (New York: Rowman & Littlefield, 2005).
15. See chapter 8 for the discussion of deliberative democracy.
16. Rutger Bregman, *Humankind: A Hopeful History* (London: Bloomsbury, 2020).
17. Jacob W. Wood, "Rebuilding the City of God: Locating the Politics of Virtue within the Politics of Sin and Grace," *Nova et Vetera* 16, no. 4 (2018).
18. Garett Hardin, "The Tragedy of the Commons," *Science* 162 (1968): 1243–72.
19. Elinor Ostrom, *Governing the Commons: The Evolution of Institutions for Collective Action* (Cambridge: Cambridge University Press, 1990).
20. David C. Rose, *Why Culture Matters Most* (Oxford University Press, 2019).
21. Rose, 151.
22. Aristotle, *Ethics*, trans. J. A. K. Thompson (Harmondsworth, UK: Penguin, 1981), bk. 1, cc. 3, 4.
23. Rose, *Culture*, 68.
24. Rose, 156.
25. Jon Elster, *Nuts and Bolts for the Social Sciences* (Cambridge: Cambridge University Press, 1989).
26. Rose, *Culture*, 83.
27. Rose, 56.
28. Edmund Phelps, *Mass Flourishing: How Grassroots Innovation Created Jobs, Challenge, and Change* (Princeton, NJ: Princeton University Press, 2013), 2.

29. G. E. M. Anscombe, "Modern Moral Philosophy," in *Philosophy* 33 (1958): 1.
30. John Finnis, *Fundamentals of Ethics* (Oxford: Clarendon Press, 1983), 82–84.
31. Luke Bretherton, *Resurrecting Democracy: Faith, Citizenship, and the Politics of a Common Life* (Cambridge: Cambridge University Press, 2015), 198.
32. Bretherton, 241.
33. Bretherton, 306n5.
34. Bretherton, 241.
35. Bretherton, 60.
36. Bretherton, 289.
37. Bretherton, 7.
38. Bretherton, 9.
39. Bretherton, 297.
40. Ernst-Wolfgang Böckenförde, *State, Society, and Liberty: Studies in Political Theory and Constitutional Law* (New York: Berg, 1991), 60.
41. Tine Stein, "The Böckenförde Dictum: On the Topicality of a Liberal Formula," *Oxford Journal of Law and Religion* 7 (2018); Olivier Jouanjan, "Between Carl Schmitt, the Catholic Church, and Hermann Heller: On the Foundations of Democratic Theory in the Work of Ernst-Wolfgang Böckenförde," *Constellations* 25 (2018).
42. Sandel, *Tyranny of Merit*, 14.
43. Sandel, *Tyranny of Merit*, 112.

EPILOGUE

The conclusion to chapter 10 could stand as a conclusion to the book's argument in favor of liberal politics serving human dignity from the Catholic perspective on common goods. It invokes the three lenses of approach outlined in chapter 1: Aristotelian practical philosophy, Catholic social thought, and political liberalism. In chapter 10, education illustrates the common good from *Gaudium et spes* as the set of conditions that facilitate the flourishing of individuals and their communities. The importance of the formation of children and the training for citizenship in enabling individual persons to flourish is illustrated, but more significantly, the impact of such formation on the quality of economic, social, and political life is addressed. That quality of life requires high levels of trust and willingness of people to accept moral constraints. But a liberal political regime is incapable of generating such trust or guaranteeing the moral formation of its citizens. It depends on the contribution of persons and communities in civil society.

The three authors invoked in chapter 10 to make the point about formation rely on Aristotelian-type arguments without invoking Aristotle's authority. The distinction drawn from Aristotle between practical and ontological accounts of common goods is shown to be useful in addressing the relationship between culture and communal flourishing.

Rawls's understanding of the political challenge of multiple communities embracing differing comprehensive doctrines building a shared life for economic, social, and political cooperation also feeds into the final chapter. Addressing problems of division and divisiveness in our experience, the chapter follows Mill's recommendation of reflecting on our history as an experiment in living, and it identifies the prospects for engagement in democratic politics.

The Second Vatican Council's idea of the common good as a set of conditions for human flourishing, without insisting on any one account of that fulfillment, complements the liberal emphasis on human freedom and the recognition of the appropriate limits to the power and authority of the state. Civil authority's respect for those limits and its reticence about enforcing any version of morality and ultimate fulfillment should not mean that consideration and discussion of ultimate goods and visions of fulfillment are excluded from public discourse. Faithful to Mill's injunction that open debate is necessary to help discover what is most conducive to the realization of human interests, such discussion should be a hallmark of a liberal democratic society. This complementarity underlines the interpretation of the ultimate common good as a *heuristic*, naming that which is not yet known but is in the process of discovery. While unknown, it is not completely unknown, since criteria and principles are available to help us exclude that which would be unreasonable and indefensible, and hence can guide the process of discovery. To that end, a liberal political community should welcome, on liberal principles, those instances in civil society—such as religious communities, churches, and academic institutions—that facilitate the broader discussion of the common good as ultimate purposes. It would not be consistent with those liberal principles but clearly obscurantist to suppress discussion of the ultimate destiny and purpose of human existence.

The life and work of the German jurist Ernst-Wolfgang Böckenförde, cited in chapter 10, exemplifies the Pope Benedict Option of engagement with our liberal regimes. Böckenförde's work contributes to chapter 10's discussion of intangible common goods. Those goods of shared meaning, ethos, values, and culture, essential if a liberal democratic state is to function well, require attention and sometimes action to sustain them. However, the state itself, with its instruments of coercive control and authoritative domination, should not attempt to guarantee these resources. Were it to do so, it would violate its own principles concerning the freedoms of its citizens.

But Böckenförde can provide another service to the argument. The main thrust of this book has been to challenge a growing tendency among Catholic authors and others to appropriate "the common good" as their slogan in their criticism of liberalism. By polarizing liberalism and a politics of the common good, they create the double impression that there is an ideology or practical project of the common good on which a political, social, and economic system can be constructed, and that it is an alternative to liberalism. An implication of this stance is that it is not possible to uphold concern for common goods and at the same time espouse a liberal political philosophy. This is the implication I challenge in this book, hoping to demonstrate that it is both intellectually coherent and defensible to be liberal in one's politics and a Catholic believer. This does not require any separation or division between the public and the private, or denial of the implications of faith commitment for political engagement.

Böckenförde exemplifies the challenges of holding this position as a defender of liberal institutions and a committed Catholic. His career spans the major transitions of the twentieth century, as Germany after the Second World War embraced liberal democracy and the Catholic church adapted itself to the challenges of modernity. He had been a student of Schmitt and engaged with Schmitt's critique of liberalism, especially recognizing the theological elements in liberalism's claims, but he denied that he was a disciple of Schmitt. He developed his own articulation of the value presuppositions of liberalism, stressing both the dignity of the human person as incorporated in Germany's constitution, the Basic Law, and the fundamental right to liberty, especially religious liberty, freedom of conscience, and freedom of speech. These are the shared values that the legal institutions of the federal republic are obliged to uphold and defend, but neither the state nor the courts can guarantee that respect for these values will be deeply rooted in the citizenry. His clarity on these values also enabled him to be critical of decisions by the courts that he considered insufficiently attuned to the fundamental values.

In the decades prior to the Second Vatican Council, Böckenförde struggled with the apparent tension between the espoused doctrines of the Catholic church and the liberal values on which the political order was to be based. Pope Leo XIII's encyclical letter *Immortale Dei* (1885) had asserted the principle that error has no rights, and modernist assertions of human liberty and its fundamental value for political order were taken to be erroneous. He attributed the church's doctrine as it then was to the adoption of a Thomist account of natural law, and the church's interpretation of this natural law doctrine he saw as contradictory to the principles grounding democracy that he was embracing as an engaged citizen and jurist. He did not avoid the challenge, but in several publications addressed the contradictions that he found. When the Vatican Council with its Declaration on Religious Liberty in 1965 overturned the church's previous political stance and embraced the principle of religious liberty, he welcomed it, but in his publications sought an account explaining how it was possible for such a change of teaching to take place. His public speeches and publications can be read as an attempt to persuade fellow Christians, including Catholics, that they could and should commit to supporting the constitution of the German state as grounded on the twin principles of respect for human dignity and the inalienable right to liberty.

His dictum that the liberal state lives from spiritual resources that it cannot guarantee to itself was interpreted by many as an argument for the inclusion of a religious element in the state, guaranteeing a moral foundation for its institutions and legal order. But while his purpose was partly to make believers aware of the scope of their action and contribution, he did not believe the moral foundation would necessarily have to be of religious origin. His commentators and defenders have insisted on this breadth of vision, preventing his thought from being hijacked for an ideological purpose. An editor of a collection of his papers in two volumes insists that his dictum be understood as a liberal principle.[1]

Some of the critics of liberalism advocate the Benedict Option—namely, to seek to construct a communal life based on the common good outside of the liberal economic and political structures. Pope Benedict's espousal of the fundamental importance of religious liberty and the other basic liberties rooted in the dignity of the human person lends weight to the proposal of a Pope Benedict Option in chapter 5 on liberalism. Böckenförde, in his life and work, committed himself to this latter approach—namely, to work in and with liberal institutions to deliver on the commitment to liberty and dignity. His remarks in a 1957 essay provide a convenient thought with which to end.[2] He cites a frequently quoted remark by Aquinas from the *Summa* that "unjust laws are outrages rather than laws" and that such laws "do not oblige in the court of conscience, unless perhaps to avoid scandal or riot (*turbationem*); on this account a man may be called to yield his rights."[3] In support, Aquinas cites the words of Jesus from Matthew's Gospel about going the second mile and giving the additional cloak. Böckenförde elaborates on these exceptions, which might make unjust laws binding in conscience after all. He notes that it is beyond human competence to bring about a perfectly just order immediately, and that the measures open to human action will be relatively limited, either toward or away from the just order. He continues:

> For that reason it may be necessary, precisely for the sake of the common good, to respect also less perfect or even contestable political structural forms, provided they do not directly contravene human dignity and divine law; and to place oneself loyally on the ground of their ethos, instead of hollowing them out from the inside for the sake of realizing absolute values and thus surrendering them to the enemies of human order. In this regard, as in all other things, the Christian must not be rigidly dogmatic, but must accept things as they are with the requisite soberness.[4]

Spanning the years of transition in the Catholic church's thinking on politics and the central role of human rights and religious liberties grounded in the dignity of the human person, Böckenförde's life shows the possibility of being faithfully Catholic and politically liberal. His support of liberal institutions is not based on any naive enthusiasm but on the reasons given by Aquinas why it might be obligatory for Catholics to give their support to a regime that falls far short not only of the ideal but also of what it has promised.

I end with this short reflection on Böckenförde's life and writings. They illustrate well the challenge faced by Catholic Christians in public life as formulated in chapter 1. We must combine and hold in tension a set of propositions: First, our faith conviction that all humans have offered to them an ultimate common good, or highest good, that is God, and the beatitude of life in God in the Resurrection. Second, the facts that the members of our political community (a) do not all accept that there is or even could be a common ultimate purpose; (b) that we do not all agree on what the common purpose is, even if we do think there is one; and (c) that we disagree on its implications for practical life, even if we agree on the ultimate purpose. Third, in the context of this plurality, we face the challenge to make and conduct a common life seeking peace, prosperity, and justice according to law. That it is possible to navigate this challenging route within a pluralist society in a liberal democratic state is demonstrated by the example of Ernst-Wolfgang Böckenförde. He shows that there are Catholic options to safeguard human dignity by means of liberal politics and liberal institutions, in service of the common good.

NOTES

1. Tine Stein, "The Böckenförde Dictum: On the Topicality of a Liberal Formula," *Oxford Journal of Law and Religion* 7 (2018): 97–108.
2. Ernst-Wolfgang Böckenförde, "The Ethos of Modern Democracy and the Church [1957]," in Böckenförde, *Religion, Law, and Democracy*, ed. Mirjam Künkler and Tine Stein (Oxford: Oxford University Press, 2020).
3. Thomas Aquinas, *Summa Theologiae*, vol. 28, ed. and trans. Thomas Gilby, OP (London: Blackfriars, in conjunction with Eyre and Spottiswoode, 1966), pt. 1–2, q. 96, a. 4.
4. Böckenförde, "Ethos of Modern Democracy," 63.

BIBLIOGRAPHY

Aghion, Philippe, Céline Antonin, and Simon Bunel. *The Power of Creative Destruction: Economic Upheaval and the Wealth of Nations*. Translated by Jodie Cohen-Tanugi. Cambridge, MA: Belknap Press, 2021.
Anderson, Elizabeth S. "Fair Opportunity in Education: A Democratic Equality Perspective." *Ethics* 117 (2007): 595–622.
———. "John Stuart Mill and Experiments in Living." *Ethics* 102 (1991): 4–26.
Anscombe, G. E. M. "Modern Moral Philosophy." *Philosophy* 33 (1958): 1–19.
Aquinas, Thomas. *Summa Theologiae*. Vol. 28. Translated by Thomas Gilby, OP. London: Blackfriars, in conjunction with Eyre and Spottiswoode, 1966.
Aristotle. *Ethics*. Translated by J. A. K. Thompson. Harmondsworth, UK: Penguin, 1981.
———. *Politics*. Translated by T. A. Sinclair. Harmondsworth, UK: Penguin, 1962.
Augustine. *The City of God*. Edited by D. Knowles. Translated by H. Bettensen. Harmondsworth, UK: Penguin, 1972.
Beiner, Ronald. *Civil Religion: A Dialogue in the History of Political Philosophy*. Cambridge: Cambridge University Press, 2011.
Berlin, Isaiah. *Four Essays on Liberty*. Oxford: Oxford University Press, 1969.
Biggar, Nigel. *What's Wrong with Rights?* Oxford: Oxford University Press, 2020.
Bingham, Tom. *The Rule of Law*. London: Allen Lane, 2010.
Böckenförde, Ernst-Wolfgang. *State, Society, and Liberty: Studies in Political Theory and Constitutional Law*. New York: Berg, 1991.
———. "The Ethos of Modern Democracy and the Church [1957]." In Böckenförde, *Religion, Law, and Democracy*, edited by Mirjam Künkler and Tine Stein, 61–76. Oxford: Oxford University Press, 2020.
Botero, Giovanni. *The Reason of State*. Edited by Robert Bireley. Cambridge Texts in the History of Political Thought. Cambridge: Cambridge University Press, 2017.
Bregman, Rutger. *Humankind: A Hopeful History*. London: Bloomsbury, 2020.
Bretherton, Luke. *Resurrecting Democracy: Faith, Citizenship, and the Politics of a Common Life*. Cambridge: Cambridge University Press, 2015.
Brooks, Rosa Ehrenreich. "Failed States, or the State as Failure?" *University of Chicago Law Review* 72 (2005): 1159–96.
Brown, Chris. "Human Rights and Human Nature." In *Human Rights: The Hard Questions*, edited by C. Holder and D. Reidy, 23–38. Cambridge: Cambridge University Press, 2013.
Brown, Roger, and Helen Carasso. *Everything for Sale? The Marketisation of UK Higher Education*. London: Routledge, 2013.
Bruno, Michael J. A. *Political Augustinianism: Modern Interpretations of Augustine's Political Thought*. Minneapolis: Fortress, 2014.
Budziszewski, J. *Commentary on Thomas Aquinas's Treatise on Law*. Cambridge: Cambridge University Press, 2014.

Burrell, David. *Analogy and Philosophical Language.* With an introduction by Stephen Mulhall. Eugene, OR: Wipf and Stock, 2016. Previously published 1973 by Yale University Press.
———. *Aquinas: God and Action.* London: Routledge, 1979.
Cahill, Edward. *Framework for a Christian State.* Dublin: Gill, 1932.
———. *Ireland and the Kingship of Christ.* Dublin: Irish Messenger, 1928.
Carney, Mark. *Value(s): Building a Better World for All.* London: William Collins, 2021.
Casey, Conor. "Common Good Constitutionalism and the New Debate over Constitutional Interpretation in the United States." *Public Law* 4 (2021): 765–87.
Casey, Cornelius J., and Fáinche Ryan, eds. *The Church in Pluralist Society: Social and Political Roles.* Notre Dame, IN: University of Notre Dame Press, 2019.
Cavanaugh, William T. "The Church's Place in a Consumer Society: The Hegemony of Optionality." In *The Church in Pluralist Society: Social and Political Roles,* edited by Cornelius J. Casey and Fáinche Ryan, 57–80. Notre Dame, IN: University of Notre Dame Press, 2019.
———. "Killing for the Telephone Company: Why the Nation-State Is Not the Keeper of the Common Good." In *In Search of the Common Good,* edited by Patrick D. Miller and Dennis P. McCann, 301–32. New York: T&T Clark, 2005.
———. *The Myth of Religious Violence.* Oxford: Oxford University Press, 2009.
Chaplin, Jonathan. *Faith in Democracy: Framing a Politics of Deep Diversity.* London: SCM Press, 2021.
Chappel, James. *Catholic Modern: The Challenge of Totalitarianism and the Remaking of the Church.* Cambridge, MA: Harvard University Press, 2018.
Chappell, Timothy. *Knowing What to Do: Imagination, Virtue, and Platonism in Ethics.* Oxford: Oxford University Press, 2014.
Chaput, Charles J., OFM Cap. *Render unto Caesar: Serving the Nation by Living our Catholic Beliefs in Political Life.* New York: Doubleday, 2008.
Congregation for the Doctrine of the Faith and Dicastery for Promoting Integral Human Development. *Considerations for an Ethical Discernment regarding Some Aspects of the Present Economic-Financial System.* 2018. https://www.vatican.va/roman_curia/congregations/cfaith/documents/rc_con_cfaith_doc_20180106_oeconomicae-et-pecuniariae_en.html.
Cooper, John. "Political Animals and Civic Friendship." In *Aristotle's Politics: Critical Essays,* edited by R. Kraut and S. Skultety, 65–89. New York: Rowman & Littlefield, 2005.
Craig, R. J., and Amernic, J. H. "Enron Discourse: The Rhetoric of a Resilient Capitalism." *Critical Perspectives on Accounting* 15 (2004): 813–51.
Crean, Thomas, and Alan Fimister. *Integralism: A Manual of Political Philosophy.* Neunkirchen-Seelscheid, Ger.: Editiones Scholasticae, 2020.
Crick, Bernard. *In Defence of Politics.* New edition. London: Continuum, 2005.
Deneen, Patrick J. "Hegemonic Liberalism and the End of Pluralism." In *The Church in Pluralist Society: Social and Political Roles,* edited by Cornelius J. Casey and Fáinche Ryan, 29–44. Notre Dame, IN: University of Notre Dame Press, 2019.
———. *Why Liberalism Failed.* New Haven, CT: Yale University Press, 2018.
Dreher, Rod. *The Benedict Option: A Strategy for Christians in a Post-Christian Nation.* New York: Sentinel, 2017.
Duff, Nancy J. "The Commandments and the Common Life: Reflections on Paul Lehmann's *The Decalogue and a Human Future.*" In *Explorations in Christian Theology and Ethics: Essays in Conversation with Paul L. Lehmann,* edited by Philip G. Ziegler and Michelle J. Bartel, 29–44. Farnham, Surrey, UK: Ashgate, 2009.

Dworkin, Gerald. "Paternalism." *The Stanford Encyclopedia of Philosophy*, Fall 2020 ed. Edited by Edward N. Zalta. https://plato.stanford.edu/archives/fall2020/entries/paternalism/.
Dworkin, Ronald. *Justice for Hedgehogs*. Cambridge, MA: Harvard University Press, 2011.
Eggemeier, Matthew T., and Peter Joseph Fritz. *Send Lazarus: Catholicism and the Crises of Neoliberalism*. New York: Fordham University Press, 2020.
Elias, J. L. *Conscientization and Deschooling: Freire's and Illich's Proposals for Reshaping Society*. Philadelphia: Westminster Press, 1976.
Ellis, J. J. *American Sphinx: The Character of Thomas Jefferson*. New York: Vintage Books, 1998.
Elster, Jon. *Nuts and Bolts for the Social Sciences*. Cambridge: Cambridge University Press, 1989.
Epstein, Richard A. *Principles for a Free Society: Reconciling Individual Liberty with the Common Good*. Reading, MA: Perseus, 1998.
Filotas, Zoli. *Aristotle and the Ethics of Difference, Friendship, and Equality: The Plurality of Rule*. London: Bloomsbury, 2021.
Finnis, John. *Fundamentals of Ethics*. Oxford: Clarendon Press, 1983.
———. "Public Good: The Specifically Political Common Good in Aquinas." In *Natural Law and Moral Inquiry: Ethics, Metaphysics, and Politics in the Work of Germain Grisez*, edited by R. P. George, 174–209. Washington, DC: Georgetown University Press, 1998.
Freire, Paolo. *Pedagogy of the Oppressed*. London: Penguin, 1985.
Gabardi, Wayne. "Contemporary Models of Democracy." *Polity* 33, no. 4 (2001): 547–68.
Gilby, Thomas, OP. "Common and Public Good (1a2ae, 90, 2)." Appendix 4 in Aquinas, *Summa Theologiae*. Vol. 28, 172–74. Translated by Thomas Gilby, OP (London: Blackfriars, in conjunction with Eyre and Spottiswoode, 1966).
———. "Law and Dominion in Theology (1a2ae, 90, 1–4)." Appendix 1 in Aquinas, *Summa Theologiae*. Vol. 28, 157–61. Translated by Thomas Gilby, OP (London: Blackfriars, in conjunction with Eyre and Spottiswoode, 1966).
———. "The Theological Classification of Law (1a2ae, 90, 1–3)." Appendix 2 in Aquinas, *Summa Theologiae*. Vol. 28, 162–64. Translated by Thomas Gilby, OP (London: Blackfriars, in conjunction with Eyre and Spottiswoode, 1966).
Girard, René. "Victims, Violence, and Christianity." *The Month* 265, no. 1564, 2nd n.s. 31, no. 4 (1998): 129–35.
Glendon, Mary Ann. "Justice and Human Rights: Reflections on the Address of Pope Benedict to the UN." *European Journal of International Law* 19, no. 5 (2008): 925–30.
———. *A World Made New: Eleanor Roosevelt and the Universal Declaration of Human Rights*. New York: Random House, 2001.
Gray, John. *Black Mass: Apocalyptic Religion and the Death of Utopia*. London: Allen Lane, 2007.
———. *Two Faces of Liberalism*. Cambridge: Polity, 2000.
———. "Where Pluralists and Liberals Part Company." In *Pluralism: The Philosophy and Politics of Diversity*, edited by Maria Baghramian and Attracta Ingram, 85–102. London: Routledge, 2000.
Griffin, Leslie. "Commentary on *Dignitatis humanae* (Declaration on Religious Liberty)." In *Modern Catholic Social Teaching: Commentaries and Interpretations*, edited by Kenneth R. Himes, OFM et al., 244–65. Washington, DC: Georgetown University Press, 2005.
Gutmann, Amy, and Dennis Thompson. *Democracy and Disagreement: Why Moral Conflict Cannot be Avoided in Politics, and What Should be Done about It*. Cambridge, MA: Harvard University Press, 1996.
Hadas, Edward. *Counsels of Imperfection: Thinking through Catholic Social Teaching*. Washington, DC: Catholic University of America Press, 2021.

Hardin, Garett. "The Tragedy of the Commons." *Science* 162 (1968): 1243–72.
Harvey, David. *A Brief History of Neoliberalism*. Oxford: Oxford University Press, 2005.
Hobbes, Thomas. *Leviathan*. Edited by J. C. A. Gaskin. Oxford: Oxford University Press, 1996.
Hollenbach, David. "Civil Society: Beyond the Public-Private Dichotomy." *Responsive Community* 5 (Winter 1994–95).
Hughes, Glenn. "The Concept of Dignity in the Universal Declaration of Human Rights." *Journal of Religious Ethics* 39, no. 1 (2011): 1–24.
Ivereigh, Austen. *Wounded Shepherd: Pope Francis and His Struggle to Convert the Catholic Church*. New York: Henry Holt, 2019.
Jenkins, Willis. *The Future of Ethics: Sustainability, Social Justice, and Religious Creativity*. Washington, DC: Georgetown University Press, 2013.
Jones, Nicolette. *The Plimsoll Sensation*. London: Little, Brown, 2006.
Jouanjan, Olivier. "Between Carl Schmitt, the Catholic Church, and Hermann Heller: On the Foundations of Democratic Theory in the Work of Ernst-Wolfgang Böckenförde." *Constellations* 25 (2018): 184–95.
Kane, Robert. *Ethics and the Quest for Wisdom*. Cambridge: Cambridge University Press, 2010.
Kingston, William. *How Capitalism Destroyed Itself: Technology Displaced by Financial Innovation*. Cheltenham, UK: Edward Elgar, 2017.
Kohn, Marek. *Trust: Self-Interest and the Common Good*. Oxford: Oxford University Press, 2008.
Kraut, Richard. Review of *The Problems of a Political Animal*, by Bernard Yack. *Political Theory* 23, no. 3 (1995): 547–51.
Laborde, Cécile. "Justificatory Secularism." In *Religion in a Liberal State: Cross-Disciplinary Reflections*, edited by Gavin D'Costa, Malcolm Evans, Tariq Modood, and Julian Rivers, 164–86. Cambridge: Cambridge University Press, 2013.
———. *Liberalism's Religion*. London: Harvard University Press, 2017.
Lehmann, Paul L. *The Decalogue and A Human Future: The Meaning of the Commandments for Making and Keeping Life Human*. Grand Rapids, MI: Eerdmans, 1995.
Legutko, Ryszard. *The Demon in Democracy: Totalitarian Temptations in Free Societies*. New York: Encounter Books, 2016.
Leigh, Ian. "The European Court of Human Rights and Religious Neutrality." In *Religion in a Liberal State: Cross-Disciplinary Reflections*, edited by Gavin D'Costa, Malcolm Evans, Tariq Modood, and Julian Rivers, 38–66. Cambridge: Cambridge University Press, 2013.
Locke, John. *Locke on Toleration*. Edited by Richard Vernon. Cambridge: Cambridge University Press, 2010.
Lonergan, Bernard. *Method in Theology*. 2nd ed. London: Darton, Longman & Todd, 1973.
———. *Verbum: Word and Idea in Aquinas*. Edited by David Burrell. Notre Dame, IN: University of Notre Dame Press, 1967.
Lucas, J. R. *On Justice*. Oxford: Clarendon, 1980.
MacIntyre, Alasdair. "A Partial Response to My Critics." In *After MacIntyre*, edited by John Horton and Susan Mendus, 283–304. Oxford: Polity, 1994.
———. *After Virtue: A Study in Moral Theory*. 2nd ed. Notre Dame, IN: University of Notre Dame Press, 1984.
———. *Ethics in the Conflicts of Modernity: An Essay on Desire, Practical Reasoning, and Narrative*. Cambridge: Cambridge University Press, 2016.

———. "Intractable Moral Disagreements." In *Intractable Disputes about the Natural Law: Alasdair MacIntyre and Critics*, edited by Lawrence S. Cunningham, 1–52. Notre Dame, IN: University of Notre Dame Press, 2009.
———. "Politics, Philosophy and the Common Good." *Studi perugini* 3 (1997). Reprinted in *The MacIntyre Reader*, edited by Kelvin Knight. Cambridge: Polity, 1998.
———. "Three Perspectives on Marxism: 1953, 1968, 1995." In *Ethics and Politics: Selected Essays*. Vol. 2. Cambridge: Cambridge University Press, 2006.
———. *Three Rival Versions of Moral Enquiry: Encyclopaedia, Genealogy, and Tradition*. London: Duckworth, 1990.
———. *Whose Justice? Which Rationality?* London: Duckworth, 1988.
Madeley, John. "The European State: Ineradicably Secular or More Than a Little Religious?" In *Religion: Problem or Promise? The Role of Religion in the Integration of Europe*, edited by Šimon Marinčák, *Orientalia et Occidentalia* 4 (2009): 107–28.
Markus, R. A. *Saeculum: History and Society in the Theology of St. Augustine*. Cambridge: Cambridge University Press, 1970.
Massa, Mark S., SJ. *Anti-Catholicism in America: The Last Acceptable Prejudice*. New York: Crossroads, 2003.
Mazzucato, Mariana. *The Entrepreneurial State: Debunking Public vs. Private Sector Myths*. London: Anthem Press, 2013.
———. *The Value of Everything: Making and Taking in the Global Economy*. London: Allen Lane, 2018.
McCloskey, Deirdre Nansen. *Bettering Humanomics: A New, and Old, Approach to Economic Science*. Chicago: University of Chicago Press, 2021.
———. *The Bourgeois Virtues: Ethics for an Age of Commerce*. Chicago: University of Chicago Press, 2006.
———. *Why Liberalism Works: How True Liberal Values Produce a Freer, More Equal, Prosperous World for All*. New Haven, CT: Yale University Press, 2019.
McGee, Owen. *A History of Ireland in International Relations*. Newbridge, Ireland: Irish Academic Press, 2020.
McGettigan, Andrew. *The Great University Gamble: Money, Markets and the Future of Higher Education*. London: Pluto, 2013.
McKnight, Stephen A. "Gnosticism and Modernity: Voegelin's Reconsiderations Twenty Years After *The New Science of Politics*." *Political Science Reviewer* 34 (2005): 122–42.
Meador, Jake. *In Search of the Common Good: Christian Fidelity in a Fractured World*. Downers Grove, IL: IVP Books, 2019.
Mill, John Stuart. *Utilitarianism, On Liberty and Considerations on Representative Government*. Edited by H. B. Acton. London: Dent, 1972.
Miller, Seumas. *The Moral Foundations of Social Institutions: A Philosophical Study*. Cambridge: Cambridge University Press, 2010.
Mitchell, Mark T. *The Limits of Liberalism: Tradition, Individualism, and the Crisis of Freedom*. Notre Dame, IN: University of Notre Dame Press, 2019.
Morris, Charles R. *The Two Trillion Dollar Meltdown: Easy Money, High Rollers, and the Great Credit Crash*. New York: Public Affairs, 2008.
Moyn, Samuel. *Human Rights and the Uses of History*. London: Verso, 2014.
———. *The Last Utopia: Human Rights in History*. London: Belknap Press, 2010.
Noonan John T., Jr. *The Lustre of Our Country: The American Experience of Religious Freedom*. Berkeley: University of California Press, 1998.

Nussbaum, Martha. *Cultivating Humanity: A Classical Defense of Reform in Liberal Education.* Cambridge, MA: Harvard University Press, 1997.

———. "Human Functioning and Social Justice: In Defense of Aristotelian Essentialism." *Political Theory* 20, no. 2 (1992): 202–46.

———. *Liberty of Conscience: In Defense of America's Tradition of Religious Equality.* New York: Basic Books, 2008.

———. *Not for Profit: Why Democracy Needs the Humanities.* Princeton, NJ: Princeton University Press, 2010.

———. *Women and Human Development: The Capabilities Approach.* Cambridge: Cambridge University Press, 2000.

O'Donovan, Oliver. "The Political Thought of *City of God.*" In *Bonds of Imperfection: Christian Politics, Past and Present,* by Oliver O'Donovan and Joan Lockwood O'Donovan. Grand Rapids, MI: Eerdmans, 2004.

O'Neill, John. *Markets, Deliberation and Environment.* Abingdon, UK: Routledge, 2007.

O'Neill, William R. *Reimagining Human Rights: Religion and the Common Good.* Washington, DC: Georgetown University Press, 2021.

Oderberg, David S. "The Structure and Content of the Good." In *Human Values: New Essays on Ethics and Natural Law,* edited by D. S. Oderberg and T. Chappell, 127–65. Basingstoke, UK: Palgrave Macmillan, 2007.

Ostrom, Elinor. *Governing the Commons: The Evolution of Institutions for Collective Action.* Cambridge: Cambridge University Press, 1990.

Perreau-Saussine, Emile. "What Remains of Socialism?" In *Values in Public Life: Aspects of Common Goods,* edited by Patrick Riordan, 11–34. Berlin: LIT Verlag, 2007.

Phelps, Edmund. *Mass Flourishing: How Grassroots Innovation Created Jobs, Challenge, and Change.* Princeton, NJ: Princeton University Press, 2013.

Plato. *The Republic.* Translated by Benjamin Jowett. London: Sphere Books, 1970.

Pope Benedict XVI. "Address to the German Federal Parliament." Berlin, 2011. https://www.vatican.va/content/benedict-xvi/en/speeches/2011/september/documents/hf_ben-xvi_spe_20110922_reichstag-berlin.html.

———. "Address to Representatives of British Society." Westminster, 2010. https://www.vatican.va/content/benedict-xvi/en/speeches/2010/september/documents/hf_ben-xvi_spe_20100917_societa-civile.html.

———. "Address to the United Nations." New York, 2008. https://www.vatican.va/content/benedict-xvi/en/speeches/2008/april/documents/hf_ben-xvi_spe_20080418_un-visit.html.

———. *Caritas in veritate,* "Love in Truth," 2009. http://w2.vatican.va/content/benedict-xvi/en/encyclicals/documents/hf_ben-xvi_enc_20090629_caritas-in-veritate.html.

Pope Francis. *Document on Human Fraternity for World Peace and Living Together.* Apostolic Journey of His Holiness Pope Francis to the United Arab Emirates, Abu Dhabi, February 3–5, 2019. https://www.vatican.va/content/francesco/en/travels/2019/outside/documents/papa-francesco_20190204_documento-fratellanza-umana.html.

———. *Fratelli tutti,* "On Fraternity and Social Friendship." 2020. https://www.vatican.va/content/francesco/en/encyclicals/documents/papa-francesco_20201003_enciclica-fratelli-tutti.html.

———. *Laudato Si',* "On Care for Our Common Home." 2015. https://www.vatican.va/content/francesco/en/encyclicals/documents/papa-francesco_20150524_enciclica-laudato-si.html.

Pope John XXIII. *Mater et magistra*, "Mother and Teacher." 1961. https://www.vatican.va/content/john-xxiii/en/encyclicals/documents/hf_j-xxiii_enc_15051961_mater.html.

Pope John Paul II. *Centesimus annus*, "On the Hundredth Anniversary of Rerum novarum." 1991. https://www.vatican.va/content/john-paul-ii/en/encyclicals/documents/hf_jp-ii_enc_01051991_centesimus-annus.html.

———. *Fides et ratio*, "On Faith and Reason." 1998. https://www.vatican.va/content/john-paul-ii/en/encyclicals/documents/hf_jp-ii_enc_14091998_fides-et-ratio.html.

———. *Laborem exercens*, "On Human Work." 1981. https://www.vatican.va/content/john-paul-ii/en/encyclicals/documents/hf_jp-ii_enc_14091981_laborem-exercens.html.

———. *Sollicitudo rei socialis*, "On Social Concern." 1987. https://www.vatican.va/content/john-paul-ii/en/encyclicals/documents/hf_jp-ii_enc_30121987_sollicitudo-rei-socialis.html.

Pope Paul VI. *Populorum progressio*, "On the Development of Peoples." 1967. https://www.vatican.va/content/paul-vi/en/encyclicals/documents/hf_p-vi_enc_26031967_populorum.html.

Pope Pius XI. *Dilectissima nobis*, "On Oppression of the Church in Spain." 1933. https://www.vatican.va/content/pius-xi/en/encyclicals/documents/hf_p-xi_enc_03061933_dilectissima-nobis.html.

———. *Divini redemptoris*, "On Atheistic Communism." 1937. https://www.vatican.va/content/pius-xi/en/encyclicals/documents/hf_p-xi_enc_19370319_divini-redemptoris.html.

———. *Mit brennender Sorge*, "On the Church and the German Reich." 1937. https://www.vatican.va/content/pius-xi/en/encyclicals/documents/hf_p-xi_enc_14031937_mit-brennender-sorge.html.

———. *Quadragesimo anno*, "On Reconstruction of the Social Order." 1931. https://www.vatican.va/content/pius-xi/en/encyclicals/documents/hf_p-xi_enc_19310515_quadragesimo-anno.html.

———. *Ubi arcano Dei consilio*, "On the Peace of Christ in the Kingdom of Christ." 1922. https://www.vatican.va/content/pius-xi/en/encyclicals/documents/hf_p-xi_enc_19221223_ubi-arcano-dei-consilio.html.

Porter, Jean. "Does the Natural Law Provide a Universally Valid Morality?" In *Intractable Disputes about the Natural Law: Alasdair MacIntyre and Critics*, edited by Lawrence S. Cunningham, 53–95. Notre Dame, IN: University of Notre Dame Press, 2009.

Rahner, Karl, and Herbert Vorgrimler. "Modernism." In *Dictionary of Theology*. Rev. ed. New York: Crossroad, 1981.

Rawls, John. "The Idea of Public Reason Revisited." In *The Law of Peoples*. Cambridge, MA: Harvard University Press, 1999.

———. *The Law of Peoples with "The Idea of Public Reason Revisited."* Cambridge, MA: Harvard University Press, 1999.

———. *Political Liberalism*. New York: Columbia University Press, 1996.

———. *A Theory of Justice*. Rev. ed. Cambridge, MA: Belknap Press, 1999.

Raz, Joseph. *Practical Reason and Norms*. 2nd edition. Oxford: Oxford University Press, 1999.

Reich, Robert. *The Common Good*. New York: Alfred A. Knopf, 2018.

Rengger, Nicholas. "Between Transcendence and Necessity: Eric Voegelin, Martin Wight and the Crisis of Modern International Relations." *Journal of International Relations and Development* 22 (2019): 327–45.

———. "The Exorcist? John Gray, Apocalyptic Religion and the Return to Realism in World Politics." *International Affairs* 83, no. 5 (2007): 951–59.

Riordan, Patrick. "Europe's Common Good: The Contribution of the Catholic Church." In *Religion: Problem or Promise? The Role of Religion in the Integration of Europe*, edited by Šimon Marinčák. *Orientalia et Occidentalia* 4 (2009): 279–94.

———. "Five Ways of Relating Religion and Politics or Living in Two Worlds: Believer and Citizen." In *The New Visibility of Religion: Studies in Religion and Cultural Hermeneutics*, edited by Graham Ward and Michael Hoelzl, 30–44. London: Continuum, 2008.

———. *Global Ethics and Global Common Goods*. London: Bloomsbury, 2015.

———. *A Grammar of the Common Good*. London: Continuum, 2008.

———. "Human Solidarity in Need and Fulfilment: A Vision of Political Friendship." In *Solidarity beyond Borders: Ethics in a Globalising World*, edited by Janusz Salamon, 65–82. London: Bloomsbury, 2015.

———. "Neither Theocracy nor Civil Religion Can Serve the Common Good." *Tambara* 32, no. 1 (2015): 85–106.

———. "The Secular is not Scary." In *The Church in Pluralist Society: Social and Political Roles*, edited by Cornelius J. Casey and Fáinche Ryan, 123–41. Notre Dame, IN: University of Notre Dame Press, 2019.

Rose, David C. *Why Culture Matters Most*. Oxford University Press, 2019.

Rousseau, Jean-Jacques. "A Discourse on the Arts and Sciences." In *The Social Contract and Discourses*. Translated by G. D. H. Cole. London: Dent, 1973.

Rousseau, Jean-Jacques. "A Discourse on the Origin of Inequality." In *The Social Contract and Discourses*. Translated by G. D. H. Cole. London: Dent, 1973.

Rubio, Julie Hanlon. *Hope for Common Ground: Mediating the Personal and the Political in a Divided Church*. Washington, DC: Georgetown University Press, 2016.

Sacks, Jonathan, *Morality: Restoring the Common Good in Divided Times*. London: Hodder and Stoughton, 2020.

Sandel, Michael. *Liberalism and the Limits of Justice*. Cambridge: Cambridge University Press, 1982.

———. *The Tyranny of Merit: What's Become of the Common Good?* London: Allen Lane, 2020.

Sands, Justin. "Introducing Cardinal Cardijn's See-Judge-Act as an Interdisciplinary Method to Move Theory into Practice." *Religions* 9 (2018): 129.

Satz, Debra. *Why Some Things Should Not Be for Sale: The Moral Limits of Markets*. Oxford: Oxford University Press, 2010.

Schellenberg, James A. *The Science of Conflict*. Oxford: Oxford University Press, 1982.

Schwarzenbach, Sibyl A. "On Civic Friendship." *Ethics* 107, no. 1 (1996): 97–128.

Scruton, Roger. *Green Philosophy: How to Think Seriously About the Planet*. London: Atlantic Books, 2012.

Second Vatican Council. *Dignitatis humanae*, "Declaration on Religious Freedom." 1965. https://www.vatican.va/archive/hist_councils/ii_vatican_council/documents/vat-ii_decl_19651207_dignitatis-humanae_en.html.

———. *Gaudium et spes*, "Pastoral Constitution on the Church Today." 1965. https://www.vatican.va/archive/hist_councils/ii_vatican_council/documents/vat-ii_cons_19651207_gaudium-et-spes_en.html.

Shakespeare, William. *As You Like It*. In *Complete Works*, edited by W. J. Craig. London: Oxford University Press, 1969.

Smith, Adam. *An Inquiry into the Nature and Causes of the Wealth of Nations*. Edited by R. H. Campbell and A. S. Skinner. 2 vols. Indianapolis: Liberty Fund, 1981.

Soros, George. *The New Paradigm for Financial Markets: The Credit Crisis of 2008 and What It Means*. New York: Public Affairs, 2008.
Standing, Guy. *Plunder of the Commons: A Manifesto for Sharing Public Wealth*. London: Pelican Books, 2019.
Stein, Tine. "The Böckenförde Dictum: On the Topicality of a Liberal Formula." *Oxford Journal of Law and Religion* 7 (2018): 97–108.
Stiglitz, Joseph. *Globalization and its Discontents*. London: Penguin, 2002.
Swift, Adam. *Political Philosophy: A Beginner's Guide for Students and Politicians*. Cambridge: Polity, 2001.
Tasioulas, John, and Effy Vayena. "Just Global Health: Integrating Human Rights and Common Goods." In *The Oxford Handbook of Global Justice*, edited by Thom Brooks. Oxford University Press, 2020. https://doi.org10.1093/oxfordhb/9780198714354.013.7.
Taylor, Charles. "Cross-Purposes: The Liberal-Communitarian Debate." In *Philosophical Arguments*, 181–203. Cambridge, MA: Harvard University Press, 1995.
———. "The Politics of Recognition." In *Philosophical Arguments*, 225–56. Cambridge, MA: Harvard University Press, 1995.
TeSelle, Eugene. "The Civic Vision in Augustine's *City of God*." *Thought* 62 (1987): 268–80.
Tierney, Brian. *Liberty and Law: The Idea of Permissive Natural Law, 1100–1800*. Washington, DC: Catholic University of America Press, 2014.
Tirole, Jean. *Economics for the Common Good*. Translated by Stephen Rendall. Princeton, NJ: Princeton University Press, 2017.
Trainor, Brian T. "Augustine's Glorious City of God as Principle of the Political." *Heythrop Journal* 51 (2010): 543–53.
———. "Augustine's 'Sacred Reign–Secular Rule' Conception of the State: A Bridge from the West's Foundational Roots to Its Post-Secular Destiny, and between 'the West' and 'the Rest.'" *Heythrop Journal* 56 (2015): 373–87.
Trigg, Roger. *Equality, Freedom, and Religion*. Oxford: Oxford University Press, 2012.
Vallier, Kevin. "Neoliberalism." *The Stanford Encyclopedia of Philosophy*. Summer 2021 ed. Edited by Edward N. Zalta. https://plato.stanford.edu/archives/sum2021/entries/neoliberalism/.
Vermeule, Adrian. "All Human Conflict Is Ultimately Theological." *Church Life Journal* (July 2019). https://churchlifejournal.nd.edu/articles/all-human-conflict-is-ultimately-theological/.
———. "Common-Good Constitutionalism." *Atlantic*, March 31, 2020. https://www.theatlantic.com/ideas/archive/2020/03/common-good-constitutionalism/609037/.
———. "Integration from Within." Review of *Why Liberalism Failed*, by Patrick J. Deneen. *American Affairs* 2, no. 1 (Spring 2018). https://americanaffairsjournal.org/2018/02/integration-from-within/.
———. "Liturgy of Liberalism." Review of *The Demon in Democracy: Totalitarian Temptations in Free Societies*, by Ryszard Legutko. *First Things* (January 2017). https://www.firstthings.com/article/2017/01/liturgy-of-liberalism.
Voegelin, Eric. *The New Science of Politics: An Introduction*. Chicago: University of Chicago Press, 1952.
———. *Order and History*. Vol 4, *The Ecumenic Age*. Baton Rouge: Louisiana State University Press, 1987.
———. *Religion and the Rise of Modernity*. Edited by J. L. Wiser. Columbia: University of Missouri Press, 1998.

———. "World-Empire and the Unity of Mankind." *International Affairs* 38, no. 2 (1962): 170–188.

Walsh, David. *The Growth of the Liberal Soul.* Columbia: University of Missouri Press, 1997.

———. *The Priority of the Person: Political, Philosophical, and Historical Discoveries.* Notre Dame, IN: University of Notre Dame Press, 2020.

Weber, Max. "Politics as a Vocation." In *Max Weber*, translated and edited by H. H. Gerth and C. Wright Mills. London: Routledge and Kegan Paul, 1948.

Williams, Rowan. "Politics and the Soul: A Reading of the *City of God*." *Milltown Studies* 19–20 (Spring–Autumn 1987): 55–72.

Wolf, Martin. *Why Globalization Works.* New Haven, CT: Yale University Press, 2005.

Wolff, Jonathan. "Democratic Voting and the Mixed-Motivation Problem." *Analysis* 54, no. 4 (1994): 193–96.

———. *Ethics and Public Policy: A Philosophical Inquiry.* London: Routledge, 2011.

Wolterstorff, Nicholas. "The Role of Religion in Decision and Discussion of Political Issues." In *Religion in the Public Square*, edited by Robert Audi and Nicholas Wolterstorff, 67–120. London: Rowman & Littlefield, 1997.

Wood, Jacob W. "Rebuilding the City of God: Locating the Politics of Virtue within the Politics of Sin and Grace." *Nova et Vetera* 16, no. 4 (2018): 1371–414.

Woodard, Colin. *American Character: A History of the Epic Struggle Between Individual Liberty and the Common Good.* London: Penguin, 2017.

Woodhead, Linda. "Liberal Religion and Illiberal Secularism." In *Religion in a Liberal State: Cross-Disciplinary Reflections*, edited by Gavin D'Costa, Malcolm Evans, Tariq Modood, and Julian Rivers, 93–116. Cambridge: Cambridge University Press, 2013.

Yack, Bernard. *The Problems of a Political Animal: Community, Justice, and Conflict in Aristotelian Political Thought.* Berkeley: University of California Press, 1993.

Young, Michael. *The Rise of the Meritocracy.* Harmondsworth, UK: Penguin, 1958.

INDEX

analogy, 26, 71–73, 77–79, 83
Anderson, Elizabeth, 178, 180
Anscombe, Elizabeth, 213
apocalypse, 136, 139, 141–42, 153, 156
Aquinas, 5, 37–39, 43, 70–82, 88–89, 117, 128, 146, 176; on analogy, 73, 77–79, 80; on conscience, 74–75, 77, 226–27; on law, 71–81, 89, 124–25
Arendt, Hannah, 144–45, 147
Aristotle, 13–19, 27, 41–45, 72–73, 86–87, 114–15, 117–18, 165, 214, 223; on the good life, 17–19; on politics, 30–38
Augustine, 5, 38, 43, 49–51, 54–61, 66–67, 100, 142. *See also* political Augustinianism
autonomy, 40, 50, 103, 109–10, 158, 160, 163, 178, 217; of the secular, 42

Benedict option, 6, 12, 50, 111, 181, 212, 215, 226. *See also* Pope Benedict option
Berlin, 137
Biggar, Nigel, 40, 152
Bingham, Tom, 31
Böckenförde, Ernst-Wolfgang, 8, 217–19, 224–27
Botero, Giovanni, 47n19, 146
Bregman, Rutger, 209, 211
Bretherton, Luke, 213–16, 219
Brooks, Rosa Ehrenreich, 31, 46n4
Bruno, Michael J. S., 51
Budziszewski, J., 80
Burrell, David, 78–79

Cahill, Edward, 94–95, 98
capitalism, 21, 94–95, 119, 183, 192, 194
Caritas in veritate, 22, 131, 157
Carney, Mark, 119, 193–94

Casey, Conor, 37
Catholic Church, 14, 19–20, 95, 104–6; and paternalism, 156–57; and politics, 42, 100–101, 106, 115, 126, 225–26
Catholic social teaching, 4, 19, 22, 26, 49, 96, 106–7, 158, 183, 197, 223
Cavanaugh, William, 11, 37, 55, 92, 124
Centesimus annus, 132, 183
Chaplin, Jonathan, 101
Chappel, James, 97–100, 103
Chappell, Sophie Grace, 164
Chaput, Charles, 50–52
church-state relations, 51–54, 61, 102, 156; Vatican Council on, 20, 102, 126–27, 130, 157
civil authority, 4, 5, 43, 50, 107, 136, 147, 224
civil religion, 55
civil society, 7, 45, 67, 89, 214–15, 219
coercion, 6, 36, 37, 38, 43, 55, 57, 88–89, 96, 115–16
common good, 5, 17, 27, 42, 130–31, 198; Aquinas on, 70–81; as set of conditions, 20, 86, 89, 126, 166, 220, 223; as ultimate end, 5, 20, 26–27, 44, 72, 81–82, 102, 105
common good constitutionalism, 37
common goods, 1–4, 6–8, 12, 15, 32, 81–87, 132–33, 136–39, 176, 218; in Catholic social thought, 19–22, 132–33, 183–84
commons, 6, 84–85, 205, 210, 212; tragedy of the, 84, 209, 212
communism, 96, 98–99, 119, 136, 138, 145, 151, 186
conflict, 4, 31, 35–36, 114; Augustine on, 56–57; as context for politics, 5, 6, 32,

conflict (*continued*)
114, 115, 127; managed not resolved, 36, 39, 114–15, 116, 133, 193; meaning of, 115, 118–21; Pope Francis on, 127, 131–32; and religion, 122–23
Congregation for the Doctrine of the Faith, 199n51
conscience, 74–75, 77, 80, 103, 226. *See also* liberty: of conscience
conscientization, 161–63
cooperation, 12–13, 18, 33, 44, 83, 86, 118, 166, 207, 212, 219–20
credit crisis, 189, 210
Crick, Bernard, 115
culture, 17, 87, 103, 121; as a common good, 216–17; dependent on self-restraint, 210–13; political, 38, 45, 114–15, 137, 194, 196; public, 3, 12; as shared values, 70, 100, 110, 182, 206, 208

dedivinization, 142, 148
deliberation, 2, 19, 33, 39, 41, 75, 130, 161, 171–72, 196–97
democracy, 18, 36, 94, 100, 126–27, 217–18; deliberative, 170–71, 173, 182–83, 197, 208; liberal, 9, 29, 55, 98, 101, 145, 149
Deneen, Patrick, 11–12, 23, 37, 50, 92–93, 145, 177–79, 181, 196
deregulation, 7, 183, 185, 187, 190–91, 192–93, 195–96
Dignitatis humanae, 97
dignity, 4, 6, 20, 23, 49, 60, 93, 97, 101–7, 111, 131–32, 176, 225–27
Dilectissima nobis, 100
Divini redemptoris, 99–100
Dreher, Rod, 50, 215
Duff, Nancy J., 124
Dworkin, Gerald, 157
Dworkin, Ronald, 163

Eggemeier, Matthew, 92, 185
Elster, Jon, 212
Enron, 189–90
environment, 49, 84, 108, 161, 165, 169, 171, 172, 182
eschaton, 139–42, 144–45, 147, 153
ethics, 13, 16, 86, 103, 168, 194, 203, 211

Europe, 3, 66, 93, 95, 97–98
European Court of Human Rights, 64–65
experiments in living, 7, 177–78, 180–82, 184, 194, 197

Fides et ratio, 134n31
Filotas, Zoli, 35, 117–18
finance, 189, 192, 210; financial markets, 177, 191, 193, 215; financial sector, 189, 192–94; financiers, 94, 188
Finnis, John, 43, 213
Fratelli tutti, 124, 132
Fraternity declaration, 124
Freire, Paulo, 161
friendship, 17; political, 209
Fritz, Peter, 92, 185

Gabardi, Wayne, 171
Gaudium et spes, 3, 13, 20, 101, 106, 126–27, 130, 136, 157, 176, 216, 220, 223
Gilby, Thomas, 79–80, 81, 85
Girard, René, 114–15, 132
Glendon, Mary Ann, 113n41, 151
globalization, 103, 184, 193
Gnosticism, 141–42
good: meaning of, 89; ontological sense of, 44, 159, 173, 207, 218, 220, 223; practical sense of, 15, 44, 165, 207, 218, 220, 223
goodness itself, 74, 81, 89
goods: club, 85–86, 205, 218–19; collective, 86, 207; private, 85–86, 204–5, 207; public, 6, 84–85, 86–87, 169, 204–5, 208, 219. *See also* common goods
government, 26, 50, 63, 101, 122, 162, 177–78, 191; and common goods, 2, 9, 60, 86–87, 128; conflict, 36, 114, 122; liberty, 6, 23, 92, 101, 111, 137, 176
Gray, John, 141, 148–50

Habermas, Jürgen, 26, 61
Hadas, Edward, 96, 186
Harvey, David, 184–85
heuristic, 5, 17–19, 27, 42, 58, 110, 130, 198, 214
Hobbes, Thomas, 44, 59, 66, 72, 114, 209–10
Hollenbach, David, 26

INDEX

human nature, 32, 39, 42, 88, 107, 109, 125, 131, 164–65, 167, 173, 209
human rights, 40, 44, 49, 67, 98–99, 105–8, 137, 139, 149–52, 160

institutions, 10–11, 38, 45, 70, 86, 100–101, 109, 131–33, 184–86; as common goods, 6–7, 15, 26, 70, 166; political, 25, 31, 65, 106, 129; reliant on trust, 212–17
integralism, 50, 68, 98, 153, 176
international relations, 46n4, 105–6, 116, 141, 149, 215
Ireland, 9, 53, 94, 95, 98, 115, 120, 188

Kane, Robert, 178
Kingston, William, 188–89, 192
Kraut, Richard, 42

Laborde, Cécile, 63–64
Laborem exercens, 21
Laudato Si', 121, 127, 161, 181–82, 196, 209
law: definition, 71–72; coercive force of, 37, 88, 89; directive force of, 72, 88, 89; divine, 76–77, 79, 80, 124, 128, 226; eternal, 74, 79–81; kinds of, 73–74; natural, 39, 73–75, 79, 88, 124–25, 225; on rights, 39–40
Legutko, Ryszard, 145
Lehmann, Paul L., 124
Leigh, Ian, 64–65
liberal-communitarian debate, 10, 24, 28, 117
liberalism, 62, 92–96, 97–98, 105, 109, 145–49; illiberal liberalism, 62, 64, 148, 150, 177. *See also* neoliberalism
liberty, 17, 24, 42, 92, 93, 109–10, 145, 163, 225; Berlin on, 137; of conscience, 40, 43, 53, 60, 64, 110, 225; Mill on, 32, 75–76, 179; religious, 4, 6, 40, 43, 66, 95, 96, 101–4, 106
Locke, John, 53
Lonergan, Bernard, 78–79

MacIntyre, Alasdair, 9–10, 12, 19, 24, 39, 55, 125
Madeley, John, 65–66
marketization, 194, 204
markets, 169, 184–85, 187, 191–95

Marx, Karl, 99, 195
Massa, Mark, 52–53
Mater et magistra, 20
Mazzucato, Mariana, 192, 194
McCloskey, Deidre, 169, 184, 195–96
Meador, Jake, 2
meritocracy, 7, 23, 119, 202–4, 218–20
Mill, John Stuart, 176–81, 194. *See also* experiments in living
Miller, Seumas, 86
Mit brennender Sorge, 100
Mitchell, Mark T., 92
modernism, 95, 98, 99, 100, 109
modernity, 5, 30, 54, 61, 96–100, 141–44
morality, 2, 11, 24, 40, 75, 87, 95, 97
Morris, Charles R., 191
Moyn, Samuel, 150–52

nationalism, 120, 142, 144
neoliberalism, 1, 4, 7, 49, 150, 184–86, 193
Nussbaum, Martha, 110, 164, 167

Oderberg, David, 167
O'Donovan, Oliver, 57
O'Neill, William R., 23–24
Ostrom, Elinor, 210

paternalism, 7, 22, 67, 156–59, 172–73
Phelps, Edmund, 213
Plato, 13, 17, 80, 120, 122, 126, 129
Plimsoll, Samuel, 187
pluralism, 11, 23, 98, 106, 148
pluralist society, 11, 45, 62–64, 67, 105, 126, 129
political Augustinianism, 13, 51, 68n7, 176–77, 216
political common good, 6, 85, 101, 136–37, 217, 220
political liberalism, 1, 5, 13, 22, 25, 27, 63, 130, 149
politics: defined 115–16, 118, 120; identity politics, 123; of recognition, 123. *See also* religion and politics
Pope Benedict option, 6, 215, 224, 226
Pope Benedict XVI, 6, 22, 97, 104, 109, 136, 158, 176; Berlin address, 107, 108; UN address, 51, 67, 105–6, 107; Westminster address, 106–7, 108

Pope Francis, 22, 62, 121, 124; on conflict, 131–32; on environment, 121, 159, 161, 176, 181–83, 196, 209
Pope John Paul II, 7, 21, 101, 104, 130, 132, 158, 183, 188, 193, 197
Pope John XXIII, 20, 97
Pope Leo XIII, 21, 95, 225
Pope Paul VI, 97
Pope Pius XI, 94–95, 96, 99–100, 101, 132
Populorum progressio, 131
practical rationality, 123
practical reason, 72, 88, 125
public reason, 25, 63

Quadragesimo anno, 95, 132

Rawls, John, 13, 22–26, 62–64, 86–87, 130, 149, 177, 223
ragion di Stato, 36, 146, 147
Reich, Robert, 3
regulation, 7, 38, 179, 186–88; of banking, 188–89, 190, 193–95, 196. *See also* deregulation
religion and politics, 55, 57, 65. *See also* church-state relations
Rengger, Nicholas, 141
Rose, David C., 210–13
Rousseau, Jean-Jacques, 76, 120, 122, 137, 201–2, 209
Rubio, Julie Hanlon, 49
rule of law, 36, 87, 93, 160, 206

Sacks, Jonathan, 2, 23, 24
sacred, 5, 50–51, 58–62, 147, 156, 177
saeculum, 50, 57
Sandel, Michael, 1, 22, 24, 119, 163, 201–4, 218–20
Schmitt, Carl, 225
Scruton, Roger, 38
secularism, 25, 62, 65; illiberal, 5, 62–63, 67, 148, 177; justificatory, 63–64
self-interest, 187, 189
Shakespeare, 140, 210
Smith, Adam, 184, 187
socialism, 12, 98–99, 142, 144, 151
solidarity, 7, 21–22, 25, 27, 156–63, 172–73, 197

Sollicitudo rei socialis, 21
Soros, George, 190
state, 10–11, 32–33, 41, 44, 55, 96, 118, 136–37, 156–57; defined, 116–17; failed, 31; roles of, 184–86
Stiglitz, Joseph, 192
subsidiarity, 4, 7, 21–22, 27, 49, 96, 158–59, 172, 186, 197

theocracy, 50, 55, 63, 68
Tierney, Brian, 71–72
Tirole, Jean, 193–94
totalitarianism, 64, 98–99, 108, 136, 138, 144, 145, 147–48
Trainor, Brian T., 55–62, 66–67, 148
trust, 88, 125, 168, 210–13, 219, 223

Ubi arcano, 100
Universal Declaration of Human Rights, 51, 61, 105–7, 151
utilitarianism, 87–88, 180, 185, 194, 213
utopia, 6, 67, 138–41, 149–53, 156

Vallier, Kevin, 185–86
value, 25–26, 63, 106–7, 118–20, 122, 171–72, 183, 193–97, 217–18
Vatican Council II, 3, 6, 10, 20, 61, 86, 96–98, 101–3, 225
Vermeule, Adrian, 36–37, 92, 145–48, 177, 181, 185
violence, 6, 114–15, 117, 131–32, 139, 151, 172
virtue, 5, 9–10, 17, 37, 42, 59, 75–76, 119, 133, 209–10; civic, 2, 18, 214, 217–18
Voegelin, Eric, 141–45, 148

Walsh, David, 103–4, 111
Weber, Max, 116–17
Wolff, Jonathan, 187
Woodard, Colin, 3
Woodhead, Linda, 62

Yack, Bernard, 35, 42, 131
Young, Michael, 202–3, 219

ABOUT THE AUTHOR

DR. PATRICK RIORDAN, SJ, a member of the Irish Jesuit province, is senior fellow for political philosophy and Catholic social thought in Campion Hall, University of Oxford. He previously taught political philosophy at Heythrop College, University of London, and, for fifteen years, at the Milltown Institute of Theology and Philosophy in Dublin, where he served as president. His book *Recovering Common Goods* (Dublin, 2017) was given the "Economy and Society" award by the Centesimus Annus Pro Pontifice Foundation in Rome in 2021. Along with his book *Global Ethics and Global Common Goods* (London, 2015), he has published articles on a wide range of topics such as human dignity, human rights, punishment, restorative justice, business ethics, terrorism, and just war theory, but always from a perspective of common goods. Visiting professorships in three of the Philippines' five Jesuit universities, in Manila, Naga, and Davao, have enriched his Irish worldview, already broadened by graduate studies in Munich and Innsbruck.

www.ingramcontent.com/pod-product-compliance
Lightning Source LLC
Chambersburg PA
CBHW030538230426
43665CB00010B/943